RAZOR 03
A NIGHT STALKER'S WARS

Dedicated to the Night Stalkers who lost their lives in the service of our country. They and their families paid the ultimate sacrifice – Their bravery and dedication must not be forgotten.

They loved to fight, fought to win, and would rather die than quit.
NSDQ!!

RAZOR 03

A NIGHT STALKER'S WARS

Alan C. Mack   NSDQ!

Pen & Sword
MILITARY
AN IMPRINT OF PEN & SWORD BOOKS LTD.
YORKSHIRE – PHILADELPHIA

First published in Great Britain in 2022 and reprinted in 2023 by
PEN & SWORD MILITARY
An imprint of
Pen & Sword Books Ltd
Yorkshire – Philadelphia

ISBN 978 1 39901 869 2

A CIP catalogue record for this book is available from the British Library

Typeset in 11/13.5 & Ehrhardt MT Std by SJmagic DESIGN SERVICES, India.

Printed and bound in the UK by CPI Group (UK) Ltd, Croydon, CR0 4YY

Pen & Sword Books Ltd incorporates the imprints of Pen & Sword Archaeology,
Atlas, Aviation, Battleground, Discovery, Family History, History, Maritime,
Military, Naval, Politics, Social History, Transport, True Crime, Claymore Press,
Frontline Books, Praetorian Press, Seaforth Publishing and White Owl

For a complete list of Pen & Sword titles please contact
PEN & SWORD BOOKS LTD
47 Church Street, Barnsley, South Yorkshire, S70 2AS, England
E-mail: enquiries@pen-and-sword.co.uk
Website: www.pen-and-sword.co.uk

Or

PEN AND SWORD BOOKS
1950 Lawrence Rd, Havertown, PA 19083, USA
E-mail: Uspen-and-sword@casematepublishers.com
Website: www.penandswordbooks.com

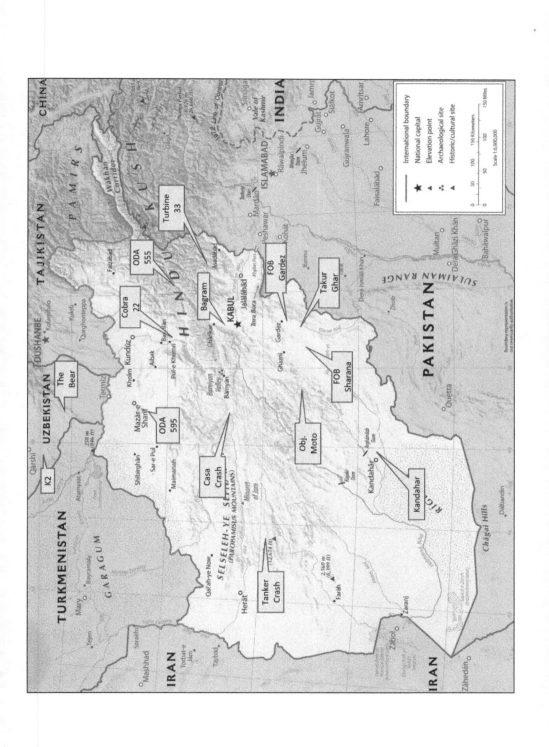

Contents

Acknowledgements

First, I could not complete this project without the support of my family, especially my sons, Stephen and Andrew, who, as 'Night Stalker Kids,' endured my long and frequent deployments, all the while knowing I might not come home – I can't believe they followed in my footsteps. As they grew, they reversed roles with me by joining the Navy and Army; Now, I had to worry about their safety in combat – I could not be more proud.

My wife Patti's persistence and positive reinforcement were crucial to my success. But, if she was the driving factor in finishing the story, I have three men in mind that truly helped make this happen.

Jim DeFelice, the NYT Best Selling Author of *American Sniper*, was the person who convinced me I could write a book. He'd just finished interviewing me for a book that he was writing and asked a simple question. "You tell a good story; Why don't you write a book?"

I didn't think I had enough experience putting words on paper that would interest others. But months later, at the movie premiere for Doug Stanton's *Twelve Strong*, Jim once again pressed me about writing; This time, he got me. The next day I started the memoir that would become *Razor 03, A Night Stalker's Wars*. His periodic reviews and comments helped shape the narrative along the way.

Steven Hartov, another bestseller, and author of *In the Company of Heroes*, looked at my work occasionally with an eye on style. His points had to do with emotion. After reading the first draft, he said, "You special operators are all the same. You make getting shot at sound like you're buying bagels. You've got to share your real emotions. Not what you said with bullets flying, but what you felt."

I took his opinion to heart and ran with it. My emotions such as fear, loss, happiness, friendship, and love are laid bare for you, the reader.

Another successful author, and editor, Chris Evans, believed in me and my work. He ultimately convinced me that I had an exciting and engaging story – He was truly the key to publishing.

Other indirect support came from the Writers Guild Initiative and Wounded Warrior Project writing workshops. Their workshop that gave me a perspective on storytelling that quite frankly made me feel good about the tales I wanted to tell. In addition, the instructors and peer writers enjoyed my vignettes enough to offer encouragement that certainly influenced my decision to continue writing.

These are my memories. The events of this book are told from my perspective as a Flight Lead and have been reviewed by the DOD Office of Prepublication and Security Review. The views expressed in this publication are mine and do not necessarily reflect the official policy or position of the Department of Defense or the US government. Though I owe a debt of gratitude to the pilots that followed me, my crew chiefs have a special place in my heart. Not only did they prepare our helicopters, but they rode into danger with no physical control of where or how I took them to a target or objective. Their trust in my abilities to drag them into potentially hellish situations and deliver them safely home is something I will never forget. Their attitude and bravery made my story possible

I don't want to forget that many others were involved. An old axiom floats around the special operations community – I don't know who said it first. "Don't determine your importance to the mission based on your proximity to the 'X.'" You may be shooting on the target, putting fuel in the helicopters, feeding the crew, making sure they got paid, or were a family member. It takes the entire unit to make missions happen. So, whether a mission consisted of fellow Night Stalkers, SEALs, Special Forces, Air Force, or Army Rangers, we were all part of something much bigger than ourselves. We represented America, stood for our service, and were there for each other in good times and bad.

Last and certainly not least, I thank God that I'm here to tell my story – Enjoy. Night Stalkers Don't Quit!!

Section I

Alea iacta est (Let the die be cast)

– Julius Caesar

Chapter 1

September 10, 2001

My left leg tingled as I shifted in the pilot's seat. My lower back ached from the weight of body armor – Chinook cockpits were notoriously uncomfortable for such a long flight. I sighed as my Night Vision Goggles struggled to amplify enough light for a clear video. It was darker than I would have liked over the bayous of Southern Louisiana. I nervously tweaked the NVG focus, hoping to improve the picture. The moon, if it were up, would have helped, but it was nowhere in sight. A quick glance across the cockpit revealed my copilot Jethro's eyes reflecting an eerie green glow from his NVGs. "Damn, it's dark," he said to nobody in particular.

The spacious cockpit was lit only by four multi-function displays on the instrument panel. My radar was on, augmented with the forward-looking infrared sensor, known as a FLIR. This was as good as it would get. So, I turned my attention to our front, scanning the horizon for navigation cues and hazards.

I was the flight leader of two Special Operations Chinooks and had a mission to finish.

I was mad about the last back-and-forth conversation on the radio.

I'd just argued with the Air Mission Commander riding in Chalk Two. He and I had distinct ways of doing things. He wanted me to abort the infil because he thought the poor weather would keep us from our intended target, and would rather cancel than fail. I took a second look at my map. We would not have a problem – I was sure.

We'd butted heads before over similar circumstances. Joe Gorst was a captain, and I was a chief warrant officer three. As a CW3, he outranked me. But I was the 'Flight Lead,' an influential leadership position in the 160th Special Operations Aviation Regiment (SOAR). Years of experience, piloting skills, talent, cult-of-personality (ego), and decision-making put me at the front of our formation, not his seniority. I was goal-oriented with an attitude to match. I'd go over, around, or through any problem I faced to complete my mission – sometimes to a fault.

I'd gone toe-to-toe with senior officers before, and mostly, I got my way. Joe was once a non-commissioned officer in SOF before attending flight school and working his way to our unit. His personality and attitude were every bit as intense as mine. Sometimes I think he just loved to argue because he never overruled me outright – this mission was no different – I'd gotten my way. So, as we pushed through the rain, the stress was all on me. If I came up short, Joe would never let me forget that he was right and I was wrong. To say we were both stubborn would be an understatement. I was the proverbial immovable object, and Joe was the rock smashing against me. But the advantage was mine, with several thousand flight hours under my belt. Our disagreements might get my ass kicked someday over a beer, but in the air we always worked things out.

I started planning for flight deviations as we penetrated the simulated enemy air defenses of the fictional country of Pineland.

Night flying can be challenging in the best of circumstances. Add thunderstorms and the complexity increases. I hoped the heavy rain wouldn't derail our riverine infil. 'Observer Controllers' from the Louisiana-based Joint Readiness Training Center (JRTC) were onboard, watching our clandestine operation. JRTC provided a realistic free-play-training environment, allowing me to exploit the strengths of my specially modified Chinook helicopter. We couldn't ask for a better venue to practice with our Special Forces brothers.

Jethro did most of the flying. The affable copilot kept his head moving side-to-side and occasionally up and down scanning the landscape for unlit antennas and power lines. Windshield wipers stroked across my field-of-view like an inverted metronome. The visibility dropped to an uncomfortably low distance. So, I ordered my wingman to drop back and pick up two minutes of separation, keeping in mind we'd still need to rejoin before arriving on target. Several checkpoints later, I brightened the aircraft's clock slightly – it was time.

Satisfied that we'd met our requirements to re-join the flight, I instructed Jethro to reverse course using a standard-rate turn to the right. I frantically searched the sky for my wingman. The risk of collision was very real. We'd need to see each other before getting any closer.

I pointed. "Over there."

Emerging from the misty dark background at my two o'clock was Chalk Two.

The MH-47E Chinook isn't the most beautiful machine in the air, but it is one of the fastest and strongest helicopters in the world. The flat-black airframe made it more challenging to see at night, but the fuselage was big, close to fifty feet long and ten feet wide. It resembled a miniature space shuttle without wings, or maybe more like a Greyhound bus with a pointy nose. The fuselage hung beneath two massive sixty-foot rotors at the front and back in tandem. The standard joke was that it looked like "two palm trees mating in a trash dumpster." But as it banked in my direction, I noted how gracefully it maneuvered through the sky.

The radios were quiet, but the intercom chatter in our aircraft picked up as the joining black Chinook passed down my right side and circled behind me. Once in position, and in formation, we turned back along our next intended heading and accelerated to make our time-on-target – plus-or-minus thirty seconds.

I craned my neck to look back into our cargo compartment to see the 'precious cargo.' A Special Forces Maritime Operations Team was asleep and sprawled over their motorized inflatable Zodiac. I divided the twelve-man MAROPS Team evenly among our two Chinooks, with each aircraft easily carrying a boat to insert. The rivers in this area cut through heavily wooded swamps and forests. And we were going to 'infil' our passengers at a pre-designated linkup location.

Waiting on the river were a pair of heavily armed riverine boats from a nearby Navy Special Boat Unit. The Army and Navy would work together in a Direct-Action assault of an enemy encampment a few miles from the river.

On the dark and stormy night, our landing zone was merely a straight stretch of river just wide enough for our large rotors to fit snugly between the tree-lined riverbanks as we conducted what we called an 'Amphib-One' approach.

An alarm sounded in my flight helmet. The distinctive 'Bing Bong' reminded me we were close to our objective. I alerted the crew, "ten minutes!"

Trained and proficient, the crew chief at the right ramp responded with "Ten minutes, aft ready."

The crew chief at the right gun position did his part, "Ten minutes, forward ready."

The SF Team leader acknowledged the time and passed it on to his men.

I needed to conduct a Before Landing Check and quickly review the 'Amphib' procedure. It was simple. We'd approach the area at eighty knots and eighty feet, looking for our rendezvous point. And once we identified the 'friendlies' and their boats on the river, we'd set up to come alongside.

At a pre-determined distance, we slowed to forty knots, then descended to forty feet, followed by twenty knots and twenty feet. Once in the correct location, Jethro slowed to ten knots; and I entered ten feet in the keypad of the Control Data Unit (CDU) near my right knee. The flight director accepted my input, and I engaged the coupler. The helicopter descended on its own to ten feet above the water and maintained a precise altitude.

Jethro adjusted our speed and heading with the help of the Integrated Avionics Suite Hover Page. The video-game-like display helped us keep our desired track along the river with minimal lateral drift.

As the helicopter descended, the foliage to our left and right parted as our rotor wash pushed most of the branches away. The trees were closer than I was comfortable with, and it wasn't long before the scent of newly shorn pine trees wafted into the cockpit. The rotor tips cut through the more rigid pine boughs that refused to move with the rotor wash.

"Jethro, we're chopping wood, slide right," I said.

"Sorry. Coming right."

If we hit a big enough branch, we could damage the aircraft, or worse, end up in the water in a spectacular crash, killing all of us.

Jethro's adjustment was enough as both aircraft settled into the flight-profile of ten knots and ten feet. The spray and mist roiled up by our rotor wash, made it hard to see, but Jethro focused on his hover page... My side window was still open, allowing my left arm to get wet from the spray. The cool water felt refreshing, and as far as I could tell, we were ready, and I wanted to get the guys in the water – So, I gave the order, "Boats, Boats, Boats." I repeated the call on our FM radio for Chalk Two to hear so they could mirror our actions.

Windshield wipers swiping back and forth improved what I could see, but not by much. I could feel the subtle shift in the helicopter's center of gravity as the boat slid off the ramp and into the water. The six Special Forces soldiers followed it into the river. I wanted them to hurry. The further we went upriver, the narrower it became; and the longer we held the profile, the more likely we'd trim trees again.

Jethro held our speed and altitude while the crew chief counted heads. "Six thumbs up – clear to come up."

With one stroke of a button, the Radar Altitude Hold function began a climb. And as we got higher, the spray and mist dissipated.

Chalk Two tucked into formation, and we began accelerating to our maximum range airspeed of 138 knots. I wanted to get back to base, to rest and reset. The infil went well, but to complete our mission, we still had to weave our way home through Pineland. I had to believe the JRTC controllers wouldn't allow us to penetrate the enemy air defense network without making our flight a learning event. To add stress and increase the difficulty, air defense systems along our projected flight path would stimulate our Radar Warning Receivers.

The MH-47E's Aircraft Survivability equipment (ASE) incorporated a suite comprised of a Radar Warning receiver, Jammers, Flares, and Radar decoying CHAFF. A small circular screen displayed symbols of Air Defense threat systems emissions detected, their location, and mode. A computer-synthesized voice spoke into my helmet, announcing a potential threat system. "S-A, S-A Six, Two O'clock, tracking."

The JRTC team placed a simulated SA-6 radar-guided missile at a nearby airport. I'd have to evade the threat to avoid being shot out of the sky.

The SA-6 was the most likely weapon we'd see on deep penetration missions other than heat-seeking MANPADs. 'Bitchin' Betty,' the female personality of our voice warning system, alerted us to our jammer's automated response: "Radar warning – Pulse Jamming Forward, Pulse Jamming Forward."

Jethro's instincts were sharp, and his moves well-practiced. His effective 'break-lock' maneuver interrupted the SA-6's ability to track us, as the JRTC observer watched intently. Things got exciting when our altitude dropped too low, causing 'Bitchin' Betty' to speak again. "Altitude low, altitude low." The radar altimeter showed that we'd descended to seventy-five feet... much too low. And I didn't want to collide with any unlit man-made hazards; I had friends in Desert Storm die that way. So, I was about to coax Jethro higher, when the crew chief on the Right Gun noticed powerlines to our front emerging from the mist – Right in front.

"Crap." I was sure they would slice through my windshield.

An excited voice pounding through the intercom pushed Jethro to action. "Climb, climb, climb!".

Jethro pulled too much 'thrust,' reaching a power limit. Betty bitched at him again, *"Torque, torque, torque."* About the time we cleared the wires, the SA-6 radar would regain its track. So, we banked again, popping a cloud of aluminum CHAFF to help break the radar lock. "That was close," I said. And the visibly shaken observer controller confirmed our maneuvers succeeded, allowing us to return to base.

I gloated about our success. I was right, and Joe was wrong... At least I was self-aware that I had an egotistical streak. But what pilot didn't?

+++

Our destination was Camp Beauregard, Louisiana National Guard base. The old state-run facility was comprised of single-story cinder block buildings. We each had individual rooms furnished with a bed, nightstand, and TV – no complaints from me. There was a downside – acoustics. The waxed tile floors and masonry walls amplified every noise along the echo-enhancing-hallways. Loud conversations penetrated the thin particle board doors effortlessly. Even soft-spoken conversations reverberated throughout the building. As members of the Night Stalkers, we worked a PM schedule – this JRTC rotation was no exception. Our days started around 11:00 in the morning with a run and workout, followed by breakfast, which was everyone else's lunch. After a shower, we'd report to the planning area to work on our next mission... replay over and over.

For now, it was time for sleep. I must have been tired because I don't remember adjusting my pillow; I just remember waking up to some loud conversations in the hallway.

"Holy crap, did you see what happened?" someone said.

"Yeah, that's messed up!"

Someone yelled further down the hall. "What the heck, guys? Be quiet!"

"Dude, you need to see the news – turn on your television!"

Curiosity drove me toward the TV. Without a remote, I had to climb out of my bed. "How primitive," I joked. The television video was slow to appear, allowing time for me to realize the air conditioning was too cold. I shivered as I read the thermostat. I squinted as I tried to make out the tiny faded numbers. I would need glasses soon. And after a suitable temperature correction, I turned my attention back to the TV. "Wow..." Now, I knew what the commotion was about; it was the same on all channels. One of the World Trade Center towers was on fire. Smoke billowed from a gigantic hole mid-way up. I stood there, dumbfounded. Within minutes, another airliner flew in from off-screen, tearing into the second tower. All that remained was an eerie airplane-shaped hole and smoke.

There's no way two impacts could be an accident – we were under attack.

The unfolding news coverage continued. There wasn't much for me to do at that point. So I did the only thing I could think of and made a pot of coffee. The aroma of the fresh brew permeated the air, adding some sense of normalcy to my morning.

It wasn't long before strong black coffee slipped over my lips, scorching my tongue, "crap, that's hot." My God, what was I seeing; was that a person? As more objects dropped from high atop the twin towers, news cameras zoomed in; those falling objects had souls. They were people making a horrific choice – burn to death or fall for forty seconds and die quickly on impact.

As I poured another cup of coffee, other guys assembled in my room to watch TV.

Then, without warning, the towers collapsed in succession. Right there – right in front of us. How could that happen? What about all those police and firefighters? How many people were inside? There had to be thousands.

What we didn't realize was that another plane had hit the Pentagon, and one plowed into an empty field in Pennsylvania. By this point, no one knew how big an operation this was. So, to be safe, the Federal Government 'grounded' all air traffic. Nothing except military fighters could fly, not even us. I did not understand how pivotal this moment would be in my life – no one did.

+++

Our battalion commander, LTC Brass, and I rented a car and drove back to Fort Campbell, Kentucky. Once in the controlled environment of the Headquarters, we'd be able to access sensitive information that might give us some direction in our preparation for war. The eleven-hour drive was silent as the colonel and I each tried to make sense of what was unfolding. The attack on our country would warrant a counterattack of some magnitude. Our unit would likely be involved in any immediate response. Rapid deployment was our bread and butter. Which is why our families had to be ready to stand on their own any day of the week. I hoped my wife, Linda was up to the task...

What if the deployment was too long for her? Or worse, what if I didn't return? Ideas, thoughts, and various scenarios bounced around my brain until the gentle hum of our tires on pavement produced a slight bout of 'road hypnosis.' We still had over six hours remaining in our drive home. The colonel and I settled in for a long, quiet ride. I was sure our unit would be part of our nation's response to the heinous attacks on our homeland. I looked forward to the opportunity.

Section II

"Each man delights in the work that suits him best."
— Homer, *The Odyssey*

Chapter 2

Flight School (1989–1990)

My childhood dream was to fly helicopters, and I was about to get my chance as an army warrant officer at Fort Rucker, Alabama. 'UCLA' or Upper Corner of Lower Alabama was the home of Army Aviation when I entered flight school in 1989. I was one of seventy-three warrant officer candidates in Class 89-16, 'Royal Blue' Flight.

Linda and the boys rented a house in the nearby town of Enterprise, Alabama, while I began my journey to adventure. Linda understood that flying was something I always wanted to do, and she supported me wholeheartedly as I was doing push-ups, polishing brass, shining shoes, buffing floors, and, oh yeah... learning to fly.

She held down the home-front, keeping both sons in line while giving me the emotional and mental boost I needed when I experienced difficulties in class. But, one thing was for sure, with her help, I would not quit.

One of the skills WOC school tries to cultivate is time management. The curriculum is designed to weed out soldiers that cannot prioritize their time or to work around problems encountered along the way. For example, I had to prepare for a barracks inspection while studying for my 'Primary' flight evaluation. So, besides prepping my room, I needed to wash my laundry with an insufficient number of provided washers and driers. As a result, I would not have enough time to do everything, and I needed help.

It wasn't long after I made a clandestine call for help from an off-limits payphone that Linda drove alongside the barracks and beeped her horn. Smiling the whole way to her car, I carried two laundry bags – mine and my roommate's. I tossed the contraband into her car, stole a kiss, and went back to studying and cleaning. I finished about the time a familiar car horn announced the delivery of freshly washed and ironed uniforms. I could have kissed her... and you bet I did.

First thing in the morning, our TAC Officers (think of drill sergeants with officer rank) woke us up with clanging garbage can lids, whistles, and screaming. We dressed quickly and stood by for an inspection, which went well, and thanks to Linda, painlessly.

+++

Flying the UH-1H Huey was a blast. As a young boy, I'd watched the evening news as these beautiful machines flew around Vietnam; and now I was piloting them. But, the first day I picked one up to a hover, I got the surprise of my life. I'd always imagined that I needed steady hands to fly helicopters, but that is far from the truth. Helicopters require control movements constantly, and every time I adjusted a control axis, it affected every other axis. My instructor pilot (IP) patiently explained what he wanted me to do.

"Okay, Mack, I want you to pick this thing up to a three-foot hover – do not drift."

I was concentrating so hard, a simple "yes sir" was all I could muster.

The 'collective' was a lever near my left thigh. Raising or lowering it changed pitch in both rotor blades equally, causing an adjusted angle of attack and new power requirements.

As I applied more power, I had to counteract the torque effect by pushing on my left yaw pedal to keep the helicopter from spinning; conversely right pedal input was necessary when I reduced the power setting. These control adjustments occurred over and over during the entire flight. As if that wasn't enough, the cyclic stick between my knees moved each rotor blade individually to provide directional control. If I moved my right hand toward my crotch, the helicopter would drift back. Pushing it toward the instrument panel, we'd move forward, and moving my hand left, and right would cause a slide to the side.

So, I tried to do as he instructed. His voice was merely background noise as he tried to talk me through the procedure. "Come on, Mack, I want you to smoothly increase power with the collective until we start to break ground, simultaneously apply left pedal as required to maintain heading. Using the cyclic, you'll maintain position over the ground allowing no drift."

"Coming up," I said over the intercom.

"Nice and easy, Mack. You've got this."

No – I didn't. As soon as my skids cleared the ground, the aircraft nose yawed right without enough correction, and then I started to drift to the left and backward. I overcorrected again and found myself somewhere around twenty feet above the ground, not the intended three feet. I was all over the place, and my IP, who'd seen this play out hundreds of times, calmly took over. "I have the controls, Mack." The Huey stopped bucking and hovered rock-steady without me flying.

I looked across the cockpit at my smiling instructor. He was flying with only his index finger on the cyclic.

"Mack, you gotta relax. Heck, I can teach a monkey to fly," he said. "let's try this again, and we'll work on your 'monkey skills.'"

I tried over and over, each time with a near-disastrous result. I didn't think I would ever learn to hover. Then, on my third flight, I somehow found the 'hover button.' Finally, I was doing it – flying was now my profession.

I had a long way to go and had much more to learn; weather forecasting, navigation, emergency procedures, and something that would come in handy many years later – the altitude chamber.

+++

My training continued, and month after month, they added more tasks to our curriculum. We had a saying, "Flight school doesn't get better; it just gets over." Every time I mastered a portion of the class, the instructors added something else. Linda, much like other guys' wives, helped me study emergency procedures using flashcards. I had to perform these EPs from rote memory, which I learned from repetition. Studying and practice paid off as I rose to be ranked number one in my UH-1 section when a CH-47D Chinook slot opened up.

Historically, flying Chinooks had been considered a reward for years of service flying other aircraft, but now, almost the entire Chinook pilot corps was retirement eligible. And the folks at the Department of the Army needed to backfill as quickly as possible. So, even though I was graduating as a lowly WO1, a Chinook slot was in my future.

Consequently, the Army needed pilots, so they turned to junior warrants like me. They'd only take the best candidates to fly Chinooks right out of flight school, and the only metric available was academic class standing. As number one in the class, I was invited to join the ranks of Army aviation's 'hookers.'

+++

I wasn't happy at first. I wanted to fly assault missions in the Air Cavalry, and I was convinced that UH-1s and the new UH-60 Blackhawks were the only way I would do that. After all, Chinooks just flew cargo from base to base. Right?

It would take a while to find out, but the Chinook is a powerful, fast, and really maneuverable machine. The first thing I learned was that it was surprisingly easy to fly. The flight controls at either pilot's station functioned the same as any single-rotor helicopter. It had two yaw pedals, one cyclic, and a version of the collective that is called the thrust control in a Chinook. The flight controls are manipulated the same as a Huey or Blackhawk, but what happens above the pilot's head is dramatically different; it is quite frankly a bit of PFM (pure frickin' magic).

The CH-47D Aircraft Qualification Course took only a few weeks, and my family and I were on our way to my first duty assignment as a warrant officer. My whole year as a WOC, I was treated like crap; it was hazing, pure-and-simple. But thousands of WOCs endured the same program of instruction before me; it created the desired attitude to go along with flying skills.

Now, as a WO1, I moved to Savannah, Georgia, to join B Company, 2/159th Aviation Regiment. Lucky for me, another WO1 preceded me by several months.

He was a hard worker and a 'good stick,' so the old guys had high hopes that I'd be the same.

The unit looked like it was going to be fun. So, Linda and I found an apartment near the airfield, and she·planned on looking for a job as soon as we got settled. Little did we know, this move was about to get a little more complicated.

+++

The Instructor Pilots (IPs) would typically have taken their time training me, but I arrived at the unit just as Saddam Hussein invaded Kuwait. It wasn't long before we were alerted to deploy to Saudi Arabia to support Operation Desert Shield; my readiness level progression hit high gear. I needed to be able to fly as a co-pilot with anyone in the company. So, I flew every day, sometimes twice a day to build experience. They had to get me ready.

We ended up flying our helicopters to the port of Wilmington, North Carolina, so we could place them on the deck of a transport ship heading to the Port of Dammam, Saudi Arabia. The parking lot near the loading dock was our destination, but it was only large enough for two CH-47Ds at a time. So, we departed Savannah as flights-of-two separated by about forty-five minutes. The timing allowed us to land, shutdown, and assist with removing all six rotor blades so the helicopters could be towed near our ship. There the 'forty-seven' could be lifted by crane to the top deck where crews were waiting to shrink wrap the large airframes for the journey across the sea.

But first, we had to get there. I was the co-pilot of Chalk Two for my first cross-country flight ever. As lead's wingman, we'd be responsible for backup navigation and following their every move. This was an excellent opportunity for me to practice formation flying, which I'd only done in UH-1Hs.

My pilot-in-command, Jim Leech, was an older-than-average CW2 who'd left the Army as a captain after two tours in Vietnam flying UH-1 Hueys and CH-47C Chinooks. He'd been recalled to active duty to fill a shortage of Chinook pilots. Even with a reduced rank, Jim just wanted to fly. He was a natural teacher and provided formation flying tips. But, roughly an hour into our flight, our lead aircraft developed a problem and had to land at a nearby airfield to check out a malfunction. We followed them to confirm a safe landing before proceeding to the port alone.

Neither Jim nor I had been paying attention to where we were along the route. The Atlantic Ocean was about twenty miles to our east. But that didn't help much in determining our precise location. Jim used this golden opportunity to train me. There was no GPS constellation like there is today. We flew using a chart, compass, and clock. Jim took the controls as he tossed the map at me. "Okay, Al, get us to the port."

I was pretty good at navigating in flight school. This couldn't be that hard. Heck, there were significant roads, towers, power lines, and airfields everywhere.

I should be able to match something up to the chart, and Jim reminded me I'd better do it soon. We'd need to call through whatever controlled airspace lay ahead, and there was plenty.

"Al, have you got us on the map yet?' Jim asked.

"Yeah, of course, I do. We should be crossing a large set of power lines in about five miles."

There were wires everywhere, and five miles was an acceptable answer for now.

Jim started to make out an enormous airport in the distance. "What airfield is that at twelve o'clock?"

I took too long to answer and was slowly rotating my map like the steering wheel of a large bus, trying to match it to the surrounding area. "Jim, I'm sorry, but I don't have a clue where we are." I hated to admit my failure, but I needed his help. I thought we were screwed because neither of us knew where we were.

Jim passed me the controls, tuned an air traffic control frequency from memory, and started talking. He knew where we were all along, and he was trying to see how I'd react. And, though embarrassing, I'd do better with some time under my belt. For now, Jim had the map, and I had the controls.

Upon landing at the port alongside our ship, the teardown teams jumped at getting a start on disassembling our Chinook.

+++

Our unit was a sixteen-ship company with a sister unit at Fort Bragg, North Carolina. They'd be joining us for the trip to the desert. The older pilots in my unit thought our Battalion's combined strength of thirty-two CH-47Ds for this fight was overkill. But we didn't have a clue that there would be over 100 Chinooks in theater before Desert Shield morphed into Operation Desert Storm.

Once everything was loaded onto the ship, we piled onto a chartered bus to go back to Savannah. One beer stop at a convenience store made the long drive home more relaxed and allowed me to get to know my new peers before we went to war.

Chapter 3

Desert Shield/Storm (1990–1991)

My first combat deployment was finally here. My son, Stephen, almost four years old, was clinging to my leg as I tried to climb aboard the bus to our airplane. "Daddy, don't leave. I don't want you to die."

"Don't worry," I said. "Let go and see Mommy. Everything's gonna be all right." I couldn't be sure I wasn't lying, but what else could I say? I was holding up the bus, and his emotional plea tugged at my heartstrings. I held back tears as I took my seat and waved at my crying son on the tarmac. *What was I getting myself into?*

Operation Desert Shield involved staging military forces into Saudi Arabia to dissuade Iraq from invading. Maybe the liberation of Kuwait would happen as well. Our mere presence was supposed to be enough to defend the kingdom, and it was. Saddam talked tough but stayed within his and Kuwait's borders.

The only certainty for us was that we did not know how long we'd be in the Middle East. So, a month into my deployment, I got a letter from Linda. She didn't know anyone in Savannah, and the kids were too young for school, so she headed North to stay at my Mom's home in Portsmouth, New Hampshire. My parents took them in for the duration of hostilities with Iraq. I didn't like that she left Georgia, but it was nice to have them with family.

Linda found a local physician that would hire her for the unknown time and hopefully short period of my deployment. Her days were busy, but she found time to organize a 'support the troops' rally. Several hundred people took to the streets, catching the attention of local news channels. Her interviews went well; she appeared articulate and beautiful. The only thing more charming was my infant son Andrew in her arms, and Stephen on her lap.

"Where is your father?" the reporter asked.

My son responded with a slight speech impediment, "My daddy is saving the good guys and shooting the bad guys."

"That about sums it up," said the reporter.

I saw that interview when a VHS tape showed up in the mail from the news channel that visited her. I was impressed and proud of her efforts, and damn were my kids cute...

+++

When the first bombs dropped on Baghdad, Dad, Mom, and Linda watched CNN as Bernard Shaw, Peter Arnett, and John Holliman reported on the military air campaign against Iraq. My father poured a cocktail and, like the rest of America, watched the war unfold live on television.

They had no idea that my unit was participating in the famous Schwarzkopf 'left hook,' moving the main assault force out into the borderlands west of Kuwait. Desert Shield now transitioned into Operation Desert Storm. The fighting would last a mere 100 hours; kind of a letdown, but also a blessing.

+++

Before we knew it, we were back at our compound in Dharan, preparing to go home. Cleaning the sand from our equipment was almost impossible. A customs unit from the National Guard was assigned the job of making sure nothing organic went back to the States. They were a little too thorough and didn't understand how to clean aircraft components. They made us pressure wash the insides of our helicopters. You can't imagine what water leaking into electrical cannon plugs does to aircraft systems. Excessive and unwanted moisture took the entire sea voyage home to dry out. But in the meantime, we had to ferry the now partially malfunctioning helicopters to the port of Dammam for their return to the States. Our maintenance folks shuffled back and forth between Chinooks as they tried to get enough waterlogged systems online for a 'onetime flight.'

Once we shuttled all fifteen of our remaining aircraft to the teardown area, we had nothing to do but wait for our flight home. Sitting around our pool reading donated paperbacks was the best way to spend our time in limbo. I couldn't wait to go home. I'd only been able to call Linda three or four times in the seven months we were deployed; letters were our usual mode of communication. I imagined my homecoming and wondered how my sons had grown.

The Army chartered an airliner to bring us to the states – we were going home.

+++

My long flight from Saudi Arabia ended when I stepped onto Stewart Army Airfield into the arms of my wife and kids. Linda returned to Georgia as soon as she knew I was headed back to Savannah. And reunification was as wonderful as I'd hoped. She put some serious thought into my return... Before I put my dusty bags into the car, she pulled a large pepperoni pizza and a six-pack of beer from the back seat. I can't think of a better way to say hello – at least publicly.

Our helicopters were on a slow boat to Wilmington and wouldn't be back in the States for about a month. There was nothing for me to do but to get reacquainted with my family. Disney offered military families, and by that, I mean me, free admission to their parks upon our return, so you know where we took the kids – Disney World.

Carefree days made for an easy readjustment, especially because our chaplains taught mandatory classes about reintegrating with our spouses. You know, "they've been running the home for the last seven months. Don't reunite and criticize," etc. It seemed to work. Linda did a great job raising the kids without a father present, and things couldn't have been better. Life went on like that for a few more years...

Chapter 4

Pushing limits – NTC and the Bermuda Triangle (1992–1993)

All the 'experts' and 'talking heads' on the news programs thought Operation Desert Storm would last months, not hours. The Army, anticipating a prolonged conflict with heavy losses, accelerated its flight program, pushing more pilots through school and recalled retired aviators back to active duty. The anticipated catastrophic loss didn't occur, and we had only a handful of deaths – unfortunately, four were ours.

When I returned from my post-deployment vacation to Disney World, I walked into the pilots' office at work to find ten new warrant officers waiting to in-process. We had to get them into the air and find flight time for them. And since most of the guys that I'd deployed with were senior to me, they chose to fly during the day, allowing me to train at night. I was hungry for flight time and could see the writing on the wall; the Army would transition into a 'fight-at-night' organization. The transformation was happening at a quick clip. So, night vision goggle qualified crews were requested for every field problem, exercise, and operation. That meant a small group of friends and I would be gone a lot. But that experience was vital to my progression as a unit trainer. And it wasn't long before I was trusted to take out the new guys.

Instructor pilots taught new techniques and skills, then handed them off to me for what we called continuation training; basically, I was a babysitter watching the other new guys practice what they'd learned. I wrote grade slips and critiqued their flights – I was having a blast.

My night flying skills improved, but my attitude needed seasoning. I can look back now, and honestly admit that my ego led me into situations that needed my talent to get me out of. There's a saying: "Good judgment comes from experience, and experience comes from bad judgment." I was gaining experience.

My friend Tim Kools and I were assigned to haul M-198 Howitzers on a gun raid. The one-niner-eight is a towed artillery piece, and it's frickin' heavy. Chinooks excelled at carrying this particular type of load. It's why the triple hook system was developed for the CH-47D.

We'd hover over the load and hook a pair of slings to the front and aft cargo hooks and fly to a firing point. The tandem hooks kept the load from spinning, and because it was so heavy, it didn't sway or swing. Upon reaching the landing zone, we'd place the gun precisely on its 'gun–target-line' and set down about 100 feet away and let out the gun crew. They'd rapid-fire approximately ten 155mm artillery rounds down-range, stow the 'tube' for travel, and re-hook it to our waiting aircraft. We'd get away from the firing point as fast as we could to evade potential enemy counter-battery fire. It was fun, challenging, and exciting, so we were looking forward to the night's mission. But before taking off, we were briefed by the Air Force forecaster that clouds and visibility would hover right around our minimums. Tim and I didn't even debate it. We were going. We had a legal forecast, though prudence dictated we cancel the flight.

"No big deal, we'll just Follow the railroad tracks to the river then to our HLZ," I said.

Tim was the pilot-in-command, so it was really his call, but I 'egged' him on as most copilots do. "Come on, Tim, we've got this. Let's go."

Before I knew it, the rotors were spinning, and the massive turbine engines hummed. The control tower granted our request to depart under Special Visual Flight Rules. That should have clued us in that if this mission wasn't vital, we shouldn't take off – gotta get experience– right?

I flipped down my NVGs and took off, turning left after departing the taxiway. The tracks we intended to follow were covered in fog. The temperature, dewpoint, and mild wind should have been sufficient indicators that we were headed for trouble. "Tim, can you turn on the searchlight? I'm having trouble seeing," I said.

"It's already on, I think its really dark. My goggles are straining to get a good picture. Maybe it'll get better near the river," Tim said.

I flew for the next four minutes, white-knuckling the cyclic stick. I flexed my hand to relax when I came to the realization that I couldn't see anything outside the helicopter. It was like being inside a golf ball or a milk jug. Regardless of what you wanted to call it, it was Inadvertent Instrument Flight conditions (IIMC). And I let the crew know. I was hoping someone else could see, we might avoid what was next – no such luck.

I started a climb to the emergency altitude of 2,200 feet, which would clear the 'antennae farm' to the north of the Fort Stewart restricted area and allow local Air Traffic Control (ATC) to pick us up on RADAR. We didn't have any problems landing back at Hunter Army Airfield. But we did have issues with the veteran pilots waiting for us in the hangar hallway. Nobody yelled, but they all had their arms crossed as we passed them on the way to the Operations office.

"What were you guys thinking?"

"Glad you guys are back safely; I hope you learned something."

Since Tim was in charge, he got a lecture about decision-making and judgment.

Within the hour, the weather improved to the point we figured we could still get the mission done. Nope – The same miserable results...

+++

Surviving stupid decisions is one of those things that make you feel invincible as a young aviator. Flying at the National Training Center in the California desert can ensure the 'superman complex' grows. One rotation at the NTC comes to mind; Our sister unit A Company, 2/159th Aviation Regiment, from Fort Bragg, North Carolina, sent two Chinooks and crews to join our two aircraft. We all got along great, but the competitive spirit was alive and well.

Who could be the most effective crew?

Cargo tonnage moved in a single day was an easy metric.

I showed up at the division support area to pick up my first lift of cargo. I was underwhelmed with the load. *Okay*, I thought, this just wasn't going to do. I didn't want to waste my time. The joke we made was that we were being asked to carry a strongly worded message in a paper bag. But I wanted my engines to strain, and the rotor blades to 'cone.'

I turned down the load and hovered over to the aircraft parking area to shut down. The Non-Commissioned Officer in Charge of the logistics area walked over to see what the problem was. "What's up, Chief?" He asked.

"That load's not big enough," I said.

He was confused. "Not big enough? I was trying to make things easy for you."

I looked around. "Does everything in the yard need to go somewhere?"

"It all needs to move," he told me.

I started picking things to carry. "Okay, let's put that pallet inside, that pallet too, and the green one as well. What's that weigh? About five thousand pounds?"

The Sergeant nodded.

I searched the freight yard for more cargo. "Alright then, let's add that tank transmission on the forward hook and that engine container over there on the aft hook."

The Sergeant was amazed. "Wow. That's about 8,000 pounds total. That'll be great," he said.

I pulled my performance planning card from my pocket, did some fuzzy math in my head, and pointed at one last piece of equipment.

"Add that generator over there to the center cargo hook."

"That's about a 10,000-pound load. How many flights will this take?" he wanted to know.

"One lift," I said. It didn't take the forklift operators long to place everything where I could get to every load. Of course, once they figured out what we could carry every lift was an impressive and worthwhile load. It wasn't long before our Alpha company brothers figured out what we were doing, and they joined in on the fun. At the end of the day, we'd set an unofficial NTC record of cargo delivered in a single rotation.

The next day was the same thing but without out using our Automatic Flight Control System. Without too much detail, the AFCS augments the Chinook's flight controls and handling qualities. It helps to hold headings, attitudes, speed, and bank angles. Pilot inputs are enhanced, and surges, turbulence, and bumps are dampened to reduce the pilot's workload, making a CH-47D a very forgiving helicopter to fly. Turning the system off meant the aircraft bucked a little, causing the pilot to stay very focused. Control inputs that the AFCS would typically make, now had to be made by the pilot along with his maneuvering inputs. That's a lot of description to say the Chinook is a lot tougher to fly without AFCS, and we were going to do it with several thousand pounds of cargo slung beneath us, at terrain flight altitudes, and we were taking off and landing in dust clouds. It couldn't get much more demanding or fatiguing.

All four crews started the day intending to last without their AFCS until we returned to base. I was proud that my crew was the only one to last the entire flight period. That day's experience was probably not prudent, but it would unknowingly save my life in early 2002 during a shootdown.

Sometimes you don't know which training will pay off...

+++

Time passed quickly in Savannah. Stephen and Andrew did well in school, and Linda thrived as a medical assistant for an allergy doctor. She loved her job and her co-workers, giving them hard work and a great attitude. Then, one day, she earned her keep with an unexpected situation at the doctor's office. A man in the waiting room passed out on the carpet. The receptionist froze; the wife didn't know what to do but shriek that her husband was dying.

Linda heard the commotion and started CPR while calmly instructing the receptionist to call an ambulance and simultaneously calming the horrified wife.

Linda's quick actions resuscitated the stricken man impressing the staff and doctor. I don't think she ever found another job as rewarding as working there in Savannah, Georgia.

+++

Life was going well. Our little family couldn't be happier. We lived near the beach, and our large group of friends gathered often. Everyone got along great, and we helped each other in any way possible. A move to a new apartment or menial jobs that needed extra hands were happily paid for with pizza and beer. We were close and trained hard. But occasionally, a premiere mission would drop in our laps. A Bahamas supply run was just the ticket. You'd think the senior pilots would take the trip, but no. None wanted to risk a long overwater journey beyond the sight of land. I couldn't wait. More experience for me.

The Bermuda Triangle is a place you read about but never think the stories are true. I might have to rethink that after a flight to the Bahamas...

My mission was to deliver replacement helicopter parts to a UH-60 Blackhawk unit in the southern islands. My copilot and dear friend, Mike Steele, occupied the right seat of our CH-47D as we departed from West Palm Beach, Florida, heading toward the Great Exumas. Our track mainly was over the open ocean, passing just to the south of Bimini. As per Army regulations, we were outfitted with appropriate overwater gear like rafts, personal flotation devices, and egress compressed air bottles. We trained to use that equipment but never thought we'd even come close to needing it…

Mike and I got an early start, hoping to enjoy as much time on the islands as possible. And we were looking forward to trading our cold, gray overcast weather for the sunny Caribbean. Our journey started worry-free as we headed out over the Atlantic, and thanks to a favorable wind, we passed Bimini cruising at over two hundred miles an hour. It was the last chunk of land we'd see until we came upon the Exuma chain. I adjusted our heading to compensate for the wind and coupled the heading select feature of the AFCS. Periodically, I verified my fuel consumption and recalculated reserve and burnout times. So far, so good… that is until about thirty minutes past our last sighted land. Then, a slight problem emerged – My Heading indicator differed from the standby compass by sixty degrees – SIXTY. Which indication was wrong?

The minor problem had significant implications. If the standby compass gave erroneous readings, I only had a minor inconvenience. But if the Heading Situation Indicator (HSI) was off, that would mean my aircraft, which was coupled to that gyro, would have traveled sixty degrees off-course at about 200 miles an hour, for at least thirty minutes. We were over the open ocean… Where was I?

Step one, figure out which compass was acting up. The standby compass was a time-tested liquid-filled ball with no electronics, just fluid, and a free-floating compass card. I could see no reason to doubt it. Consequently, the HSI received its input from a directional gyro that was reliable and ordinarily accurate. Next, I checked the HSI control panel on the overhead console. There, a tiny needle indicated gyro problems, which meant we'd been pulled off course.

I stared at my map – I could be anywhere in an area roughly the size of my open hand. I needed to make an educated guess where the nearest land might be, and I needed to do it soon. Unfortunately, we didn't have much fuel to play with, and if I guessed wrongly, we'd get to use the emergency overwater gear stowed neatly in the cargo compartment.

I tried the radio first to get a RADAR fix – nobody answered.

Even though we were far from land, I should still be able to talk to Flight Service, and if not, overflying airliners routinely respond. But none answered my calls. I resorted to old-school navigation, but the cloudy gray overcast kept me from using the sun to determine cardinal directions. No doubt about it, we were in a pinch. My transponder failed when I selected emergency mode. Nothing electronic was working; what the heck…

Would we end up as footnotes in the news as just another missing aircraft in the Triangle? I was no longer at the top of the food chain, so I wasn't about to quit and end up in the ocean.

I had to think...

Our non-directional beacon (NDB) was a nearly obsolete navigation aid, but like my standby compass, it was time-tested. I tuned two different NDBs, several hundred miles away. The tension was building as I completed a cross-fix. I estimated my position and decided to turn several degrees to the right – just an educated guess. Now, we just had to wait and see if land appeared. If it didn't, we were screwed.

The northern tip of the Great Exuma island chain came into view in about fifteen minutes. Mike banked further in their direction, and once we approached the shoreline, we followed it to the south. So, you'd think our little adventure was resolved, but now the fuel gauge needle and quantity indicator began to spin, making it impossible to determine how much gas remained in the tanks. So now I'd have to consider a precautionary landing in the middle of nowhere, well short of our destination. But, at least it would be overland.

Maybe I should push on, relying on my last fuel burnout calculation; by the way, I was never very good with math...

We made it this far. Why quit now?

When our tires touched the destination runway, the fuel gauge stopped spinning, showing that we had about eight hundred pounds of fuel in the main tanks, the equivalent of about twenty minutes' worth of flight remaining.

Needless to say, the beers went down easy that night – probably not the last toast to cheating death.

Chapter 5

Instructing at Fort Rucker (1993–1995)

A tremendous opportunity fell into my lap. The Army asked me if I wanted to become a CH-47 Instructor Pilot. Becoming an IP was a dream of mine since flight school. Now I had to convince Linda that we wanted to go to rural Fort Rucker, Alabama – she was receptive.

Two things appealed to her: First, I wouldn't deploy at all – no TDY trips and overseas deployments. The second selling point for her was that the beaches in Panama City and Destin were only an hour away; she loved everything about going to the waterfront. So, this would be an excellent assignment and an effective emotional reset after our recent year-long separation while I was in Korea.

Within weeks Linda rolled into Enterprise and found a rental house outside the gates of Fort Rucker. The location was great; my drive to work was a short twenty minutes, and the property was fun for my sons.

Our home was on the side of a hill – big enough for them to swoop down the slope in their little red wagon. The only way to stop hitting the trees in the wooded area below was to bail out just before impact. I suppose it would be like 'trapping' the three-wire on an aircraft carrier. Maybe that's where Stephen got his calling to join Naval Aviation. Unfortunately, his little brother was usually the victim of a late escape, meaning Stephen would hang in till the last second before jumping. Andrew, situated in the front of the wagon, couldn't egress until his brother cleared the way. Guess who plowed into the trees for a sudden stop more than once...

Life was going to be fabulous – I just had to get past my instructor, who did not like me.

The Instructor Pilot course was not easy for me. My 'IP,' CW4 Dave Martini, thought I was too junior to work at the Cargo branch. And he made me miserable, trying to force me to quit – he came close.

The very first part of the course is MOI, which stands for Method of Instruction. This is where the IP tells a student how to conduct a maneuver while simultaneously doing it. For example, simply picking the helicopter off the ground to a ten-foot hover:

"With the before takeoff check complete, release the brakes and smoothly increase thrust so that all four landing gear leave the ground at the same time. Maintain your position over the ground with the cyclic and heading with pedals. Continue up to an altitude of ten feet – aft gear height, or roughly fourteen to fifteen feet on the radar altimeter." Every maneuver sounded something like that. Slopes, landings, takeoff, and emergency procedures.

As you learn to speak and fly at the same time, your flying goes to hell until it becomes second nature. In the meantime, your altitude gets away from you, or airspeed slips out of parameters, and I was no exception. Dave was all over me; constantly berating me. He said I wasn't capable, and I started to believe him – I wanted to quit.

By the time Christmas break rolled around, I was convinced I sucked and couldn't instruct. And I was thinking of resigning from the class. Thank God for the time off; otherwise, I'd have failed the course. The two weeks away from purely negative remarks allowed me to have fun with my kids and remember that I wasn't a loser after all. My batteries were recharged, and by the time I returned to school, I was a different man. I was ready to fight.

Dave and I started my first flight back with a simulated Emergency Procedure on the way to the takeoff pad. No problem, I reacted quickly and professionally. He left me alone for most of the flight and observed my maneuvers. I was nailing it that day, enough that he seemed content to just watch me. Finally, the flight period was nearing its end, and I felt ready to test my newfound confidence...

So, I casually slipped my hand to the center console while Dave was flying and discreetly flipped the number-one engine emergency trim switch to manual – he hadn't noticed. Then, I pressed the rocker switch with my finger, causing the number one engine torque to decrease rapidly, and a corresponding increase in the number two engine to pick up the rotor load. The L712 turbine engines were powerful but not strong enough to compensate without pilot intervention – I caught him off guard.

Dave's startled expression was priceless.

I waited for his response as he diagnosed the problem. He quickly figured what I'd done. And a mean-spirited smile spread across his face as he purposely reacted incorrectly.

But I was ready. My hand was in a position to block incorrect control inputs. Then I calmly explained how to respond to a 'low side,' and I recovered the engine, ending the EP.

He never messed with me again.

I guess he just wanted to make sure I could deal with assholes like him without getting flustered. I was going to make it, no doubt about it.

+++

Teaching new aviators how to fly a Chinook was fun at first. My first four students were enjoyable to teach and receptive to my instructional style. And I enjoyed every minute with them, whether flying or engaging in 'table talk.' *I could do this forever*, I thought. *Linda was doing well, and my kids couldn't be better.* Then came the older pilots from the National Guard…

Each guard unit flies a particular airframe suited for its mission. The CH-54 Sky Crane had reached its end of life and was being retired. Of course, the only suitable replacement was the CH-47D Chinook. The pilots from the National Guard were much more senior than me, with far greater experience, and they weren't the least bit interested in operating a Chinook. Nor did they want to learn from me…

My students complained about their unit changing aircraft as if I had something to do with their plight. These guys got through the Aircraft Qualification Course (AQC), not because they wanted to, but because they had to. I hated every minute I spent with these guys. I needed to make a change, or I'd go crazy. *Maybe flying nights was the answer.*

I'd been a Night Vision Goggle Unit trainer in Savannah and Korea. If I could switch from mornings to the night section, I'd at least enjoy the schedule. So, I lobbied our Standardization Instructor Pilot (SIP) to make the switch. I couldn't have been luckier. CW5 Jake Stevens, one of my mentors, had just arrived from Korea and took the SIP job, making him the Chief Pilot. And thanks to him, I was assigned a new desk in the night section as soon as I finished my current set of students.

What a change. I loved flying in the dark. The schedule during the summer was fantastic. I didn't have to report until 6:00 PM (18:00), allowing me to spend the day at the pool with my sons. The Officers' Club pool opened around 09:00, and the boys swam while I napped on the lounge chair nearby – I know, lousy parent.

I appreciated the lifeguard on duty. I don't know how many times they may have saved my kids from drowning, but they're still around. So, get off my back.

Life at Rucker was slow and easy. I suppose it couldn't get any better, but I was still feeling unfulfilled – bored, really. Schoolhouse instruction was something that I probably would have enjoyed if I'd had more time in a field unit – that opportunity was about to present itself…

+++

The Spring of 1995 was to be the beginning of an incredible life-changing journey. I needed to drive from Fort Rucker to Hunter Army Airfield in Savannah, Georgia, to help the tenants of my rental property with the air conditioning.

The six-hour drive started with a rainy day in Enterprise, but as I crossed the Chattahoochee River into Georgia, the clouds parted as if on cue. I felt like God was reminding me there were better times ahead. Memories of the good times we had in Savannah popped up as I drove along. And when I pulled up in front of my home, a flood of emotions poured over me. I was glad to be out of this house, even though I loved it. But opportunity knocks where you least expect it…

After fixing the renter's air conditioning, I went to the Post Exchange on Hunter Airfield; and ran into a friend from my time in the 2/159th. He'd moved next door on the flight line and joined the 160th Special Operations Regiment. There were two Chinook Battalions in the 160th, one in Savannah and one at Fort Campbell, Kentucky. I'd thought about trying to join them several times in my career but didn't think I was good enough. Pilots that I considered better than I got turned down. Quite frankly, I was scared of rejection. My friend let me tour one of their MH–47D AWC helicopters. The AWC, or Adverse Weather Cockpit, had an air refueling probe, a sophisticated navigation system and was armed with M-134 Miniguns. I didn't think I'd be impressed, but I was.

I needed to investigate the requirements to join as soon as I got back to Rucker, and most importantly, I'd have to get the whole idea past Linda.

+++

A brief history lesson: April 1980, Operation Eagle Claw failed miserably. The move to rescue the American hostages held by Iranian revolutionaries led to the creation of a Joint Special Operations Task Force. Shortcomings in the failed mission would be addressed before the second attempt, known as Operation Honey Badger, kicked off. A dedicated helicopter force needed to be created. This paragraph from the 160th SOAR's website describes the beginning:

> The unit originally formed from attachments of the 101st Airborne Division. It immediately entered into a period of intensive night flying, quickly becoming the Army's premier night fighting aviation force and the Army's only Special Operations Aviation force. Task Force 160 was officially recognized as a unit on 16 October 1981, when it was designated the 160th Aviation Battalion. Since that time, the 160th has become known as the "Night Stalkers" because of its capability to strike undetected during the hours of darkness and its impeccable performance around the world.

The unit was created along with ground and communication elements, to name a few, then prepared to rescue the hostages. But Iran released their captives as soon as President Ronald Reagan took office from President Carter, rendering the need for a rescue unnecessary. The Department of Defense realized the unit needed to stay together for potential future operations.

For the most part, the 160th has been cloaked in secrecy since its inception. Some high-profile events forced them into the light. Probably the most infamous incident was the Blackhawk Down situation in Somalia.

These soldiers were fierce, dedicated, and professional – I wanted to be one...

Chapter 6

Assessment for the 160th
7 Years before 9/11

Though life at Fort Rucker was quite good, I couldn't take the overly laid-back lifestyle. I needed something more. *I should be happy. Right?* You'd think so. After eight months serving in Operations Desert Shield and Storm and a year away from home in Korea, my wife deserved the break Rucker offered – I knew it and so did she.

Linda and I married young. We were only twenty years old when we tied the knot, and the first of our two sons was on the way within a year. Ten years had passed since we first laid eyes on each other in an El Paso dance club. As I think back to those days, we were so naive to the ways of the world. Eighteen-year-old Linda May VanAssen joined the Army in 1982 to escape Los Angeles. She'd been in and out of foster homes because of abusive and dysfunctional parents. The military was a noble way to escape and make a positive change.

She wasn't the strongest or fastest recruit, but she had heart, her eye-hand coordination was something to boast about, and she could shoot. Linda achieved an expert rifle badge, though shooting would never be a big part of her career path as a medic.

After training in San Antonio, she ended up at William Beaumont Army Medical Center in El Paso, Texas, which is the city where we'd eventually meet and marry. Linda was young and pretty. She cleaned up nicely and wore a flattering white nurse uniform to work, which drew the attention of the young doctors. Beaumont hospital, you see, was a training unit; the young officers were mostly single and on the prowl for a pretty enlisted girl. Who wasn't? I know I was.

+++

I arrived a Biggs Army Airfield via a tour of duty in the Republic of Korea. My time in the ROK lasted a year and was my first duty assignment. I, like Linda, joined the Army immediately following high school. Our reasons for enlisting were drastically different. She was escaping, and I wanted adventure.

Growing up in the small coastal city of Portsmouth, New Hampshire was a blast. Back when I was young, we had no cell phones, computers, or cable TV, so my friends and I were always looking for something to do, to include minor mischief. We loved a good chase, but skiing, cycling, and camping were high on the list of fun. Other than that, we ran track and cross country.

The same Army recruiting slogan of "be all that you can be" that enticed Linda grabbed me too.

Regardless of how we met all those years ago, one thing was for sure – we enjoyed being together, we loved each other, and adored our sons, Stephen and Andrew. Now, I sat at the kitchen table making the case to join the 160th. I knew Linda wanted to stay at Rucker, but like many men have done throughout history, I put my desires for adventure ahead of her wish for domestic bliss.

I ran my right hand nervously back and forth across the smooth oak tabletop. Each imperfection in the surface provided a slight distraction. Even though I knew she'd rather not move, I kept up the pressure and the 'puppy dog eyes.' I could see she was considering my request. She was wavering.

Yes! She said yes.

She was supportive and maybe even a little curious about life at Fort Campbell, Kentucky. The next day I finished the application to try out for the Army's only Special Operations Aviation Regiment (SOAR) and mailed it to their recruiter before Linda could change her mind.

Within a week, I got a call back. They wanted me to come to Fort Campbell in a month for Assessment Week; I thought it would be at least six months, maybe even a year. My company commander wouldn't be happy, neither would Linda. *"Oh well,"* I thought, *"no worries, I won't get accepted anyway, but it'll be fun trying."*

+++

Now I needed to prepare for the grueling week of tests and activities. Lucky for me, I was on a night schedule, ideal for training. Each morning I went for a two or four-mile run, then took my kids to the Officers' Club pool to practice swimming. I heard the swim test was especially grueling, especially the underwater portion. I practiced treading water with no hands and then without using my feet.

My role as an instructor pilot kept me in the books, so technical aviation questions shouldn't be a problem. I was nervous, but confident and was as ready as I could be for the experience that lay ahead. So, I headed to Kentucky for my tryout.

Nashville airport had a simple layout and was easy to navigate, making it quick to grab my bags and a rental car. The Sunday afternoon drive to Fort Campbell took only forty-five minutes. I found my way to the Night Stalker recruiting office to sign in and receive my instructions for the week. The schedule of events packed a lot into five days.

Bright and early Monday, I had to be at the running track for a standard Army PT test. My first quandary, believe it or not, was what to wear. There were indications that maybe civilian workout clothes were more appropriate than Army 'PTs.' "The heck with it," I thought. If they didn't want me because of my choice of clothing, then I didn't want to be there. Though, I must admit, I hedged my bet and brought along my Army clothing. Just in case.

The grader wouldn't tell me how much time remained during the three events and refused to count my repetitions out loud, which added some stress. I completed the push-ups, sit-ups, and a two-mile run with no problems. After the PT test, we drove to the "Cav Country" pool for the swim test. I considered myself a strong swimmer. But wearing a flight uniform combat boots, helmet, and flight vest made things harder. I was feeling great until the underwater swim. No one would confirm how far we had to go, and I struggled as my flight helmet buoyed me to the surface. I climbed out of the pool, unsure if I'd gone far enough.

I felt like I failed.

Oh, but there was another chance – the grader strolled up from behind and whispered. "Sir, you are having fun?"

I lied. "Yes, I am."

"Did you get to do the underwater swim twice?"

Twice? How the heck could I do that more than once? "No."

"Sir, no problem. Get back in line for your second run."

I must not have gone far enough. My heart was racing, I was still out of breath from my first attempt; there was no way I was going to make it. I approached the edge of the pool and waited for the signal to enter the water.

A whistle sounded, and I stepped out into the cold water.

I stroked harder than before – I was hungry for air, but I couldn't quit. I was going to push until I blacked out. At least I could say I gave it everything I had.

Someone tapped my helmet. I'd made it all the way to the other end.

I showered, slipped on a dry uniform, and headed to the testing station where I had the pleasure of taking two different psych questionnaires; one had six hundred questions, and the other, three hundred. My pencil was dull, and I was tired of filling in bubbles. And as I flipped over the last page, an evaluator tossed a general-aviation knowledge test on to my table. The fifty-question test asked specifics about threat-weapons systems, general FAA facts, and aeromedical questions regarding fatigue, physiology, and hypoxia. Then I was whisked to my psychologist interview – I was most afraid of this.

One reason Fort Rucker had been such a good deal for Linda and me, was because of a problem that reared its ugly head during my previous assignment to Korea.

The doctor wanted to know what happened.

"Our geographic separation laid bare Linda's little secret – depression."

He looked up from his pad of paper, adjusting his eyeglasses on to the bridge of his nose. "Okay," he said. Then quietly stared at me – no – through me.

I started to sweat but mustered the courage to reveal our issue. "As soon as I left the States, Linda withdrew from our friends and ignored invitations for parties, barbeques, and other social events. She wouldn't leave the house, refusing to socialize."

I was blissfully unaware of her self-imposed isolation, and I had no reason to believe there was a problem.

"So how did you find out her sadness was beyond self-recovery?" he asked.

"She called me in the middle of the night." I paused for a second as I searched for the words I needed. "Linda woke me to say she was sorry. She said she was going to kill herself. I remember shaking the cobwebs of sleep away as I tried to clarify what she'd said."

I noticed the doctor scribbling his notes – he seemed to write a novel.

"She sounded drunk or drugged as she explained how much of a failure she was. Failure was something she couldn't abide – another unwanted gift from her abusive mother.

What the hell was I to do? It was 2:00 AM, and I was over 7,000 miles away in Korea. I tried to talk her out of suicide, but I was too late. She'd already taken pills and overdosed. As I saw it, I had two choices. The first was to stay on the phone so she wouldn't die alone. The second, and more-like-me option, was to let her know I loved her and hung up. Then I called the Savannah police department through the international operator. Police officers entered our home and saved her life."

"And she was okay?" he asked.

"Yes... well, physically. After retrieving Linda from the hospital, we found a therapist to help us through our experience. Seven years we'd been together... this behavior was new. Linda's depression and fragile emotional state were now exposed. She got better quick; her rebound was immediate." I still wondered if she was fixed or just re-masked. The Army had seen this kind of thing before and offered me a compassionate reassignment. I didn't have to go back to Korea and could stay in Savannah, assigned with my old unit. But Linda would have none of it. Once she recharged mentally, I had to go back.

"I couldn't believe her. She really thought I could go back to the other side of the world and function. I knew I would worry about her always. We disagreed on how to proceed and recover. Her desire to toughen up and get through our separation was strong. She insisted that I would be responsible for her failure if I stayed in the States. In her mind, I had to go back for her to succeed. This simple approach to controlling me worked time-and-again throughout our twenty-six years together."

I must have stopped talking for too long and the 'Shrink' asked me why I thought it was okay to believe her.

I raised my water bottle but didn't drink as I tried to think of an answer. I needed one that he would accept, but I wasn't even sure how I felt. "Well,"

I said. "After consulting with her psychologist, I was convinced against my better judgment to let Linda try to work through her issues.

"So, you went back?"

"Yes, I did. I went back even though I had my doubts. And she made it. Not only did she not have any more meltdowns while I was away in Korea, but she came back stronger than ever.

"Either she was better, or she was hiding her feelings. To me, it didn't matter – I had my wife and best friend back."

He kept writing.

I was open and forthright; they needed to see me, warts and all. By the end of my session, I'd bared my soul. And I felt that if anything was going to torpedo my chances, this was it.

+++

About an hour later, I received my navigation target. And because I was a Chinook pilot, I would fly in the MH-47E instead of an MH-6 'little bird.' My flight evaluator introduced himself and handed me a briefcase full of aviation publications, maps, and charts. I had until the next night to plan a one and a half to two-hour flight to a small unlit grass airfield in Kentucky.

The hotel I chose was convenient for assessment but was a total dump. I ignored the nasty surroundings and got down to business planning my route. As the night went on, the map blurred. Fatigue set in. I needed sleep. Three hours of sleep wasn't enough, but I woke up excited and a little nervous. I grabbed a fast-food breakfast and headed to meet with my evaluator. He began the session with an 'oral' evaluation. My experience as an instructor pilot made this part easy.

The MH-47E was an impressive machine. It had double the fuel capacity of the Delta models I was used to flying. The air refueling probe was intimidating at first, but eventually I got used to seeing it. The 'wow factor' was through the roof when we powered up the APU, and the instrumentation came to life. All the flight information was displayed on four Multi-Function displays (MFDs) on the instrument panel. I suddenly felt like my 47D was a toy compared to the machine I was about to fly.

We started out with standard check ride items.

The evaluator knew I was an IP, so he asked me to demonstrate my Method of Instruction (MOI). So, I started describing everything I was doing as I picked the helicopter off the ground to a hover:

"With the Before Takeoff Check complete, release the brakes and smoothly increase thrust allowing the LCTs to retract. All four landing gear should leave the ground at the same time. Maintain position over the ground with the cyclic and heading with pedals. Continue up to an altitude of ten feet aft-gear height, or roughly fourteen to fifteen feet on the radar altimeter."

Much like my IP evaluation at Rucker, years before, he made me do the same routine for every maneuver – slopes, landings, takeoffs, and emergency procedures. I flew a couple of traffic patterns, followed by a simulated engine failure and subsequent roll-on landing, two-wheel taxi, and AFCS-off-flight. And once it was dark enough, we departed with only a clock, compass, and map as my tools. Along the way, my evaluator realized that my route and target were already engulfed by thunderstorms and asked for my map. He folded and unfolded it as he searched for a reasonable substitute.

He found one, told me where to go, and asked for my estimated time of arrival.

I ran some 'fuzzy' math in my head and told him to turn along a path that I thought would ensure my success. I didn't compensate for the unexpected storm wind, and I blew right past my navigation target. I missed it by several miles. I couldn't place my location. *Oh Crap*, I thought. I started to rotate my map like a steering wheel to match the terrain, roads, and lit antennas, but it was not good – I was lost.

The ride was over; time to head back to base.

As we shut down the helicopter, he offered me the opportunity to fly the next night to try again. I'd be able to use my planned route.

I was bummed that I got lost, but I had nothing left to show. They either saw potential in me, or they didn't. Heck, the family situation was probably going to be the nail in the coffin, anyway.

I still had to explain how a Chinook flew by teaching a class on tandem rotor attitude and heading control. So, I scribbled some aerodynamic figures on a sheet of poster paper and headed for what was probably the toughest portion of the assessment week – the board.

I'd sit in front of my flight evaluator, the psychologist, the personnel officer, the recruiter, and the regiment commander, a job interview on steroids.

I sat in my dress uniform while the panel of officers grilled me on the results of my assessment. They were stern and aggressive, trying to get me to crack a sweat, but I was only dreading questions about Linda's suicide attempt. They fired question after question. But no matter how mean or tricky, I was relieved that my personal life wasn't under the scrutiny I expected. And at the end of my grilling, I was accepted.

Months later, Linda and I packed our possessions and moved to Tennessee for a new adventure.

Chapter 7

Desert Fox and the Gorst Games (1998-1999)
3 Years before 9/11

Years passed, and my time with the 160th was enjoyable and rewarding. Linda and I were having the time of our lives. Temporary Duty Assignments, known as TDY, were frequent and fun for me. We often went to Virginia Beach for ship landings. The mountains of Colorado were like a second home. And the desert – well, we never seemed to get enough of sand and dust. Everywhere we went we refueled in the air from MC-130 tankers to maintain our proficiency in Helicopter Aerial Refueling (HAR). The flying and training were second to none; days and weeks on the road help you get to know the guys in the unit. We spent long hours in planning cells and the cockpit. The times we didn't fly or crunch numbers, we spent talking about our families. Guys shared everything about themselves, their experiences, their likes and dislikes. It's also when you found out how people think, what their wife is like, how their kids behave, and occasionally how they behave when drinking. Cell phones weren't in widespread use at the time, so you got to share phone time in a hotel with your roommate. Happy times and spousal fights – nothing was secret.

The unit did business a certain way. The tribal elders ensured we stuck with time-tested procedures. Things had been done this way since the inception of our unit. What I didn't know, though, was that life as a Night Stalker was about to ratchet up a notch.

Military life is cyclical in nature. It starts with Basic Training, which transforms a civilian into a soldier; then, Advance Individual Training builds on those skills. For example, infantrymen learn more about combat, medics learn more advanced treatment techniques, mechanics learn their trade, and pilots learn to fly. None of these basic courses or schools entirely prepares someone for war. Only soldiers who have served in combat have the experience to know what training to emphasize or prioritize. Unfortunately, in a peacetime military, those lessons and opinions are generally relegated to war stories over a beer. Some crusty old warrant officer or non-commissioned officer can share a story of how things were done in their conflict. The stories usually begin with, "There I was…".

I'm going to respectfully describe Captain Joe Gorst as an anomaly, even in the Special Operations Community. We used to joke that the expression, "In case of fire, break glass," needed to be modified with Joe: "In case of war, break glass." He was a warrior through-and-through. He graduated from Green Platoon and came to B Company, 2-160th SOAR, sometime around the mid-to-late 90s. Once an enlisted Ranger and SOF operator, he decided to try his hand at flying. Nobody, including him, had any idea what kind of positive mark he'd leave on the organization, not as a pilot, but as a leader and trainer.

Upon his arrival, he was treated no differently than any other young captain. The 160th is a warrant-officer-centric organization. The colonels and majors give guidance and missions to the regiment flight leads and senior NCOs who make things happen. A new platoon leader, like Joe, is often dismissed until he proves himself capable of fitting in. The existing structure of the 160th was established in the early 1980s and is still mostly intact from those formative years. And Joe wasn't about fitting in. He'd become a Night Stalker to meld his SOF experience with the flight skills, equipment, and attitude of our aircrews. He hoped to take a group of highly sought-after aviators and make them, meaning us, better.

Late 1998, he was about to get his wish. Saddam Hussein, the President of Iraq, was quarreling with the United Nations regarding the implementation and monitoring of resolutions passed after the 1991 Gulf War. Our Battalion deployed with the Air Force's Special Operations Helicopter unit, the 20th SOS. Their four MH-53s and our four MH-47E Chinooks made up the Rotary-wing component of a Combined Joint Special Operations Task Force based out of Ali Al Salem airport in Kuwait. Both models of aircraft were capable of air refueling and were equipped with a suite of specialized radar jammers allowing penetration of Iraqi air defenses.

To extend our fuel range, we were joined by three MC-130 Talon aerial refueling tankers. Our air package was robust for high-risk Personnel Recovery Operations. The ground force consisted of members of the 5th Special Forces group and the Australian SAS. If coalition aircraft were shot down during the bombing campaign, we'd be called upon to retrieve the crew, no matter the threat.

Saddam backed down within days, and the offensive operation was curtailed and returned to the enforcement of United Nations No-fly zones. Iraq capitulated, so most of the troops and equipment that had been brought to bear left the region. Our task force remained in place just in case Saddam reneged.

Instead of just sitting still, our small task force was re-designated to support Operation Southern Watch with Personnel Recovery (PR) coverage. PR, by its nature, is exciting when it happens but is boring while you wait for some poor sap to get into trouble. So, instead of just sitting around, we found something to do until called into action – Bring on the 'Gorst Games.'

+++

Practicing for conflict and war was an everyday thing for Gorst. No days off – his idea of a non-workday was to keep a lighter-than-normal schedule. He figured that living and working with such a precious commodity as MC-130 crews was a chance not to be wasted. Joe had us fly virtually every day, and if we were in the air, we were 'plugging.' Helicopter Aerial Refueling (HAR) was a maneuver that required practice to stay proficient, and we were getting it. Whether or not we needed to take fuel, we hit the tanker, made a couple of contacts, then went about our business.

Target practice and shooting were next on Joe's list of essential things to do.

Joe's history as a SOF Operator came in handy as he worked with us to refine our shooting skills. He had us at the rifle range, any day we couldn't fly, and sometimes in addition to flying. One of the benefits of training in Kuwait was there were plenty of open areas to shoot. Sometimes we'd take off from Ali Al Salem airbase, hit a tanker followed by a pass or two at Udari aerial gunnery range, then we'd land in the middle of nowhere to simulate a shootdown.

Shootdown scenarios vary. An aircraft might not be able to fly for any number of reasons. How you end up on the ground makes all the difference in your actions. Crashes, hard landings, or set downs to prevent loss of life have one thing in common – you're no longer flying and on the ground. Whether you are in enemy territory or under direct fire or not, set your immediate priorities for survival. Each training iteration, or 'Gorst Game,' as Joe called them, was different. He tried to expose us to every situation he could reasonably imagine happening.

He made sure our land navigation skills and first aid skills were tight. Everything we did in training ended with some type of shooting event. Joe taught us techniques for breaking contact with the enemy. And everything we did was 'live fire.' I'm kind of surprised we didn't shoot each other. I've got to admit, our training was fun, and it helped pass the time.

+++

The biggest challenge to flying in a desert is landing a helicopter. The dust cloud can make a routine landing "sporty." CW4 Chuck Grant, our 2nd Battalion Standardization Instructor Pilot (SIP), joined us in Kuwait two months into our deployment with a plan. He'd developed a procedure that allowed MH-47Es to land using hover symbology in a safe and repeatable technique. He named three methods as 'Alpha,' 'Bravo,' and 'Charlie' – each had their purpose. The Charlie was pretty much the same as any old dust landing. Stay ahead of the cloud, then touch down about twenty miles per hour. But upon reaching the ground, the pilot would focus on keeping the hover page velocity vector straight. There wasn't much use for that method once you see the other two.

The Alpha was the easiest, but slowest to perform. The pilot came to an out of ground effect hover above the dust cloud. As soon as the helicopter was stable and not drifting, the pilot on the controls would announce to his crew that he was inside, focusing on his MFD. The multi-function display became his virtual world. If the little circle stayed over the video's center crosshair, the aircraft was not drifting. The pilot would lower the thrust to achieve a three hundred-foot per minute descent until he landed. The only downsides to this maneuver was that it was harder to land multiple aircraft in a small area. It was deliberate and slow, possibly exposing an aircrew to enemy fire.

The Bravo was a much more coordinated approach. The pilot chooses a slightly steeper angle than a standard approach and begins to descend and decelerate like a standard approach to the ground. One of the goals is to get lined up with the landing direction as soon as possible, then continue decelerating and descending on the desired glide path. Once the altitude hits 80 feet above the ground, the ground speed should be roughly half. So, 80 feet and 40 knots, 40 feet and 20 knots, 20 feet, and 10 knots, and just before touchdown, 10 feet, and 5 knots. Theoretically, the helicopter should be barely moving forward as it touches the ground. It works well most of the time.

I say most of the time because repeatability was difficult: Out of every ten 'Bravo' dust approaches, three would be great – you almost didn't know you were on the ground. Five would be okay, but nothing to write home about – they could have been better but could also have been much worse. Then there's the two that sucked; maybe the pilot misjudged the angle or didn't correctly bleed off excessive speed before hitting the ground – your teeth were rattled, and you thanked God that you still had your landing gear.

Our time in Kuwait allowed us to practice and refine the procedures. These techniques made all the difference several years later in TF Dagger. We didn't damage any helicopters in our entire seven-month deployment. We had plenty of opportunities to 'clean' the landing gear off the bottoms of our Chinooks, a feat that other units couldn't claim.

+++

After redeploying back to the States, we had opportunities to try the dust landing techniques in the snow and mountains of Colorado and New Mexico with significant results. Then Saddam repeated his actions from the year before, requiring us to deploy again. Without realizing it, we were immersed in a desert training program that was unmatched by any other. And our successes in the early days of Afghanistan especially the 'Horse Soldiers' infil and Tora Bora, can be directly attributed to these Desert Thunder/Desert Fox deployments.

Chapter 8

The 'Bravo Project' and 'Gorst Games' – Phase two (2000-2001)
1 Year before 9/11

After returning from Kuwait, Joe Gorst was out of my hair for a while when he was reassigned as a platoon leader in A Co 2-160th. He didn't want to go, but it was necessary for his career progression – ironic, because Joe didn't care about moving up. He just wanted the 160th to be perfect, at least in the mold that he saw it. He didn't stand much of a chance of changing minds in his new unit. The rivalry between Alpha Company and Bravo Company was fierce at the time, so, when Joe tried to express his unconventional ways, they were viewed as B Co views; he was rebuffed and told to sit in the corner until he was told what to do. He kept his mouth shut, biding his time until he had an opportunity to command – that's when he'd make his changes. No one knew it, but Gorst's positive influence would be felt for years...

+++

Joe took command of B Company 2-160th at Fort Campbell, Kentucky, just as our eleven-ship company was shrinking to six. Both Companies in Second Battalion were giving up aircraft and personnel to form E Company 160th SOAR. The newly formed Echo Company would take six aircraft and deploy them to Korea. The new Asia-based unit would service the Pacific region, such as Thailand, Japan, the Philippines, and of course, their home base, Korea.

Alpha Company had to remain at full strength to support SOCOM Crisis response, which left Bravo Company with only six helicopters, and five were in phased maintenance. For a short time, we had one aircraft to fly until the others had their phased reset. Lucky for us, one of the five was about to return to service, giving us two to fly. With more than one aircraft, we could train and practice multi-ship flights and, of course, downed aircraft drills. We hated the shoot down scenarios. Joe and his henchman aka operations officer, CW5 Gil Gordon, could dream up the most miserable settings for our training. I spent a lot of time walking in the woods or evading in an urban environment. Was I a pilot or a 'Ground guy?'

I often grumbled to fellow Flight Lead Arlo Standish, and our First Sergeant, Dave Garrity. We needed to bring the unit's focus back to flying.

I thought hard about how to sway or steer Joe in a direction we wanted to go. Then it hit me – I had a plan but needed Joe to buy in; so, I went to his office to present my idea.

Our burly commander sat behind his desk, wondering why I was bugging him.

"Sir, I need to bend your ear for a minute."

"Come on in, Al."

His deep southern drawl could be intimidating. I was a bit nervous as I stepped in front of his desk. "Sir, we need a new mission." I paused for effect...

"Okay...?" He said.

"Look, we had eleven aircraft now we have five."

Joe was already closing his mind; I could see it in his face.

"Our Company is too small to be relied on to keep the Middle East as our Area of Responsibility (AOR); Third Battalion is picking up that role. And we'll never get a C-5 to take us overseas for training. Heck, even Alpha Company can't get invited to the overseas Joint Readiness Exercises. So, forget us going anywhere interesting... unless..."

I had Joe's attention. "We need to shift our mission-set to Central and South America. Let's offer ourselves up for supporting 7th Group. We could conduct counter-drug or counter-insurgency operations. Those guys never get any Helo support except from D 160th, and there aren't enough of them for quality support." I could see the wheels turning.

"We'd be able to self-deploy without any need for air force support. We could call this program the Bravo Project." I spoke some more about how and why we could make this happen, and it looked like I had him.

It turns out I hadn't made my case. "Al, get out of my office. That's the stupidest thing I've ever heard." He gestured toward his door with a flip of his hand. "We've got better things to do. Nice try but leave it up to me to figure out what direction we'll take."

So, just like that, he unceremoniously threw me out of his office. I was pretty bummed. I figured I must have misjudged Joe's intentions. We were fucked. He was just going to keep pushing us to become Ground Force wannabes.

The following morning Joe called a company meeting. We gathered around the planning table, and all eyes were upon him. He addressed us with his southern drawl. "Gentlemen, I'm sure you guys have realized we don't have much of a mission since giving up our other helicopters to Echo Company, but I have a plan." He paused long enough for us to look around at each other curiously.

He continued to lay out his thoughts for The Bravo Project. I couldn't believe my ears. He changed his mind overnight. By the way, to this day, he and I dispute who coined that name. It doesn't really matter, what we did next was his method to execute my idea. 'Gorst Games' went into high gear and now included air-related adventures. Somehow, Joe got permission from our Battalion Commander, LTC Jake Brass, to carry weapons on every flight. Not only did we carry our rifles and pistols, but we mounted our M-134 Miniguns with blanks. Now we had to figure in test fires to all our timelines. Familiarity with our weapons would be essential. Especially if we ended up in the mountains and jungles of South America.

+++

CW5 Don Tabron and I flew out to Fort Bragg, North Carolina, to speak with 7th Group representatives in person. We were making a sales pitch for our services – they didn't even know they wanted us. But once we told them what we could do and wanted to do, they were onboard. Their S-3, which is the section that plans operations, instructed us on what paperwork to send them. They'd include us in the next Ops Cycle in the Terms of Reference with the US Southern Command, SOCSOUTH. Don and I were ecstatic. It didn't take much to get their buy-in.

We brought the good news back to our headquarters at Fort Campbell. But our Operations officer looked like he'd just bitten a lemon when we gave him the details of our trip.

"No," he said. "No, you're not going to South America. That's not your AOR." I was confused. The S-3 approved of our trip and knew our intentions. "Sir, you knew what we were up to. There should be no surprise," I said.

"Yes, but I didn't think you'd be successful."

Again, I was surprised. "My job as a Flight Lead is to deploy worldwide at a moment's notice. I'm supposed to be able to convince any ground force that they need us, then educate them into how best to utilize us."

He apologized and gave us a compromise. "Okay. I'll tell you what. I'll permit you to go to Central America first since there is already a Chinook presence in Honduras. If that deployment goes well, we can talk about South America." I brought the news back to the Commander. Joe was happy with the compromise. He continued to think up scenarios that we could practice. Some of his ideas from years past were now coming out. But this time, he was in charge, so he couldn't be told to shut up and sit down. Our procedures were evolving with our equipment. Instead of relying on the good checkpoints of basic navigation, backed up with GPS or Inertial Navigation, we used the latter as our primary method; this was sacrilege in our Regiment. We'd use points-in-space as turning points adjacent to prominent terrain or other features customarily used for air navigation.

Our formations would be looser and slightly extended to ensure our Aircraft Survivability Equipment wouldn't interfere with the rest of the flight. Usually, we'd fly tight and disciplined, but this style was far more functional than pretty. Joe always had a motive to make us respond to contingencies. Maybe an aircraft wouldn't show up at a rendezvous point while the flight was short of fuel or time. Do you go back along the route and look for a missing aircraft, do you wait longer, or do you break radio silence? All possibilities were explored. Sometimes Joe would tell a pilot-in-command in private, what to do or not to do.

"Okay, Arlo, after the flight splits, don't respond to any radio calls. I want you to go directly to our destination and go to our hotel."

The rest of the flight would be unaware that we'd be missing an aircraft until we attempted to rejoin. Other times, Joe wouldn't send you forward, he'd pass you coordinates for a landing area where he wanted you to set down – you'd been notionally shot down.

Once on the ground, you'd be met by Joe's henchman, CW5 Gil Gordon, with an envelope of instructions. It might include sterilizing the helicopter to abandon it, followed by evasion instructions. I hated being on the ground, though later during Operation Anaconda, I'd find this training useful.

+++

Not only did we tweak our flying techniques, but we re-evaluated what we considered threats to our aircraft. We'd always been wary of missiles, radars, and AAA guns, but now Joe wanted us to think about unguided weapons, like tanks and rocket launchers. I was hesitant to worry about tanks until we visited an armor unit in Pinion Canyon, Colorado. I flew out to link up with a tank commander in the middle of the Fort Carson training area. There in the center of a wide valley sat a lone M1 Abrams tank. I landed a short distance from the mean-looking machine, and met the crew.

A young staff sergeant gave us a tour of his tank. I was surprised. It wasn't anything like I'd imagined. The tank was well lighted, clean, and roomier than expected. Our tour guide was sharp, well-spoken, and passionate about destroying helicopters. The young tank commander was proud to say that not only was taking out an aircraft possible, but it would be easy. They trained for counter-air often. "Think about it," he said. "What is the biggest killer of tanks on the battlefield other than artillery?'

"Other tanks?" I answered, but half-asked.

"No," he said. "Helicopters."

That made sense. To demonstrate the tank's capability, the sergeant had me look through the main gun sight, then told me to twist the turret control all the way to the stops. The turret spun quickly. Surprisingly, the optics never blurred or went out of focus. The gun could be brought to bear much faster than I expected. He went on to explain how deadly his 120mm smoothbore main gun was to a helicopter hovering, and in cruise flight. I was still a bit skeptical and was about to 'take him to school' with a 'face-off.' The contest was simple – he'd sit right where he was, and I'd try to get past him. I'd know if he had a simulated kill because his targeting laser would show up with my Aircraft Survivability Equipment (ASE).

My crew took their places as we began the start-up. First one engine and then the other. Our double-headed rotors spun-up to operating RPM. I took a last look around the valley to see where I could conceal myself long enough to get past our new enemy. We took off, cleared the dust, and headed toward the far end of the valley. Joe called "game on," over the radio, and I disappeared from the tank commander's view. He told me later that he had no idea a Chinook could fly so low or was so maneuverable, though it didn't do me much good.

I descended to roughly twenty feet and kept my speed around eighty knots to provide maximum surplus power and increased maneuverability. I zigged and zagged around the small rolling mounds as if I were skiing a mogul field in the winter, then as I popped into view, I accelerated to one hundred fifty knots to sprint past the tank.

I caught the tank crew entirely by surprise. They'd heard me, but the sound reverberated and bounced around the valley, masking my direction. In the blink of an eye, I was on them, then past. I swerved, veered, and 'jinked' lightly to throw off their aim…

"Laser, laser, six o'clock. Laser laser six o'clock." The APR-39VA1 computerized voice let me know I'd been shot. They must have got lucky. I swung around to the West for another run.

"Laser, laser, eight o'clock." Damn, same result.

Another try; "Laser, laser, five o'clock."

I could sneak up on them, but I couldn't get past them in open terrain – what an eye-opener for me. I needed to re-think what could bring me out of the sky.

+++

'Gorst Games' continued, but I wasn't always stuck on the ground as the survivor. As a matter of fact, one of my favorite training events was when we deployed to Fort Bragg, North Carolina. The A-10 unit at nearby Pope Air Force Base loved conducting PR coverage in their local Military Operations Area. The MOA allowed for them to fly combat maneuvers in the FAA controlled airspace. Their unit would place a downed pilot somewhere in the area, and we'd have to find him with A-10's assistance. They'd conduct a 'talk-on' to get us in the vicinity, then vector us directly toward the survivor. As we came close, we'd simulate taking fire, and the A-10s would 'daisy chain' from their overhead 'wagon wheel.' In other words, they'd take turns passing just past my right side to engage a simulated enemy. There were four A-10s in the flight. To keep the pressure on the bad guys, the Hawgs would pass me, then pull up aggressively at the survivor's location, indicating the landing zone. Then they'd circle around me and do it over and over until I recovered the downed airman. It was really an impressive display of flying and firepower.

So, one time, in particular, I got near the downed pilot. He flashed a mirror in my direction and held up an orange cloth panel marker. I turned to the right and made small adjustments to my approach angle. I slowed to land over a freshly plowed and limed field. The dust cloud that erupted was denser than I'd expected. The thick brown obscuration made it almost impossible to see. Out of the corner of my eye, I saw a farmer sitting on his tractor.

Too late to abort.

I continued my landing and picked up the survivor to return him to Pope AFB before continuing on to Bragg.

Was I in trouble, though?

I totally dusted the farmer. He had to be pissed, and I thought I should apologize. So, after talking with our Air Force liaison, I got the farmer's phone number. Fully expecting an ass chewing I called to make amends.

"Hello, this is CW3 Alan Mack from the Army's 160th SOAR. Is this Farmer William Brown?" I asked sheepishly.

"Yup, call me Bill," he said with a North Carolina drawl.

He didn't sound mad at all.

"That was one hell of a show you guys put on today," he said.

"Yes, about that…" I started to apologize. "Sir, I'm sorry about the dust cloud and your field. I…"

He cut me off. "Son, there's no need to apologize. I knew what you were doing, and I loved every moment of it. You can do the same thing any time you want. Just give me the privilege of watching. God bless you and your crews."

Oh my gosh, I couldn't believe my ears. Not only was I NOT in trouble, but the farmer loved our encounter – a true patriot.

+++

Joe's ideas kept coming.

We trained in small cities like Milwaukee and larger areas like Los Angeles. We walked and patrolled in the woods. Every mission ended at the rifle range to empty a few magazines. We increased our mountain flying in Colorado using supplemental oxygen, and we air refueled at high altitude as often as we could. Our aircraft availability improved, and before 9/11, we had access to all five of our company's Chinooks. We were in good shape as an organization. A trip to the Joint Readiness Training Center (JRTC) would prove how far we'd come since our restructuring and initiation of the 'Bravo Project.'

Little did we know that we would not conduct operations in Central America after all. We had unwittingly trained for similar conditions in Afghanistan's Operation Enduring Freedom. The timing couldn't have been better for us. We had peaked in proficiency, and we'd need it while conducting business in Northern Afghanistan.

Section III

"Let me not then die ingloriously and without a struggle, but let me first do some great thing that shall be told among men hereafter."
— *Homer, The Iliad*

Chapter 9

Response to 9/11 (Sept 2001)
Days after 9/11

Several days after 9/11, commercial flights and even most military aircraft were still grounded as I drove to Tampa, Florida. I made the twelve-hour drive with a small contingent of planners. The long, surreal trip ended at MacDill Air Force Base in the Central Command's Special Operations Headquarters. Within minutes of arriving, we were ushered into a secure planning area for a briefing.

Al Qaeda was the culprit for the 9/11 attacks. And their leader Usama Bin Laden, was our target. Many of our guys had never heard of him. I was familiar with his name because we planned a helicopter assault to kill or capture him in 1998. But President Clinton canceled the hit because of a perceived slim margin for success. We weren't allowed to go after him with direct action. Instead, the Navy threw seventy-five Tomahawk cruise missiles at him.

In hindsight, a helicopter assault against Bin Laden in Jalalabad might not have gone well. The performance numbers for our helicopters in the extremely high Afghan mountains were on the boundaries of undoable. I'm not so sure we would have succeeded without losing aircraft and crews to the terrain and weather. But by 2001 several changes to equipment and training, such as the Gorst Games would make the difference.

At least I hoped they would.

+++

Getting to Bin Laden would be tricky. The Taliban regime, led by one-eyed Mullah Omar, protected him. They were well armed with Soviet Equipment left over from the 1980s. The biggest threat to our aircraft was a large quantity of MANPADS. The man-portable heat-seeking missiles were plentiful and deadly. The Soviet air force suffered crushing losses to mujahideen forces using similar US-made Stinger, heat-seekers. There was no reason to expect to face anything different.

We formed two Task Forces (TFs) to cover as much of Afghanistan as possible. One TF operated from an aircraft carrier in the Arabian Sea and would fly into southern Afghanistan to kill or capture a senior Taliban leader. Our group,

TF Dagger, staged far to the north at Karshi Khanabad. Our mission would be to conduct Personnel Recovery (PR) and, unbeknownst to us, unconventional warfare. The Air Force and Navy would drop bombs against the Taliban and Al Qaeda in support of both TFs.

I had no idea what the long-term campaign looked like. In my mind that was because it had to be compartmented and very secret, but frankly, no one knew because it was still being worked. Eventually, we'd conduct special operations that were, at this point, still in the planning phase. But one thing we all knew was that getting past the Taliban was the key. They protected Bin Laden and held all the critical terrain, towns, and cities. The only way through them was either a massive invasion or a much more nuanced approach – unconventional warfare (UW).

Special Forces teams would be sprinkled throughout the countryside where they'd join forces with either the local population or, in this case, regional warlords of the Northern Alliance. Army Green Berets trained routinely for this type of mission. They trained and led indigenous forces to fight as a partner or proxy. The goal was economy of force, hopefully keeping US ground forces out of the wider conflict. But we'd still have to provide Combat Air Support (CAS) such as fighters, bombers, and helicopters. But to be clear, the preponderance of fighting would be conducted by our allies, the Northern Alliance.

+++

My responsibility in the opening days of OEF was to rescue downed aircrews in enemy territory. I ran the numbers for helicopter performance again and again, but they weren't shaking out the way I hoped.

I was very experienced flying Chinooks in mountainous terrain but couldn't believe how limited we'd be in Afghanistan. It was mind-boggling to comprehend that the mighty Chinook could only carry a fraction of its usual load due to the extreme altitudes of Central Asia.

+++

What I didn't know at that time was that planners from the 5th Special Forces group were putting the final touches on their unconventional warfare plan. They'd rely heavily on us and our helicopters but didn't involve us in the preliminary planning. They had no idea helicopters, even the powerful Chinooks would be so limited in performance. Other aircraft, like the Air Force's MH-53, could go virtually nowhere near our operational area. We could have helped in shaping their plans had they brought us in during the early stages. But 5th group was following the Cold War model for missions. The teams isolated themselves from anyone without the need-to-know their goals and methods to ensure operational security. The SF teams felt that the helicopter crews, aka taxi-drivers, only needed to know where and when to take them. In their eyes, there was no need for us to know any more than necessary.

The planning at MacDill finished and the SOCCENT Operations Officer sent us back to Fort Campbell. On the way out the door, he reminded us to maintain operational security (OPSEC). He told us not to speak of the operation's codename outside of secure areas. Ironically, during the drive home, we tuned in to a Pentagon press conference on the radio. The spokesman announced Operation Infinite Justice was in motion – so much for OPSEC.

The operational codename was changed the next day to Operation Enduring Freedom (OEF).

+++

Our team, Task Force Dagger, comprised four MH-47E Chinooks and three MH-60L DAPs. The original transportation plan required seven or eight Air Force C-5s. The Regiment had been moving MH-47s around the world in C-5 Galaxies for at least twenty years. The loading and unloading of helicopters into the large cargo plane had been perfected long ago. Standardized load plans were well established to carry two Chinooks and their buildup equipment. Redundancy was built into the plan. If only one cargo aircraft showed up at the destination, the helicopters could still be built up, test-flown, and ready to fly within hours. In this case the Air Force worried that the C-5s would be too vulnerable to MANPADs. They decided the newer, more maneuverable C-17 Globe Masters would take their place. The C-17 planes were definitely more suitable for the threat environment but had less lift capacity.

Not a problem, just use twice as many airplanes, right? Capacity-wise, that's true, but a tactical failure. The C-17 could only carry one Chinook and a mix of build-up team and aircrew but didn't leave room for the mobile crane used to move and assemble the helicopters.

As much 'smack' as I might like to talk about my rival service, I can honestly say the Air Force impressed me with this post 9/11 deployment. We all worked together as one big team. Our C-17 crews were talented and maintained an attitude that helped us adapt and cram our equipment into their cramped cargo compartment. At some point many months after our first transport to OEF, we collaborated to improve transit equipment and procedures.

During the early days of our post 9/11 deployment, it took three C-17 aircraft to make up for one C-5, pushing our travel requirements to twenty-one C-17s. The revised air movement plan added additional complexity, reduced our redundancy, and delayed our departure by several hours. My biggest frustration at this point was waiting to leave. I always had the fear in the back of my mind, that at any moment, our mission would be canceled, just like the Usama Bin Laden raid of 1998.

Once everything was loaded, I had time to focus on my family. I just needed to know they supported me and that they'd be okay. Linda and the boys made me feel like they'd be fine. I was certainly going to miss them and the comforts of home. I felt the draw of battle and the need to fight.

My eyes met Linda's as I left the house. I drew her close and kissed her, maybe for the last time.

Chapter 10

K-2

3 weeks after 9/11

By 4 October 2001, we were in place at our new home in Uzbekistan. Karshi Khanabad, nicknamed K-2 was a couple hours of flight time away from Bin Laden. Several hundred miles and dedicated Taliban fighters were in our way. We'd need to pass through them and fly over the mountains to get him.

An entire air campaign was waiting on our ability to 'stand up' a two-aircraft team ready to recover any downed aircrew from fighters, bombers, or reconnaissance airplanes. Our task force commander didn't want the bombing to start until all Chinooks were ready to fly. Having all four gave us flexibility, redundancy, and more firepower. Our wishes were just that... wishes. As soon as we reported to CENTCOM that a team of two MH-47Es was built up and fully functional, the response to 9/11 began in earnest...

+++

The Uzbek military hosted us at K2. They donated an abandoned portion of their former Soviet airbase to our cause. The taxiways and hardened aircraft shelters were in disrepair from years of post-cold war neglect. Living conditions were primitive and dirty. No showers, toilets, or beds. And until those niceties arrived, we slept on dirty concrete floors within those nasty Hardened Aircraft Shelters – we called them 'HAS.'

Our discomfort just made us cranky and more determined to make the Taliban and Al Qaeda miserable for years to come. In hindsight those minor degradations were nothing compared to the conditions in New York, where men and women were working feverishly on the rubble pile that was once the World Trade Center.

+++

Far from Ground Zero, our planning area was nothing to write home about. I shared a small room, almost a closet, with the C-130 navigator and Arlo, Gold Team's Flight Lead. Our laptops sat on planks supported by sawhorses; not elegant, but functional.

Along with distinct mission tasks, we had to keep up with minor administrative chores – one of those was choosing callsigns. CENTCOM sent us a list of computer-generated available radio callsigns. Arlo looked over my shoulder as I read the list. I pointed to one, and we both loved it – 'Razor.'

We'd be 'Razor 01, 02, 03, and 04.' Now, we needed one for our MH-60 DAP brothers. They weren't in the room during selection. And we laughed at the look on their faces when they got 'Sponge 01 and 02.' Everyone wants a cool callsign, like Maverick, Thunder, Basher, Maxim, or Razor. They might as well have been called 'unicorn' or 'pillow.' They took the goofy callsign in stride and good humor.

+++

As soon as we set up, Central Command (CENTCOM) wanted to rehearse downed-aircraft procedures. So, a simulated bomber crash set our process in motion. The operations officer gave Arlo and me a location to fly to. Using our laptops and old-fashioned performance charts, we struggled to quickly come up with a route that avoided enemy troops, usually over terrain requiring supplemental oxygen.

Arlo and I ran through multiple scenarios and settled on an advertised response time. We concluded that we could wake up, plan, brief, fuel the Chinooks, and get in the air within forty-five minutes – so, N+45. But that wasn't fast enough. The Airforce MH-53 helicopters based in Pakistan were claiming they could launch at N+30 minutes, forcing Arlo and me to find a faster process. We knew that if an aircraft went down in Afghanistan, whichever Task Force could respond the quickest, was going to get the rescue mission.

We wanted to be those guys.

We practiced, again and again, trying to trim time. We couldn't shorten the process in good conscience – we 'hit a wall' and could go no faster.

But it turned out that we didn't have to.

Our liaison in Riyadh, CW5 Don Tabron, called to explain a discrepancy he'd found.

"Apples and Oranges" were his first words to us.

I didn't understand what he meant. "Don, what the heck are you talking about?"

"You guys are talking apples and oranges with the Air Force. I figured it out at my last meeting at the Rescue Coordination Center."

I was exhausted and losing my patience. "Please, just tell me what you figured out, Don."

"The Air Force says they can launch N+30 minutes, which we know isn't really possible with our operational constraints..." He let his comment sink in.

"Are you saying, they consider the 'N' to be a different point than us?" I asked.

He was elated that I was starting to grasp his message. "Yes. They consider the 'N' sequence to begin after planning their route and confirming they'll conduct the mission. Then they notify the command and take thirty minutes to launch."

I couldn't believe my ears. The two Task Forces were computing time differently.

"Don, how long using 'our math' will they take?"

"About ninety minutes." He said.

There was no comparison. We were much faster than the Air Force. Thanks to Don, we could knock another problem off-the-table. It was a good reminder that even in the modern joint environment terminology misunderstandings could still cause confusion.

+++

Our work/sleep cycle was atrocious, adding to the ever-present stress of the need to succeed. Sleep was a difficult-to-achieve commodity – Ambien became our fickle friend. The sleep-aid worked wonders if you swallowed it and went right to bed. What we didn't know was that it had undesirable side effects if you stayed awake, as I found out the hard way.

One day we had nothing on the schedule, and I needed sleep. I took two Ambien pills and crawled into my sleeping bag. I was deep asleep thirty or forty minutes later. My copilot Jethro woke me for a frivolous and impromptu class – they should have left me alone. Medicated with Ambien, I struggled to remain awake during the presentation about malaria and the importance of Doxycycline.

Captain Gorst would come unhinged if I fell asleep in front of the troops, and I was losing the battle. I began to sway, and my peripheral vision dimmed. Not only was I going to hit the floor, but I was going to throw up on the way down.

I needed water, and I needed fresh air – NOW. I got up from my seat and left without a word. I wobbled like a drunk as I passed through the door into the cool autumn air and fell to my knees outside of the Hardened Aircraft Shelter. The fresh air felt good, but it didn't stop me from throwing up.

Two medics and Gorst followed close behind.

I was leaning over, hands on my knees, barfing the contents of my nearly empty stomach onto the ground.

Kyle, the lead medic, was first to speak. "Al, are you okay?"

That's a reasonable first question, but at the time, I was dumbfounded. "NO! I'm not alright." And another round of puking ensued.

"What's wrong?" Kyle asked.

"I'm puking, that's what's wrong. Leave me the fuck alone."

Kyle realized I'd taken Ambien, so he asked two pilots to put me to bed. Jethro and Dave Gross each grabbed an elbow and guided me back to my cot. My last memory was slipping into my warm sleeping bag. I woke up in much better shape, though a little embarrassed. I never used Ambien again without confirming I'd have uninterrupted rest.

+++

The infrastructure evolution of K2 was a slow process. It wasn't long before a morale phone capable of calling to the United States sprouted up near our compound. The waiting line to call home was always long, snaking through the camp, no matter the hour. The calls were being monitored for OPSEC, and our families still didn't know where in the world we were calling from. I was too busy to wait in line to say something like: "Hey, how are things? I miss you guys. The weather is cold, and I'm well. How are things there?"

My wife would respond with: "Hi. The boys and I are fine. The weather is cool here. And the house is holding up. Take care. We love you." I'd have a similar conversation with my sons, Stephen and Andrew. Needless to say, I didn't call often.

Some of our guys had more time on their hands and called every day, which caused friction as other wives wanted to know why the rest of us weren't. We had to have a talk with our frequent communicators. "Either ease up on the calls or tell your wife not to gloat that she's talking to you every day."

Once everyone adhered to that rule, the drama at home stopped.

+++

The phones got better before our food. Army field rations were getting old. I ate less and less, ultimately losing thirty pounds. Eventually, our Air Force support folks provided us with a dining tent. Better yet, they put up showers and toilets. And not long after the food improved, so did our living quarters. We moved from the nasty hardened aircraft shelters into temperature-controlled tents, improving our quality of life dramatically, though we barely noticed. We were still entirely focused on operations.

We organized into two teams – Gold and Silver. Our armed MH-60L DAPS would accompany whichever Chinook team launched. The Direct-Action Penetrators (DAPS) typically outfitted with 30mm cannon, 7.62 Miniguns, Hellfire missiles, and 2.75-inch folding fin rockets, were limited in performance just like us. They had to balance their choice of munitions for a trade-off in speed and fuel endurance. Each mission required a specific fuel load adjustment to get more bang for the buck.

There were many places the DAPS couldn't follow us. Not only did they have less power to fly at the necessary altitudes, but their radar wasn't capable of terrain following, a significant disadvantage in the mountains of Afghanistan. Their limitations reminded me of World War Two B-17s headed deep into Germany, and their fighter support didn't have the same fuel range, requiring them to turn back at the crucial point of the mission – the vulnerable bomb-run. Our '60 guys, much like the fighters escorting B-17s, just couldn't stick with us, no matter how badly they wanted to. They could follow us to the mountains, and when they could go no further, they'd hang around and wait for us to re-emerge and escort us home to K-2. That is, if we came back.

+++

The weather worsened as Fall transitioned into Winter. Cloud-shrouded mountains, sandstorm whipped dunes, and ice-fog would be our nemesis, probably more dangerous than the enemy.

Every munition in the world has a 'probability of kill' ratio or 'PK.' For example, a heat-seeking missile may have a PK of 70%, meaning it has a seventy percent chance of destroying its target, so with that being said, pilots consider the ground, mountains, and trees to have a PK of 100%. At all costs, you cannot run into terrain. And this is where MH-47E Chinook stands head and shoulders above its peers. Its Multi-Mode Radar (MMR) has several capabilities, the most important in the early days of Operation Enduring Freedom is the Terrain-Following mode. The radar, mounted in a pod outside the left cockpit door, looks ahead, mapping terrain, which is processed through a series of black boxes and displayed to the pilot as a terrain-following command or cue. The TF cue provides airspeed, steering, and power commands for the pilots to maintain a desired terrain clearance altitude, selectable by the pilots to fly at 100, 300, and 500 feet above the terrain ahead. Flying through the enormous mountains and valleys of Afghanistan was a stressful endeavor, especially when the visibility dropped, and the pilots couldn't see further than the end of the roughly ten-foot-long air refueling probe. Radar was the only tool that was likely to get us through passes or over the mountains.

The MMR, while an impressive piece of equipment, had its flaws. It couldn't see through heavy precipitation because it saw it as an obstacle to be climbed over. The worst flaw was the occasional rebooting that sporadically occurred. You never knew when, but out of the blue, the Integrated Avionics System would have a slight hiccup and stop processing terrain data. Without terrain presence to compute climbs or descents, the fail-safe was to command the pilots to apply full power and climb like your life depended on it – because it did. The full-climb-command, as it was called, had to be followed without hesitation to avoid potentially crashing into the terrain ahead. Remember what I said about the PK of the ground – 100%.

Flying in these conditions would be a decision for the commander, or as we later encountered, the Secretary of Defense. The risk vs. reward ratio had to be high for our command to allow us to launch into lousy weather, relying solely on the MMR to avoid terrain. We'd never used it in the clouds or in the mountains for real, only simulations; frankly, we weren't confident it would work as advertised. Its performance was terrific, but its reliability was in question.

+++

One of the logistical problems with the 1998 plan to get Bin Laden in this same area, was the altitudes that we'd need to conduct aerial refueling. At the time, the commonly held belief was that 6,000 feet was the highest altitude that the refueling maneuvers could be safely performed. Our opinion was that helicopter maneuverability above 6,000 feet feels mushy and sluggish. Minor control inputs to the rotors seem delayed or feel like they don't occur at all, and air refueling requires constant movements to maintain a position on the tanker aircraft.

The MC-130P tankers had a refueling speed range between 110 and 140 knots, but at some higher altitudes, the Chinooks may only be able to cruise at 110 knots, which doesn't leave much room to maneuver. I'll explain helicopter aerial refueling (HAR) later. For now, it's only essential to know that we were concerned about our ability to couple with the tanker and receive fuel in the air over enemy territory.

We concluded that the only way to be sure was to go out and verify flight conditions and handling at various altitudes. So, I rendezvoused with a C-130P about sixty miles north of K2. Multiple test 'plugs' over the unpopulated mountains would confirm if our equipment configuration and gross weights allowed us to take gas at various high altitudes. If it didn't work well, we might collide with our tanker, which would produce a very long fall to our deaths. Tables, charts, and basic math said we shouldn't have any problems, but all the army's previous HAR accidents occurred above 6,000 feet – every one of them.

I preferred to sit in the left seat, even though the right was easier for HAR. Jethro would make first contact with the hose. The big West Virginian was a natural at air refueling. He might even be better than me – no. Not better than me.

Regardless. He made the initial 'plugs.' No problems at 4,000 feet. I took the controls and made a few plugs to warm up. It was time to push things a bit. We moved from four thousand feet to six thousand, our perceived edge-of-the world. The movement-to-contact with the refueling drogue, if done too aggressively, requires the pilot to slow his forward speed and avoid drifting into the C-130, which at the higher altitudes might be harder. We couldn't go further, or could we?

Up we went – 8,000 – 9,000 – 10,000 – 12,000. The aircraft heater couldn't keep up with the cold. My toes were starting to ache, but we didn't encounter any problems. I snapped my oxygen mask into place. It obstructed my view of the probe tip slightly; I'd just have to keep that in mind. We kept movement to contact to no faster than five knots. It seemed that as long as we were smooth on the controls, there were no problems taking fuel at even the highest altitudes.

I was satisfied, and the tanker crew was happy that they didn't have to push any uncomfortable limits to accommodate us. We returned to base, excited to share our findings with the others. I was now more confident than ever that we could get into and out of Afghanistan safely – now we just needed to do it for real.

God only knows, we were about to get the opportunity.

+++

The air campaign was successful and nearing its end. The Taliban radar-guided air defense weapons lay in piles of rubble thanks to laser and GPS guided munitions. Enemy AAA was now limited to heavy guns like the ZPU 23-4 and ZPU 23-2, which were manually aimed and fired weapons systems. Arlo, the Gold Team flight lead and I, were summoned to discuss the next phase of Operation Enduring Freedom – Special Forces ODA Teams linking up with and assisting Northern Alliance forces.

Unconventional Warfare (UW) missions required the SF teams to be inserted by helicopter to the various friendly Afghan war lords scattered around the country. Joe Gorst selected Arlo's Gold Team to infil the first SF Team, ODA 555. I was relegated to the second mission. I wondered if this is what Buzz Aldrin felt like as second man to walk on the moon.

Chapter 11

The Horse Soldiers
5 weeks after 9/11

Roughly one month after 9/11 it was our chance to take the fight to our nation's enemies. We were ready to go.

As flight leads, Arlo and I were peers. Our qualifications and certifications were similar. We were both in our mid-thirties with prior enlisted experience in army aviation. I'd flown Chinooks in Desert Storm and Arlo was a Cobra pilot before joining the 160th. My experience in 'forty-sevens' pushed me up the chain. I was promoted to 2nd Battalion Headquarters two weeks before 9/11. Arlo took my place as the B Company standardization instructor pilot (SIP). By moving up, I vacated my seat, leaving it to Arlo. And as the Bravo Company SIP, he was entitled to the first infil. I've got to admit, I was envious. No, more like jealous.

Arlo and Gold Team would fly the first helicopters into Afghanistan. Their mission would be to carry SF ODA 555 for a link-up with Fahim Khan, the understudy of Ahmad Masoud, the famed and unfortunately recently assassinated Northern Alliance Commander. Fahim's insistence that he receive the first Americans, drove the schedule for all other missions. Arlo's helicopter landing zone (HLZ) was high up in the Hindu Kush, where terrain and weather were expected to be his biggest problem. I probably pouted for a few minutes but then received my mission into North-Central Afghanistan – Northern Alliance General Rashid Dostum would receive SF ODA 595 near Mazari Sharif.

Weather and extreme elevation wouldn't play as large a role in my mission as they did in Andy's. My biggest problem was penetrating large troop concentrations. The Taliban held all the key and desirable terrain between K-2 and Dostum's HQ. In other words, Arlo would likely die running into a mountain in poor visibility, and I would meet my end at the tip of a surface-to-air missile or AAA fire – both endings had the same result. Neither was desirable...

+++

Gold and Silver teams were both hard at work preparing – national pride was on the line. Although we were tactical planners, our missions held strategic importance, and we knew it. Our cell poured over maps and scoured aircraft performance charts to find acceptable routes. We needed to strengthen our chances of survivability and maximize load-carrying capacity.

Arlo and I slipped away behind closed doors to talk. What I had to say was for his ears only.

I knew we were both feeling the pressure of pulling off missions, that on paper, didn't look too promising.

"Arlo, do you have any more bourbon?'

"Yeah. A little."

Words weren't necessary as he unzipped a gym bag. He moved it into the light of a single light bulb and withdrew a half-full bottle of Jack Daniels.

"That's a sight for sore eyes."

Arlo poured two fingers into a pair of foam cups. "What do you think, Al?"

"I think we're gonna die pretty quick," I said.

He nodded in agreement. "Yeah, I think we're fucked... If the terrain and weather doesn't get us, we'll get our heads cut off in some shoot down."

"Well, there's not much we can do. We've got to get those teams in. Don't you think?"

"Yup," was all he said as he raised his cup to toast. "Shit... Night Stalkers Don't Quit."

We tossed back the amber liquid and agreed to keep our doubts to ourselves. We were going, no matter what. No need to stoke negativity, which I'm sure would have been contagious.

We knew our two missions would jumpstart the whole ground campaign. No sense moping around waiting for the Taliban to give up. We were the key to the Afghan north. We were the only way the SF guys were going to get to the Northern Alliance and topple the Taliban.

Battles and campaigns that might have taken years might now only take weeks. And with Taliban forces out of the way, we could go after our primary target – Usama Bin Laden

+++

The next day, ODAs began asking questions regarding their flights into Afghanistan. The teams were in a sub-compound dubbed the ISOFAC, which was an isolation facility meant to segregate them from everyone not intimate with the details of their entire mission.

Just like earlier in the planning stage, no one in the SF community felt the pilots needed to know much more than where to take them and what time to arrive. We were just 'taxi drivers' in their eyes. In many conflicts and environments, that would be acceptable and functional, but not in Afghanistan. I can highlight a reason why pilot input in planning is essential. One year earlier, our regiment was conducting mountain training in Colorado. And one of the Chinooks had an engine power droop while on final approach to a 12,000-foot mountain top. The rotor RPM slowed so much that the main electrical generators kicked offline.

Consequently, the pilots slammed the aircraft onto the snow-covered pinnacle luckily, avoiding damage to the helicopter. Without electricity, the instruments went dead. They sat in their darkened cockpit counting their blessings and wondering what had happened.

The voice warning system didn't kick in, and they had no instrument indications of a pending problem – everything was within limits. What could have malfunctioned?

When the sun came up, our maintenance team recovered the helicopter and downloaded the 'black box,' technically called a VADR. The Voice and Data Recorder chronicled their approach and near disaster. And with the data printed out, it was obvious what happened.

They'd exceeded maximum power available, but not in a way the Integrated Avionics System recognized. Therefore, 'Bitchin' Betty' did not alert the pilots.

It turned out that their gas producer turbine, measured in NG, had no warning designed into the software. I was sure there was a mistake. Boeing engineers wouldn't leave out such a rare but crucial notification. I asked our Battalion commander to let me recreate the scenario. I wanted to verify our theory.

I must say, he was less than thrilled with my test plan. But I assured him that I'd be safe and maintain numerous 'outs' in case we successfully recreated the anomaly. I replicated identical environmental conditions at 12,000 feet. It was easy to simulate an approach to a mountain top. As I slowed below effective translational lift, my power requirement increased as expected.

I handled the controls lightly as I eased in power to arrest my descent. Then demanded a smidgen more than I needed. There it was... the rotor slowed quickly and quietly. No warnings, cautions, or advisories.

If we were near a mountain top for real, we'd be screwed. But since we were only replicating the conditions, I was able to decrease the power and descend, allowing the rotor to smoothly increase and regain its normal RPMs.

Lesson learned: NG 'top-out' was a thing we needed to pay more attention to in the mountains.

+++

Math, the subject I hate the most, was going to rule the day in the mountains of Afghanistan in the form of Performance planning. The taxi drivers, that's us, were going to have to stand firm when the ground forces pressured us to carry more of a load. I could see this was going to be a problem. Many years of exercises, training events, and missions, the MH47E Chinook could carry virtually anything a special operations organization could want.

For example, the Rangers could load around seventy men into a single Chinook. It was crowded but not even close to a performance limitation. SF teams could pack all twelve men from an ODA with any gear or vehicles they wanted. To make it worse, we propagated the issue for years. If we told our ground forces that they could only take specific loads, they'd come back just before takeoff and ask for something more than we said we could carry. In our minds, they were the 'customer,' and we were there to support. We'd allow the extra weight – every time. Our saying was, "there's always room for one more Ranger."

Afghanistan changed all of that. The guys we flew fought us tooth and nail for more space on the helicopters, and we did NOT give in – we couldn't. As a matter of fact, our LNOs made the passengers bring everything they wanted to take along and place it on scales to verify the weight. This was not well received, but it worked.

+++

I finally had a face-to-face meeting with my team leader, Army Captain Mark Nutsch. We exchanged pleasantries as he laid out a 1:50,000 map on the table. A hand-drawn 'X' marked his intended infil site. Our conversation, as I remember it, was down and dirty –

"I'd like you to take us here," Mark said as he pointed to the 'X'."

"How many men, how much equipment, and what do you guys weigh?" I said.

We went back and forth with my questions and his answers.

"If we only have one aircraft, maybe due to maintenance or a crash, do you want to continue with your infil or pick up survivors and return home?"

He looked at me like I had a third eye.

"Why would we only have one aircraft?" he asked.

We were flying into enemy territory. The bad guys were armed with missiles that could easily take us out of the sky if our countermeasures failed. The weather looked atrocious, and who knows what else could force us into one helicopter.

"Just take me there. I don't care how."

"Okay," I said. Then we sat down to work through more contingencies, as I thought them up. Mark was a good sport and worked with me, balancing his priorities with my needs. In about an hour, we had a solid plan as long as the weather held.

He and his guys grudgingly got on the scales, as I re-ran the performance numbers. I didn't like what I saw, but it wasn't going to improve, no matter how many times I recalculated.

Nothing was going to change. What was, was.

We parted ways until mission night.

+++

We didn't have much downtime. When we did, there wasn't much to do. We could write home, read books, or watch movies. I'm not sure where our limited supply of

VHS tapes came from. Not much to choose from before a Blockbuster franchise sent us a couple of boxes of tapes. One that played heavily into conversations and jokes was George Clooney's *O Brother, Where Art Thou.*

The comedy, set in the 1920s, was an artistic rendition of the *Odyssey* by Homer. I won't go into details about the story other than George's character Ulysses Everett McGill is in a burning barn set on fire by pursuing lawmen. He keeps comedically repeating, "Damn, we're in a tight spot." I tend to recall some of the most obscure lines or references from movies. This one would be heard again.

Regardless of how we tried to take our minds off the possibility that our flight would be one way. I had to clear my mind, but make sure my family knew I was thinking of them. So, before my first mission, I took the time to write one of those in-case-I-die letters for Linda and the kids. Some guys didn't like to write them but I looked at it as a final goodbye. Maybe it would help with their grieving process should I meet a tragic end. I figured the reason why unexpected fatal accidents are so emotionally traumatic to families is because you don't have an opportunity to part ways with intention.

I'm glad my letter never needed to be read.

+++

Operation Enduring Freedom was about to ratchet up a notch as we put the first American Special Forces onto Afghan soil.

I sat through Arlo's air mission brief. And I've got to say his mission was tough. He'd fly his two helicopters over the Hindu Kush mountains at an altitude of 21,000 feet. Supplemental oxygen would be needed, and his aircraft was stripped of any non-critical equipment to save weight. He'd start by hitting an air refueling track immediately after crossing the first mountain range, nicknamed the 'Bear'. 'The Bear' was a 10,000-foot-high line of mountains perpetually shrouded in clouds. On a map, it had the shape and color of a Russian bear. He was concerned that he might not break out of the clouds for air refueling. In order to continue the mission without a tanker, he'd need a FARP. He commandeered my wingman as a contingency Forward Arming and Refueling Point.

CW3 Dave Gross configured his aircraft with an internal fuel tank capable of passing fuel to Arlo's. Dave would land in an open and relatively flat area, drag out a fuel hose and give gas to the two Gold-Team infil birds.

I watched Arlo with pride as he walked to his helicopter. He was about to take the fight to the enemy. 9/11 was still raw and fresh to us. We were hungry for payback.

I said a quick prayer and hoped he'd have a successful infil and come home, safe and sound.

+++

Arlo departed as scheduled, linked up with his tanker, but started to encounter poor visibility as he approached Afghanistan. Captain Joe Gorst rode in Arlo's jump-seat as the air mission commander. His calls over the SATCOM radio, coupled with a tracking device mounted to his helicopter, allowed us to follow their progress.

They didn't get far into Afghanistan.

A sandstorm was raging in the vicinity of the Hindu Kush mountain range. Gold Flight slowly worked their way up to about fifteen thousand feet for their first go at the terrain. Arlo would have to climb much higher eventually. His goal was to get close to the top then creep along the terrain closely following the slope up and over the mountains.

Their efforts fell short as they ran into a dead end. They couldn't climb any higher without being able to see. With rock walls on both sides, there was nowhere to go.

If they continued, they would die – there is no doubt.

Arlo had the presence of mind to have Dal, his wingman, turn around first.

Once Chalk Two completed their turn and was on their way in the opposite direction, Arlo made his turn, hopefully to safety. I watched in the Tactical Operations Center (TOC) as their tracking beacon moved along a computer monitor. They transitioned southward getting about halfway across the Hindu Kush. The GPS 'breadcrumbs' stopped.

Had their beacon stopped working? It shouldn't be stationary.

Suddenly it retraced its path back to Afghanistan. I should have been worried about them, but instead, I'm embarrassed to say I was pissed. Their failure meant my flight would be delayed twenty-four hours until Arlo tried again. Selfish is the only way I can describe how I felt; but I can't help how my mind works. I was afraid that we were about to repeat the 1998 Bin Laden raid cancelation if CENTCOM or the SECDEF considered Afghanistan's mountains too tough for us. They might call us off, before I had my crack at the problem.

Arlo and his guys were shaken up by their encounter with the mountains. But honestly, there was nothing he could do differently that would have made a difference. His do or die attitude was admirable. He wouldn't quit.

No. With revenge on his heart, he COULDN'T quit.

They'd try the next night.

+++

The second attempt didn't go any better. Nothing changed from the previous night. I should have been an understanding and supportive teammate, but instead I met Arlo in the planning area to confront him. I offered ideas of how he could have made it over the top. Still rattled from his near-death experience, he didn't want to hear my suggestions. The more I pushed, the more he pushed back. The discussion heated up and we began to shove each other.

We were going to fight. A no kidding bare knuckle brawl. I think I heard a line from *Doctor Strangelove* as someone tried to defuse the situation. "Gentlemen, no fighting in the 'war room.'"

Arlo was bigger and stronger than me. If our scuffle escalated, I was sure to get an ass-whooping. Dave Gross, arguably the toughest man I know, slid in between us. The barrel-chested freedom fighter parted us like the Red Sea. The situation died down right away. Tensions were high. We just didn't know who to take our frustrations out on. Arlo had to try a third time, and I was delayed another day, maybe longer. The weather forecast was still crappy and would be for the next several days.

The sun was rising. Time to go to bed. We'd deal with this during the next period of darkness (POD).

+++

Major Mark Henry worked the day shift in the Joint Operations Center (JOC) while the night crews slept. He couldn't wait for us to report for duty the next night. He had a story to tell.

Mark answered the main JOC phone for a call that changed everything – everything. The woman on the other end spoke calmly and businesslike. "Is this the TF Dagger Operations Center?"

"Yes, it is. How may I help you?"

"Please hold for the secretary," she said.

Mark wasn't sure what she meant. What secretary? He was surprised by the gravelly voice that now filled his ear.

"This is Donald Rumsfeld. Who am I speaking to?"

The conversation was one-sided as the Secretary of Defense explained that he didn't care what the weather conditions were. He knew we could work through our problems. He instructed us to infil both ODA 555 and ODA 595 to their respective warlords – that night.

I woke up to a whole new scenario.

+++

Arlo's team would repeat their previous attempt with some minor modifications, and I would take ODA 595 to meet General Dostum with just my single MH-47E, and the MH-60 DAPs for support. The commander told me that for political reasons, Gold Team had to infil thirty minutes ahead of me, so Fahim Kahn could gloat that he got his Americans before Dostum. This was no joke.

It was time to finally do what I'd been training for all my adult life. The reality sunk in, as my stomach twisted in knots. The pressure to succeed was crushing.

I had to get my mind on the task at hand.

+++

Darkness approached. The pre-mission madness began with the Chaplain's rousing prayer for protection and success. I walked out of the TF Dagger OPCEN and I passed through a wall of sandbags and concertina wire. The night was cold and crisp. I thought I smelled the onset of snow, but the sky was clear when I looked up.

I wanted to remember this night.

The area around K-2 had little-to-no cultural lighting, allowing the stars to sparkle brilliantly. I appreciated the dark, clear sky as my eyes adapted, making constellations easy to identify. I fixated on Orion. For no particular reason, that group of stars has meant good luck for me. To this day, I'm always comforted by its presence.

The gentle groaning of an aircraft tug caught my attention. I looked to my left and saw ground crews pulling my MH-47E from its parking spot. I walked along, keeping pace with the slow-moving tractor on the mud-covered taxiway. It was surreal. I strode past onlookers lining the taxiway. I got goosebumps as I looked into their eyes.

Before long, my aircraft was in place and ready for takeoff. Steam from my breath reminded me that the flight was going to be cold as I walked around the helicopter. With flashlight in-hand I checked that all compartments were securely fastened and covers removed. I ran my gloved hand along the right-side fuel tank, then down the full length of the refueling probe. I had the right mindset. Now I just needed a ground force to transport.

The SF team rolled up in the back of a cargo truck. I was shocked to see not uniformed soldiers, but a group of bearded men dressed like they had just jumped off a Caspian Sea fishing trawler. Their clothing was intended to help them blend in with General Rashid Dostum's Northern Alliance faction. Remember, he was an Uzbek, not an Afghan.

The team had no idea the clothing was incorrect and based on crappy intel. The Northern Alliance dressed in traditional Afghan garb, not Russian. But since no one really knew what to expect, flexibility would be the name of the game. Needless to say, they adjusted once on the ground in Afghanistan. They were so flexible they ended up riding horses with Dostum's forces. Think about how wacky that sounds – they rode horses in cavalry charges while lasing enemy targets for aircraft overhead with deadly precision. These guys, known as the 'Horse Soldiers,' would assist the Northern Alliance. Not only would they take Mazar-e-Sharif but the capital city of Kabul.

Gold Team had already departed and was encountering the same crappy weather as the other attempts, but with two previous tries under their belts, they anticipated the adjustments needed to get over the mountains.

Man, I had to pee. I tapped my heel nervously to pass the time.

The SF Team was getting situated in the cargo compartment of my aircraft when a familiar face appeared at the ramp. Our task force commander Colonel John Mulholland climbed aboard to wish us luck. I can't describe the feelings of nervous energy coursing through my mind or the butterflies pounding my stomach.

Starting up an 'echo model' Chinook is a detailed process – crew coordination is vital. I read steps from a checklist in order, and either Jethro or my enlisted crew would respond with their action. It sounded something like this:

"APU to start," I said.

"APU clear to start," a crew chief responded.

The Auxiliary Power Unit spooled up with the high-pitched whine of a small turbine engine. It provided electrical and hydraulic power until the main engines were online.

"APU generator – On." I flicked the switch on the overhead console and the instrument panel lights illuminated, and our four Multifunction Displays (MFDs) came to life. The nine-inch by nine-inch cathode-ray displays defaulted to their highest brightness. I dimmed them to the lowest useable level.

"Power Transfers – On," I said, as a hydraulic valve opened.

Jethro automatically ran the flight controls through their full range of motion. A Chinook's controls require hydraulics to move. The check ensures smooth operation and no binding; both important to flight.

"Can I have power to the guns?" my flight engineer asked.

I armed the M-134 Minigun selector switch so the gunners could finish their final gun checks. The M-134 is a 7.62, six-barrel, Gatling-style rotating machine gun. These guns made by General Electric had a high rate of fire of 6,000 rounds per minute or could be fired on low rate equaling 3,000 rounds per minute. According to Wikipedia, the 'Mini' in the name refers to its comparison to larger-caliber designs that also use a rotary barrel design.

Regardless of the name, the gun was driven by two electric motors. A feeder de-linker that pulled ammunition through a flexible metal belt and one on the ammunition can that pushed ammo along.

His checks were done. "Guns are good. You can turn off the master switch for now," he said.

We continued to plod through the checklist, finally getting to the best part – Main engine start. Since I was sitting in the left seat, the job would be mine. I opened the fuel cross-feed and turned on the fuel pumps...

"One to motor," I announced.

The crew chief standing outside by the left side, or number one engine responded, "One clear to start."

Moving the engine condition lever to the ground detent, I pushed the start switch to motor allowing the Gas producer turbine to get moving. At 10% NG, I pushed the switch all the way forward, allowing fuel to enter the combustion chamber. From that point on, the engine was on automatic and self-modulating. The six thirty-foot-long rotor blades held in place.

"Okay, we've got a good start on number one. Release the rotor brake."

"All clear, release rotor," called the crew chief at the forward cabin door.

Jethro reached out to a lever roughly at eye-height and an arm's length away. "Releasing brake."

No sooner had the lever stowed in its housing, than the blades began to spin. The drooping main rotor blades became rigid as they picked up rotational speed. The aircraft started to sway and shake until all six blades were in phase. I repeated the process on the second engine, finished our mechanical checks, and readied ourselves for taxi.

Since nobody wanted us to fly alone into Afghanistan, our two MH-60 DAPS would come along to babysit me as my Chalks Two and Three. I checked-in on the inter-flight radio frequency to see if they were ready to go.

"Sponge 01, Razor 03 on Fox Mike," I said.

They responded immediately, "Razor 03, Sponge 01 is ready for taxi.".

"Alright, guys, let's do this."

"Clear to taxi, Sir."

I released the brakes, and we started to roll forward. The Chinook drives like a truck on its four-wheeled landing gear. The power steering is controlled by a small knob using my right hand, and I managed our speed with the brake pedals. I was as ready as we were going to be as the American controller in the tower cleared us onto the runway for departure.

Jethro increased power, and we rose to a steady ten-foot hover – the DAPs did the same. I compared the torque gauge reading with our predicted power usage. It was spot on, and that was important to me because it meant we weighed precisely what we planned. We'd have the power needed to clear the mountains with plenty to spare.

Within seconds of our hover check, we were on our way as a flight of three.

+++

I finished our cruise checks, set our lighting, radar, and aircraft survivability equipment (ASE) and settled in for a long flight. Everything looked good. All systems were operational with instrumentation all in satisfactory parameters. In training I'd play with buttons and practice flight computations, but here in the show, everything was set. There was nothing to do, which was unnerving. Out of habit, I nervously tweaked my NVG focus and cockpit lighting for the tenth time.

My copilot CW2 Jethro Freed was on the controls in the right seat. He was young for a fully mission qualified aviator. I considered him one of the best. A big man, maybe two hundred and forty pounds of solid muscle, he spoke with a distinctive accent from the Hollers of Appalachia. He was cool under pressure and a great pilot. I thought about how far we'd come from JRTC, and I was glad to have him at my side. Now we were making our final preparations to cross the border with our team, aka 'precious cargo.'

The inter-crew communications system (ICS) was silent. Radio discipline was tight. Every turn, every movement and speed change were either pre-briefed or utilized light signals between helicopters. My crew periodically roamed the cabin checking the airframe for unwanted vibrations or leaks. Everything was operational as our lone Chinook carried the entire ODA and their equipment. The mission was supposed to involve both Silver team Chinooks. Since we only had one, we needed to strip it of any equipment and extra fuel to accommodate the now excessive passenger weight. That meant we'd need to take gas from our MC-130P on the inbound leg to get the team to their destination, and we'd need it again outbound to get out back to K-2 – so much for the comfort of fuel redundancy.

Our weather forecast improved from the previous outlooks, so I figured our biggest challenge was getting past enemy defensive positions without getting shot down. I keyed my mic for the intercom to speak a prayer from America's first astronaut in space, Alan Shepard. It was simple and to the point: "God, please don't let me fuck this up."

I hoped God was with us.

+++

The rotors tracked smoothly at one hundred twenty knots, roughly equaling 138 miles per hour. The ceiling and visibility were excellent, and I glanced up to look for Orion. The cockpit lighting made that difficult, so instead, I refolded my map and ran through border penetration control checks. Our external lights were off, and we now swooped through mountain passes blacked out.

I announced a test fire for all guns over the radio. The M-134 Minigun has a very distinctive noise, unlike any other machine gun in the world. It's difficult to describe it – instead of a rapid-fire "rat-a-tat-tat," like in the movies, it made a growling and roaring noise, sort of a loud "Brrraaaaaaaaaaap"! The six barrels were connected at the muzzle by a flash suppressor that helped dissipate the two–foot-long orange and yellow flame. Miniguns are impressive to watch. Normally the stream of bullets looks like a laser beam, but at this point, we were loaded with low-light tracers, making them difficult to see without the use of NVGs.

Each gunner checked in when complete – all our guns were operational.

The distinctive smell of expended ammunition wafted through the cockpit as I craned my neck to look to my left. The DAPs were still shooting.

The forward-facing 30mm cannon mounted on the right side of the Blackhawks was loaded with 30mm High Explosive Dual Purpose (HEDP) rounds. I watched as their impressive guns fired into a nearby hill. If someone took a shot at me, my gunslinging companions would protect me by delivering explosive violence and mayhem – good friends to have.

+++

One thing is for sure, it was cold. Our doors were open to allow the use of the Miniguns. That meant the heater, no matter how high I turned the knob, would not keep us warm. I checked the Free Air Temperature – yup, cold: -5°C or 23°F. I knew the passengers didn't want to sweat in the back, but this was crazy. They were freezing right along with us.

With my cockpit housekeeping chores complete, I began to notice more of the outside foliage and fauna while waiting for our tanker rendezvous. I looked out my chin bubble and I saw a mountain goat pass by. I laughed as I thought of the Gary Larson Far Side Cartoon of a goat within view of two airline pilots who comment, "What's that mountain goat doing up here in the clouds?" Then Jethro, the big man with the tiny bladder, had to pee. I asked him to hold it, but no joy.

I took the flight controls while he relieved himself using a small sponge-filled container called a piddle-pack.

With Jethro feeling more comfortable, I passed him the flight controls and got ready to meet our MC-130P tanker. Like every task, we had another series of checklists to get through before we did anything. First, there was the Rendezvous, then the join-up, followed by the observation checklist. All of them followed the same crew coordinated format of call and response.

If you've never seen it, the air refueling rendezvous is an impressive maneuver. The tanker and the receivers meet at a single geographic point called the Air Refueling Control Point (ARCP). We'd arrive at the CP at the Control Time (CT) or up to one minute early at the join-up altitude and track heading, at a speed of 110 knots.

The tanker flew a reciprocal heading toward us. We weren't quite head to head. They offset one-half mile to our left and flew 300 feet higher than us.

They'd arrive at the CP at the CT or up to one minute late.

I paid close attention to our air-to-air TACAN navigation system, as it counted down the mileage between us.

"Guys, the tanker is at twelve o'clock, thirty miles," I said.

"Roger, thirty miles, searching," was the response.

The tanker closed rapidly.

Once within five miles, I started the join up checklist and watched as he passed down our left side.

As he disappeared from my view, he turned left and passed up our right side, slightly higher than us.

Once he positioned himself at our two o'clock, we climbed to join him. Jethro moved into the observation position so we could look the airplane over. And as usual, right about the time we finished our checks, the observer in the jump door flashed a green signal-light letting us know that we were clear to cross over to the right-wing, leaving the left hose for the two DAPs. LTC Jake Brass, our commander, sat quietly in the jump seat, between and slightly behind us.

Jethro's view from the right seat gave him the best-unobstructed look down the refueling probe. It stuck out quite a bit from our airframe but was still about six feet underneath the forward rotor disk. Air refueling can be fun, or it can scare the heck out of you. That night, the air was calm, and the doughnut-shaped para-drogue was stable and easy to plug. I watched the 60s getting their fuel on the left-wing – no problems there.

I looked back to our front and adjusted the upper Infrared Searchlight on the tanker's right-wing to illuminate the hose markings for Jethro.

The hose and probe were aligned, and only ten feet separated our probe tip from the drogue and coupler.

"Movement to contact," Jethro announced. His well-practiced technique was on display as he pushed forward on the cyclic stick between his legs with a corresponding increase in power.

The aircraft nose dipped, and the helicopter accelerated.

Jethro made minor adjustments as we moved to contact. We were rewarded with a satisfying thump as the probe tip contacted the drogue coupler.

"Contact," he announced.

The retainer springs held the fuel coupler on our probe tip, allowing us to maneuver as needed to maintain the proper distance from the C-130.

The hose is controlled by a pressure sensing reel. If we backed up, it let out. Of course, the opposite was true if we moved closer. While this little dance is going on in midair, we were taking fuel. All I could do while Jethro flew was to make sure the IR searchlight stayed on his wing cues and monitor the fuel level. We couldn't top it off because we'd be too heavy when we arrived in the mountains. The DAPs were already done, and we weren't far behind. We hit our number, disconnected, and crossed back over to re-assume lead of our flight-of-three into enemy territory.

The tanker pulled away with only a handwave from the ramp observer, and we descended back to our low-level flight profile. There was no cultural lighting as we approached the river dividing Uzbekistan and Afghanistan. It was dark. And it didn't help that we might have some type of obscuration in the air. I couldn't tell if it was rain, fog, or haze. No precipitation showed on the radar, so I double-checked, the settings – all good.

The DAPs closed-up tight. One flew on my left, and the other to the right. Visibility dropped rapidly as we crossed our first set of rolling sand dunes. I'd given Arlo such a hard time about not being prepared for bad weather, and here I was having trouble seeing. I thought maybe my NVGs were out of focus, so I rotated the focus ring in an attempt to clear up my view. It wasn't the goggles. I flipped on the Infrared Searchlight. Holy shit; a sandstorm.

The DAPs tucked in uncomfortably close to maintain sight of us.

"Razor 03, Sponge 01 on 'Fox Mike.' Be advised, we can't see your aircraft, only the heat of your engine exhaust. Say speed and heading."

If they could only see the heat from my engines, that meant we would probably have to abort soon. Jethro started complaining that he couldn't see anything, either. Choices were diminishing. The MMR might make this possible.

"Jethro, follow your cues. TF mode active, Clearance Altitude set for three hundred feet."

"Roger, Right Seat is inside and on the cue."

The DAPs noticed immediately.

"Razor 03, Sponge 01. Are you TF'ing?"

I didn't want to tell him, yes, but he needed to know. "Sponge 01, Razor 03, affirmative. TF, three hundred feet clearance altitude. Proceeding direct to aerial checkpoint ten."

About that time, Sponge 02 lost sight of both helicopters, so he backed off and climbed away from the flight to avoid collision.

"Flight, this is Sponge 02, 'Blind Alley.' I'm climbing at this time."

"Sponge 02, Sponge 01, we see your wheels. Descend now, and you'll be back in the flight." He complied and was right back where he was supposed to be. But how long were they going to be able to keep this up? These guys had balls the size of watermelons. Well, maybe not... moments later, they couldn't take it anymore and requested to break away and return to base. LTC Brass approved their return. What were we going to do? I really wanted to get our passengers to their link-up site.

The Colonel was first to speak. "Al, what do you think?"

I already had my response thought through. "Sir, I think we can make it. We'll just TF all the way."

I guess that's what he wanted to hear because he didn't have to think about it before letting me proceed. We were now completely alone. We had no other rotary-wing aircraft with us and nothing overhead – no fighters or bombers. My heart was racing at the thought of being genuinely single ship. The TF radar was the mission wild card. We'd never used the damn thing in real Instrument Meteorological Conditions (IMC). Oh sure, we used it in the mountains as long as we could safely see, but never in a true obscuration.

As we flew along in TF mode, all of us were quiet except for absolutely critical conversations. I started to giggle as I thought about the *O Brother* movie and spoke George Clooney's line: "Damn, we're in a tight spot."

Jethro, realizing I was trying to break the tension, joined in. "Yup… we're in a tight spot."

And for the next hour, he flew without being able to see anything outside; instead, we focused on the tiny radar TF cue.

"Al, we've got a turn coming in one minute," Jethro announced.

"Roger, right turn in one minute," I repeated.

Jethro turned at a standard rate… Then unexpectedly, the radar gave us a surprise full-climb command and obstacle warning. Bitchin' Betty started alerting: *"Warning, Warning, Warning – Terrain ahead – Obstacle."*

This wasn't the typical radar-reboot problem – this was a no-kidding life or death emergency. We were heading toward a mountain that we couldn't climb over without immediate correction.

Jethro slowed to our best climb airspeed and pulled maximum power. The Vertical Speed Indicator was 'pegged' with the helicopter climbing at over four thousand feet per minute. The terrain ahead was my primary consideration, but I also noticed ice forming on my windshield. If it were also building on the rotor system, it would affect the lift of the blades, making the climb more difficult. I desperately cycled my MFD digital map through different scales to see if I could determine what we were facing. There… at about eight miles, was a twelve-thousand-foot peak. Our weight prevented us from gaining enough altitude to clear the terrain ahead, so I suggested a slight heading change to the north. Not much, but just enough to get the mountain out of the radar's command corridor. I swear I could taste adrenaline as we waited to see if our adjustment worked.

Success.

The TF cue commanded a descent, allowing us to eventually resume our route.

The VWS timer chimed. *"Bing Bong, Bing Bong."*

I flexed my fingers, pushing the tips further into my gloves, and I alerted my sleeping passengers that we were close to landing. "Ten minutes."

The crew responded. "Ten minutes – Aft Ready."

"Ten minutes – Forward Ready."

We were nearing our destination. I reminded everyone that the one thing we could not do, under any circumstance, was to go beyond the HLZ. We were going to approach from the south to north and land on the southside of a small hill. That hill was the only cover we had to shield us from a known ZPU 23-4 anti-aircraft gun. The four-barreled 23mm gun would tear us to pieces if they got a bead on us.

But we still had to get out of the clouds to identify our landing area, and we were now six minutes out. At four minutes, foggy wisps and 'sucker holes' began to appear. At three minutes, we crossed our release point, and I could see the valley below. Jethro slowed to eighty knots, and I selected a lower TF cue, using

100 CALT to continue out of the clouds. I nervously tapped a heel and pulled my flight gloves snug for the twentieth time.

There it was. We crested the final ridgeline. The HLZ was right in front of us, but still five thousand feet below. The hill masking the ZPU was obvious and easy to ID.

I knew immediately how I wanted to get on the ground. "Jethro, you're gonna have to do 'S' turns and increase our rate of descent."

"Al, I'm not sure what you're asking, and I don't want to screw this up. Why don't you take the controls?"

"I have the controls – coming hard left guys, and I'm increasing rate of descent."

"Clear down and left."

About ten seconds later, I banked hard in the opposite direction. "Clear down and right."

"Clear down and right."

The VSI showed a four thousand-foot per minute rate of descent, but I needed to drop faster. So, I kicked the aircraft out of trim to increase fuselage drag, consequently increasing the rate of descent. I made another turn to the left and glanced at the radar altimeter. We were low enough to begin our approach, but I couldn't see the landing area from my side of the cockpit. "Jethro, can you see the HLZ?"

"Yup. Got it right out my door."

"Sorry to do this to you, but you have the controls."

I caught him by surprise, but he rose to the challenge and started the final descent.

"Al, I have the controls – guys, the landing area is the open area at twelve o'clock and half mile – lining up now."

"Sir, Right Gun has landing area in sight. Continue forward."

As Jethro slowed and continued his approach, we entered the dense dust cloud roiled up by our rotor wash. He transitioned inside to his instruments focusing on the hover page vectors. The crew chief at the right ramp could see the ground and was calling out heights.

"Thick dust cloud at the ramp – we're at forty feet."

Jethro made a minor adjustment to his speed and rate of descent.

"Thick dust mid-cabin – twenty feet."

I called out Jethro's ground speed. Ideally, it should be half of his altitude.

"Thick Dust at the cabin door – ten feet."

"Too fast. Slow down," I said.

Jethro raised the nose to slow us down. In the dust cloud, I couldn't see movement, but I felt like we were going backward. So, I commanded a 'go around.'

I could feel Jethro starting to raise the thrust but heard the crew chief still counting down.

"Five feet, four, three, two, one contact."

The aft landing gear contacted the ground, and I changed my mind. We just touched down, we weren't about to go back up and try again. I jumped on the controls with Jethro and pushed down hard on the thrust and fought his attempt at going around. Once all four gear were on the ground, Jethro knew what I wanted, and he let the controls settle and applied the brakes.

There we were!

Even with minor route tweaks, we were on the ground at our HLZ on time.

As the dust cloud dissipated, armed men dressed in traditional Afghan garb and carrying AK47 rifles became visible. They surrounded us. Could this be a trap? If so, we were screwed.

The flight engineer lowered our ramp. ODA 595 walked out into the night and shook hands. Mark and an Afghan hugged, followed by a gesture to unload. I wasn't about to shut down this close to the Taliban. I left the engines running and we proceeded with a 'hot download' of their gear. Mark came up to the cockpit, tapped the Plexiglas chin bubble and gave me a thumbs up.

Time to leave him to his business. I tasted the grit and dust as we climbed into the air. Now, we'd just have to repeat our journey in reverse to get home.

The return flight had no new issues, and I no longer had the stress of arriving on time – on target with my SF team. While flying home I realized that if I couldn't see the mountains, no one on the mountains could see me. That meant nobody could target us, especially with MANPAD missiles. The heat seekers would never get a lock on us in this crap. Who'd have thought: bad weather equals safety. At least that's how I looked at it.

An hour later we crossed the northern dunes and approached the Amu Darya river, which represented the border between Afghanistan and Uzbekistan, my heart raced. Visibility was improving, and the Tanker's TACAN readout started counting down from about sixty miles. He was out there, ready to extend my range. I really loved the 8th SOS. This had to have been the best tanker support ever.

The rendezvous and refueling went well. And our last challenge was to re-cross 'The Bear' and get back to K-2. The clear starry sky reappeared after we got back into the Karshi valley. And as the lights of the airfield came into view, I coordinated with the control tower for my landing. Everyone was waiting for us. Arlo and his team beat me back by about thirty minutes. My aircraft was the last Task Force Dagger element out doing our nation's business.

My God, I was spent.

I can't find the words to describe the mixed emotions of success, stress, and physical fatigue. And better yet, I was going to have to do this same type of mission again and again with other teams. Then we'd need to resupply them as well.

Jethro and I sat quietly in the cockpit, contemplating our success while our ground support crews hooked up the tug and towed us into parking. Just like our departure, spectators lined the taxiway.

I looked over at Jethro and gave him a backhanded tap on the shoulder. "Damn, we're in a tight spot."

+++

My first flight, of hundreds-to-come, was now in the books. But back in my uncomfortable HAS, I used the pot belly stove to heat water for some yummy, powdered Cup of Soup mix. The hot liquid burned my tongue, but it felt good – it meant I was alive. A little chicken noodle soup in my belly was a nice way to end the day. I slipped into my sleeping bag and reflected on what we'd just accomplished.

Time for a well-earned rest.

Our two TF Dagger teams were the first real effort to get Bin Laden. Bombing sent a message but boots on the ground would be the true measure of America's Response.

Now that we proved we could fly into the Afghan mountains that once tamed the Soviets, we'd bring hell in the form of SF ODAs. The Taliban would fall, allowing us access to Bin Laden.

I ignored the cold damp air as I drifted off to sleep.

Chapter 12

Unconventional Warfare Continues
The Winter after 9/11

Arlo and I flew every other day, giving us each time to work on our next mission. Each night we'd share lessons learned. Conditions at Camp Stronghold Freedom improved incrementally. Eventually, more phones were installed, reducing the wait time to call home. Linda was doing surprisingly well, though I still couldn't tell her where I was. We were not officially in Uzbekistan, and the OPSEC managers closely monitored our communications. The conversations were always about the weather, the food, and requests for packages. I needed more shelf-stable food products. For the most part, I survived on Hickory Farm's Summer Sausages and packets of Cup-a-Soup. Weight loss was imminent.

One of my furthest infils was to the town of Farah, several hours to the south-southwest along the Iranian border. My next trip was to the mountain pass of Bamiyan, where the Taliban destroyed several giant and very ancient Buddha statues. And by the time I put a team near Pol-e-Khomri in northeastern Afghanistan, things were getting routine. We'd take off as a flight of two MH-47s with our MH-60 DAPS in tow. Then we'd cross 'The Bear,' hit our tanker, and cross the Amu Daria River into Afghanistan. As soon as we crossed over the northern dunes, we'd fly through the customary sandstorm. Once past the weather, we'd encounter AAA fire, usually from 14.5mm and 23mm guns. Occasionally Rocket Propelled grenades (RPGs) or heat-seeking MANPADs sped by as a near miss. No hits... I started getting used to getting shot at. We'd arrive at our HLZ, infil a team, or drop supplies, before turning around and heading home. The movie *Groundhog Day* where actor Bill Murray's character was forced to live a single day over and over again until he got it right sounded familiar as the nightly grind churned out mission after mission. The excitement and exhilaration of the earlier missions were giving way to fatigue.

Rules of Engagement are put in place to authorize when a soldier can shoot at the enemy, and what level of force can be used. Up until this point, we were operating under the rules that we needed to be the recipient of a hostile act. If we weren't being shot at, we shouldn't be firing. This level of absurdity was about to change based on a mission to infil an ODA to a hilltop that was surrounded by enemy light armor and artillery.

Taliban forces were lobbing Soviet BM-21 Rockets on to Northern Alliance soldiers waiting for me to deliver SF to the top of that hill. I'd been told a Navy F-14 was overhead with eyes-on the weaponry and was asking permission to destroy the rocket launcher firing on friendly positions.

CENTCOM disapproved the requested fire-mission because no US forces where being engaged. As soon as I found out about the situation, I asked for the enemy positions to be struck so I could get onto the HLZ unopposed. CENTCOM again denied the strike. It could only be destroyed if I got fired upon during infil. That's absolutely insane – one nearby rocket or artillery round would literally clean me off the mountain.

Our Task Force Commander, Colonel John Mulholland, summoned me to discuss our options; he didn't mince words. "Chief, can you get the team onto the hill?"

I took a moment.

"Yes Sir, I can get them in. But, if the BM-21 is still in place, the only way I can surprise them is to approach from the cloud-shrouded mountains using the RADAR. I've gotta tell you, it'll be 'sporty.'" Then added, "Look, all they've got to do is let the F-14 that's already on site, take out that launcher, and I can guarantee success."

"Thanks, Chief. Go get ready to go. I've got a phone call to make."

Joe Gorst was in the room when Mulholland called CENTCOM to argue the rules of engagement. He wanted the enemy rocket launcher destroyed, or he wouldn't allow me to depart K-2.

Minutes later, Colonel Mulholland told me "stand down." There would be no infil under those circumstances. I went to bed, wondering how things might have gone. I was getting good at sneaking past AAA guns and enemy positions – maybe another night.

+++

Donald Rumsfeld got wind of the ROE 'buffoonery' at CENTCOM and directed a change that benefited us. From that point forward, anything that could affect the safety of helicopters to include ingress and egress routes was now a legitimate preemptive target, eligible for attack. It wasn't long before a nearby B-1 bomber obliterated the BM-21s that stopped us the night before. No more rockets threatening infil.

Any delay had cascading effects on infil schedules. Arlo was supposed to deliver supplies to ODA 595, and I would infil the hilltop ODA. Instead of trying to coordinate separate tankers and border crossings, we combined into a single flight-of-four. I would lead the flight to a common release point, then we'd each do our individual tasks, rejoin, and return to base.

The mission itself was straightforward and uncomplicated. But like many of our missions in the early days, Mother Nature had a vote. The weather forecast included moderate icing, which would keep us from going. I argued that the forecast models, based on years of erroneous Soviet data, were way off. We unnecessarily leaned toward the worst possible conditions. We'd even canceled a couple of flights, based on inaccurate forecasts. I went round and round with the Air Force forecaster, who insisted that we COULD have icing. I agreed. We could have a tornado too, but it was unlikely, just like the ice. I proposed a compromise. Since there were no clouds over K-2, I'd circle the flight in a corkscrew-like climb in clear conditions to twelve thousand feet, which was three or four thousand feet higher than the expected tops of clouds over 'The Bear.' If we could let down to the air refueling track without penetrating clouds, I'd continue; if not, we'd abort and return to base. Everyone agreed to give it a try, even the forecaster.

The pre-flight ritual of sorting maps and packet material is different for each pilot, but they remain consistent either out of superstition or efficiency; maybe both. Guys are usually quiet while they go about their work, but this night was different.

Fear and feelings of misgiving were lurking below the surface until one of the co-pilots mumbled something about not going out because of icing. I kept quiet as I made notes on my map. One thing I have learned leading troops in combat is that negativity and fear are contagious and gain momentum quickly.

CW5 Gil Gordon cleared his throat and addressed the group. "You know what guys; I think this flight is a bad idea. The weather is going to be terrible, and I just don't think we need to be out in it."

I could hear some under-the-breath grumbling. I needed to do something to quell the potential uprising. My only recourse... I exploded with anger. I backed him up to a wall, ready to punch him in the mouth. "I'll knock your teeth down your throat if you say another word!"

The room was silent...

"You sat through the damn briefing and agreed that everything was fine," I was on a roll. I emphasized how serious I was with one final dig.

"If you don't want to go, say so right now. I'll put you on the LNO desk and get Greg to fly in your seat. Now, what's your fucking answer?"

He didn't want to be stuck behind a desk. We were fighting a war.

"I'll go," he said.

Everyone, maybe a little embarrassed, went back to work.

I reconsidered my plan and my behavior. I shouldn't have lost my temper, and what if someone died because of me, and I had shamed the group into going. I tried to apologize before we left 'the wire.' "Look, guys, I'm sorry for..."

A loud bang got our attention. Joe Gorst pounded the table with his fist – "NO!" Al, you're in charge. It's your plan. Right or wrong, they'll follow you. Do not apologize." He grabbed his bag and stomped out of the room.

I looked left, right, and behind me to make sure Joe was gone. "Sorry, guys. I shouldn't have yelled. I apologize for being an asshole." They grumbled but accepted.

Off we went.

The helicopters started on time and taxied for takeoff. The American Controller in the tower cleared us for departure. "K-2 tower, Razor flight, a flight-of-four on runway one-six, ready for departure. Be advised, we're going to start a climb to twelve thousand over the field – on course heading is 140 degrees."

"Razor flight, wind calm QNH 29.88, from runway one-six, clear for takeoff."

We were on our way, and as soon as I cleared the trees at the end of the runway, I could see the mountains to our east. 'The Bear' was clear, there were no clouds at all. There was no rain, snow, or fog, and nothing showed on the storm scope or radar. The weather forecast was a bust, eliminating the need to climb over any obscurations. Empowered with good weather, we pressed on to tanker rendezvous.

I noticed a sea of dunes as we crossed the river into Afghanistan, because the usual sandstorm was nonexistent.

Our aircraft were spaced widely in an extended free cruise formation, giving each pilot maximum room to maneuver. Our NVGs amplified the ample ambient light provided by the moon and numerous stars. Visibility was fantastic, and I had maybe the best picture my goggles had given me since we'd arrived. We zig-zagged across the northern dunes, passed through the first set of mountains, and flew loosely in and around the terrain. My God, it was fun. You'd never know we were in enemy-held territory until a stream of 23 mm tracers snaked across the sky in our direction. The large-caliber AAA drew closer until we descended into the dunes, masking our position. Flying among the gigantic dunes felt like skiing down a snow-covered slope full of moguls. Once past the deadly fire, we relaxed and climbed back from contour to low-level flight. At the Release Point, Arlo split off to drop a diverse load of supplies for ODA 595: ammunition, saddles, tack, food, and two John Deere Gators.

In the meantime, I dragged my wingman to a snow-covered hilltop HLZ. The BM-21 rocket launcher was nowhere to be seen. It had been blown to bits earlier in the day. I dropped off my half of the team, then radioed Razor 04 that I was lifting off. Dave, in Razor 04, was inbound with the other half as I took off. Heavy-caliber tracer fire snaked in front of and then behind him. His right Minigun opened fire and I dropped behind a nearby hill. The last I saw of Dave was the stream of 7.62 leaving his guns. I didn't know if he was hit or struck the enemy. The radios were quiet until he rejoined the flight.

Mission accomplished – SF ODA linked up with their Northern Alliance counterparts and 'Horse Soldiers' resupplied. Within minutes our four aircraft were reformed and returning to K-2.

The flight may have been one of the most enjoyable flights of TF Dagger. As a matter of fact, that mission was presented as a vignette to the Deputy Secretary of Defense during a visit. Occasionally, I see FLIR footage of the ingress route on documentaries and historical briefings. Everything had gone well. Even the near misses with enemy AAA weren't all that scary, but we still needed to get home. And as we crested 'The Bear' heading west, I gasped at the cloud cover below us. A thick, all-encompassing fog bank covered everything below nine thousand feet. Landing at K-2 was going to be a challenge. The cloud cover caught us by surprise. Fog limited visibility to less than 50 meters as measured on the runway. We had nowhere to go – no alternate landing locations.

Time for another first: we were going to auto-land our MH-47Es in zero-zero conditions using a self-generated approach. If everything went well, we'd sleep in our own cots that day, but if not, we'd die from impact with the ground. Remember the ground? PK 100%.

When we first arrived at K2, Greg Calvert, one of our Instrument Flight Examiners, dug out a TERP manual for designing instrument approaches. The complex formulas calculating angles and altitudes were not for the faint of heart. Yet Greg sat at his desk, crunching numbers for a self-generated GPS approach to runway 16. Once the data was double and triple checked, we flight tested the approach during day Visual Meteorological Conditions (VMC) to verify safety margins were adequate for our equipment. Now, in the heat of the moment, while IMC, we were betting our lives on math. Were our calculations accurate? We'd know for sure in about three minutes; I'd go first, and we could only land one aircraft at a time. The urge to pee that I so often felt before doing something scary or stupid came upon me. Nothing was going to stop us from getting to the ground. I had only two choices; I could delay the inevitable, running out of fuel and being dragged to the ground by gravity, which wouldn't end well. Or I could try a controlled approach into the fog, betting on the mighty MH-47E. I knew what had to be done. So, I tapped my heels nervously and flexed my fingers deeper into my flight gloves before entering the approach data into my CDU.

The navigation points entered in a specific order, funneled me toward the runway. At a pre-selected point, my Integrated Avionics Suite (IAS) calculated a glide path to the first one-third of the runway. The Chinook was coupled to the flight director, so it was doing all the work – we just sat back and nervously monitored our progress. My stress level increased exponentially as the radar altimeter kicked on at fifteen hundred feet. Our proximity to the ground was now apparent as it began counting down rapidly.

The flight director speed cue slowed us to a stationary hover forty feet above our landing point. I still couldn't see anything outside. We were still in the proverbial golf ball. I took a deep breath and typed zero into the CDU altitude field. The aircraft descended on its own at three hundred feet per minute.

My flight engineer eventually saw the runway as we got closer. "Sir, I've got the ground. We're off twenty feet, now ten, five, four, three, two, one, aft gear contact, forward gear clear down. Three, two, one, contact; Ground Contact lights on."

I was ecstatic. The self-generated approach was another capability we'd never been allowed to do for real.

"Razor Flight, Razor 03, I'm on the runway. My overt lights are on. I'm taxiing forward to clear the runway."

Each helicopter repeated my actions. I thought the guys would be mad about needing to recover this way, but they felt like me – total adrenaline rush.

We still hadn't had a shower since arriving, but because of our successful night, I went to bed stinky but smiling...

+++

A couple of days went by, and General Dostum and the 'Horse Soldiers' took Mazari Sharif from the Taliban. We joked around, wondering if the infamous warlord rode in on his shiny new Gator instead of his horse. Either way, he took the town and airport in a pitched cavalry battle supported by US laser-guided bombs. We couldn't believe he did it so fast. The best estimates figured he'd be lucky to take Mazari Sharif by spring, and here we were just weeks into the UW campaign. What was next?

The ODA 595 commander informed TF Dagger that Dostum intended to move on Kabul. It's the main reason he took the little northern town. It stood in his way to the capital. He wanted to go now – not in the Spring. Our command went nuts, trying to figure out how to keep the general from moving toward Kabul. But buoyed by his recent success, he expected the Taliban to fall if he attacked. And he was going on the offense with his timeline, regardless of what we wanted. It came as a surprise when he made his move while we slept. He rode into Kabul with light resistance. The Taliban ran away, not wanting to fight Dostum and his US bodyguards. Their withdrawal from Kabul left it wide open for the Northern Alliance and, by association, to us.

Chapter 13

Letters from Home (November 2001)
2 months after 9/11

Time between missions typically involved planning for the next. I tried to stay focused on work. Thinking of home could bring a smile but, more often than not, I missed my family. Communications with Linda were still limited in quantity and quality. Operational Security software monitored our phone calls and emails. Say the wrong words and a nasty OPSEC violation would hit the commander's desk. It was not uncommon for a soldier to be sent home for unwittingly revealing classified or sensitive information. That's why the calls were normally so bland, and emails were no better. The only way to maintain some semblance of privacy with your wife was to use the old-fashioned postal system. Letters to and from home cost nothing – no postage required. You just had to make the time to sit down and put pen to paper.

I missed my sons. When home, I spent a lot of time with them. They were independent and self-starting. If there was a way to have fun, they'd find it. I cherished the artwork they sent and words of encouragement. They missed me, but not too much. Though the holidays were nearing and that might change things a bit.

Linda was holding things together on the home front. I don't know how she did it. She dealt with both boys and resolved household problems like a leaky pipe or clogged drain. She wrote often. The military transported free packages the size of a shoebox. Linda sent a box a week. I loved coming back to the HAS or tent to find a shoebox and a letter or two on my cot. The boxes and their contents were tangible memories of what we'd left behind. The satisfaction of opening a letter or box that someone took the time to acquire and fill lovingly with items they wanted you to have is heartwarming.

School children from across America sent 'any soldier' mail. Letters and packages poured into Afghanistan with words of support and gratitude. Our Chaplain received the mail and distributed it among the unit. All he asked was that they all be opened, and if you opened one, you wrote a return letter; not always an easy task when business picked up. But all in all, it was nice to be thought of.

+++

Linda's letters were mostly upbeat. I was amazed at how well she was doing. I thought about her depression and subsequent suicide attempt many years before. I couldn't be prouder.

Her hobbies were something you wouldn't expect. While I was deployed, she bought a tile saw, a do-it-yourself book, and materials to re-tile the kids' bathroom floor. Without anyone's help, she taught herself how to use her new tools and produced a professional looking tile floor. She sent photographs of her completed project to let me know she was making do, and I should focus on my task at hand, and come home alive.

Her selfless support reminded me how much I loved her. She was mine, I was hers, and together, we could accomplish anything.

Chapter 14

Hindu Kush Rescue and Hypoxia (November 2001)

2 months after 9/11

Arlo Standish's first mission to infil ODA 555, aka 'Triple Nickle,' was the closest any of us had come to running into a mountain. He'd pushed his aircraft to the absolute limits of its performance. The altitude required to get over even the lowest available saddle was nearly twenty-one thousand feet. Supplemental oxygen kept his crew coherent and healthy while battling the physiological hazards of extreme altitude.

Not long after infil to the Panjshir Valley, one of 555's members succumbed to altitude sickness. Staying in place would kill him, but the valley was surrounded by some of the highest mountains in central Asia. The Taliban blocked one end and the other end terminated in a box-canyon, leaving helicopter evacuation as the only option.

Arlo made the first attempt at rescue. He and his flight were greeted with the same nasty mountain storm that caused him to turn around during infil of 555. Rain, ice, snow, and fog made it almost suicidal to continue across the Hindu Kush mountains. Discretion won the day; Arlo aborted. The rescue would have to wait.

The Air Force southern rescue task force salivated as they watched Arlo's tracking beacon turn around to the north.

Before the war, the 20th SOS was our primary rotary-wing competition, but these elevations were just too much for them. Though they hadn't yet accepted that fact; they wanted to get their MH-53s into the fight from their base in Pakistan.

The Air Force figured rescuing a single patient from the Panjshir valley was within their performance envelope; and if someone didn't get to him, death was imminent. The problem was that the weather pattern was extensive and covered the entire area of operations. Anyone approaching from north or south was going into a nasty winter storm.

The Air Force prepared to launch as Arlo made his way back over 'The Bear.' They took off when he touched down at K-2.

Arlo heard about their attempt. He couldn't let them head into the teeth of the winter storm and tried to warn them. They didn't stand a chance of making it in and out. Rivalry can be a strong motivating factor in any endeavor, but this life or death competition was about to run its course.

The MH-53 pilots knew they had performance and weight issues just like us, but worse. It can't be simpler; an aircraft that's too heavy at Afghanistan's elevations will have insufficient power and crash – plain and simple. The 'fifty-three' pilots tried to limit their cargo and passenger loads like we did, but they weren't empowered to turn people away. Everyone wanted to go.

The Rescue PJs added redundant people and equipment in case they crashed. Their philosophy was that they needed to be ready for any possibility. Unfortunately, by disregarding the pilot's calculations, all they did was inadvertently ensure their helicopter was too heavy. Straight and level flight was okay at their planned altitude and cruise airspeed, but as they encountered the storm and turned around, problems developed. Their helicopters didn't have enough power to use their TF radar. Without that magic hardware, the pilots needed to navigate the storm the old-fashioned way – slow down and strain to look out the window.

At some point, they slowed too much, the engines struggled to maintain rotor rpm.

The pilots knew they'd met their match in the Hindu Kush. And as they turned to abort, the rotors drooped, leaving them only one choice – lower the collective to regain RPMs. Gravity can be a bitch, and the ground met them before they could get their helicopter back into its needed flight parameters, and they crashed. The aircraft was destroyed as it impacted the ground – remember my rule of thumb, ground equals PK 100%.

Though the helicopter was a total loss, the good news is that everyone survived the impact and were rescued by their wingman. The bad news – the CASEVAC failed.

After dumping fuel in a weight tradeoff, the lone MH-53 emerged from the storm and limped back to Pakistan.

Ironically, during their after-action review, the PJs complained that they didn't have enough backboards to move injured crewmembers after the crash. Think about it. The only reason they crashed was that the pilots had been coerced into taking more equipment than they wanted to carry. Yet, here were the same people wanting to add more weight for future missions. These lessons continue today in the mountains of Afghanistan and Pakistan. Math doesn't sound sporty or cool, but in Central Asia, performance planning dethrones the artillery as the king of battle.

+++

Altitude sickness would still kill the soldier without advanced medical care.

I got the call the next night; my turn to CASEVAC.

The previous night's storm had moved several hundred miles away while we slept. I launched at first dark to cross the Hindu Kush and pull him out. My

Chalk Two aircraft had a maintenance problem, so I took CW3 Dal Deetman, Arlo's wingman, for the attempt. My dual-purpose flight started like any other as we crossed 'The Bear,' but this time I flew due east into Tajikistan to pick up the SOCCENT commander. In addition to transporting the patient, I delivered the admiral into the Panjshir. He wanted to assess the situation on the ground and speak with the Afghan warlords in person.

Arriving at Dushanbe Airbase was a trip. The air traffic controller spoke perfect English, but his thick Russian accent made the visit surreal. We assumed a civilian callsign, NB-123 to semi-conceal that we were military.

I made my approach to the main runway and was met by a 'follow me' truck. He led me to a parking ramp to meet my passengers and their cargo. Like the Air Force PJs that overloaded the crashed MH-53, this group didn't heed my weight restrictions either, which was about to bite us in the ass big time.

+++

I zigzagged across the rolling foothills finally reaching the big mountains of Afghanistan. I was already wearing my oxygen mask and reminded Jethro to don his. The masks were uncomfortable, and he wanted to wait until he needed it. Against my better judgment, I allowed him to put it off.

We slowly gained altitude to get across a 21,000-foot ridgeline. Once on the other side, we could let down to about 9,500 feet to land along a river in the Panjshir Valley. Unlike any of Arlo's attempts, the visibility wasn't bad, but the temperature was below freezing. Not only was it cold in the back with the doors open, but one of our pitot tube heaters failed. Usually, that wouldn't be much of a problem, but at that altitude and temperature, the failures were about to compound themselves.

The Inertial Navigation Unit (INU) froze and failed. Not only was the INU a backup navigator to the GPS, but it was an attitude source for the cockpit to include the inputs for the vertical speed indicator. The VSI operated inversely without the INU. When the helicopter was climbing, the gauge showed a descent. I noticed the discrepancy and announced it to my crew, all of them acknowledged... But did they?

Jethro was having difficulty maintaining a proper airspeed and climb. Every time I pointed out his shortcomings, he'd overcorrect, causing the rotor to droop. He didn't notice the RPMs fall off, which could kick our main generators offline, so I took the controls from him and banked left away from the mountains and lowered the thrust to regain the precious RPMs. My trade-off of altitude for rotor rpm put us in a descent, trading the valuable altitude we'd taken several minutes to gain. I gave Jethro back the controls and started to diagnose our system malfunctions. Then he did it again – rotor decay due to sloppy flying.

I took the controls, and again I descended to put everything back into safe parameters.

I scolded Jethro, "What the fuck, man. What's with you? Your flying sucks."

His slurred speech said it all. "I dooon't knooow, Al – I'm woooorking on it."

Oh no... I'd been to the altitude chamber with him and partied many nights during our travels – either Jethro was drunk or hypoxic.

"Jethro, check your oxygen mask. I think you've got a problem."

He fiddled with his mask while I relinquished lead.

Dal tightened his turn inside our orbit and picked up lead as I fell into trail.

My flight engineer announced that the Helicopter Oxygen System console, or HOS, was empty on Jethro's side of the aircraft. Anyone on his console had been without supplemental oxygen for an undetermined amount of time. By the looks of things, it had been a while.

A quick check indicated my HOS was fully operational. Still, it wouldn't provide enough O_2 for the entire crew. We decided that one crew chief and I would share my console. Everyone else would deal with hypoxia. It reminded me of the story of Odysseus in Homer's Odyssey. He lashed himself to the mast of his ship, ordering his men to ignore his incoherent orders and pleas while they passed the island of the Sirens. The guys in the back of my aircraft would be similarly useless until we got below ten thousand feet, maybe even six thousand. I'd ignore them while they listened to the song of the proverbial Sirens.

Knowing that my crew was less than themselves, Sergeant Bill Loucks and I had to do everything for a while.

Then I got the surprise of my life as my cyclic and yaw pedals moved rhythmically without my input. "What the heck?"

I didn't know what to make of the movements. Had we lost some type of actuator. A melody began to hum in my helmet earcups. I glanced at Jethro, sitting in the right seat. He was lightly moving the controls to an imaginary beat that only he could hear.

"Jethro, are you on the controls?"

"Yup."

Jethro outweighed me by about fifty pounds and was all muscle. If he decided to fly the aircraft there is no way I could stop him. I needed to keep him busy with something that wouldn't interfere with my ability to control the helicopter.

"Jethro, you got your E6-B 'whiz wheel?'" I knew he did. We all carried the old-fashioned circular slide rule in our map bags.

"Yup."

"Good, I need you to do some calculations."

Without the IAS functioning properly, I didn't know what the max climb airspeed was. If I could figure it out, we'd climb faster.

"What do you want me to do?" His slurring was getting worse.

Above: 2001 – The aircrew of MH-47E 'Razor 03' during Operation Enduring Freedom. This aircraft carried ODA 595, aka 'Horse Soldiers' from their staging base in Uzbekistan into Afghanistan to link up with Northern Alliance General Abdul Rashid Dostum. Note the M134 'Minigun' mounted in the right cabin door, the external rescue hoist, and the air refueling probe. (*Photo provided by Alan Mack, 160th SOAR*)

Right: 2008 – Proficiency is a must for special operations missions. The 160th trains in all environments such as overwater, arctic conditions, mountains, and, as seen here, in the desert. This MH-47G is equipped with large external fuel tanks ('fat tanks'), Multi-Mode Radar (MMR), external rescue hoist, and aerial refueling probe. (*Photo provided by Boeing Helicopters taken by Bob Ferguson*)

The crew chief in the right cabin door, known as 'Right Gun,' has a picturesque view of a US Air Force MC-130 tanker. The pilot moves forward to obtain an 'Observation Position' where he will visually verify the condition of the tanker while the entire crew runs through the 'Observation Checklist'. Note the M134 'Minigun' in the foreground. (*Photo provided by David Burnett, 160th SOAR*)

This MH-47E cockpit utilizes four Multi-function displays, known as MFDs, to display relevant flight and mission information. The pilot enters data or queries the Integrated Avionics Suite (IAS) utilizing the two Control Data Units (CDUs) on the canted console. Note the rotor brake handle near the right seat pilot's window frame. (*Photo provided by Alan Mack,160ᵗʰ SOAR*)

The MH-47G leverages five Multi-function displays (MFDs) to display more information at one time, improving the pilot's situational awareness. Technological improvements provide improved graphics and additional mission calculations not computed by the older MH-47E. (*Photo provided by Alan Mack, 160ᵗʰ SOAR*)

The MH–47G 'Hover Page' provides critical flight information to the pilot in a visually obscured environment such as dust/snow landings and low overwater hovering. The MH–47E had a similar display with less information. Both versions provide power required, altitude, speed, and lateral drift trending. Using only this page, the pilot can maintain a stationary hover or desired drift. (*Photo provided by Alan Mack, 160ᵗʰ SOAR*)

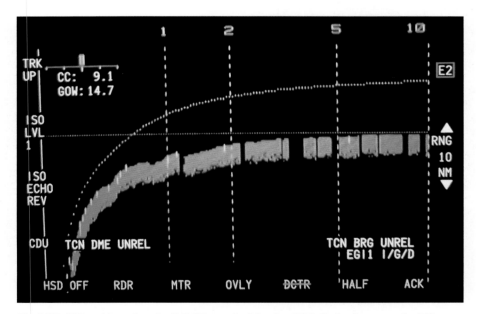

The MH–47G multi-mode radar (MMR) terrain-following (TF) display, known as the 'E2' page. Much like the MH–47E, this profile view depicts what terrain the MMR sees for TF commands. Marked using an exponential scale, the thick fuzzy line indicates terrain presence out to 1,2,5, and 10 miles. The dynamic curved-dotted line referred to as the zero–command line (ZCL) represents current engine and radar performance. (*Photo provided by Alan Mack, 160ᵗʰ SOAR*)

Be ready for war by training. An MH-47E conducts a two-wheel landing on a mountain ridgeline overlooking a desert valley. Chinooks have been performing this maneuver to load and unload passengers and cargo since their introduction to the US Army. (*Photo provided by Dave Gross, 160th SOAR*)

2008 – MH-47E and G are armed with four defensive weapons – two forward and two aft. Shown here are the dual 7.62 MM, M-240 machine guns. 160th SOAR door gunners benefit from training on the most extensive aerial gunnery range in North America (Red Rio, NM). In this photo, note the two Fast Rope Bars (FRIES) mounted at the cargo compartment entrance. (*Photo provided by Boeing Helicopters taken by Bob Ferguson*)

An MH-47 lands in the desert at night using night vision goggles (NVG). The photo captures a moment just before the pilot's visual cues are obscured by the dust cloud. This particular helicopter was fired upon with rocket-propelled grenades (RPG) from three points of origin, a common occurrence for SOAR crews. (*Photo provided by Frank Mancuso, 160th SOAR*)

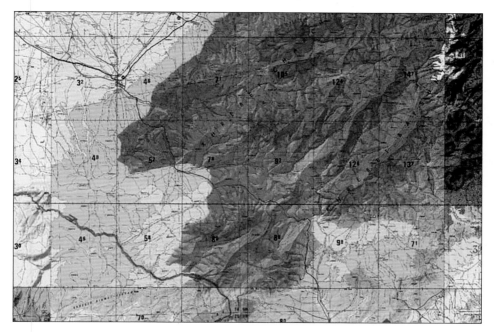

This visual phenomenon, nicknamed 'The Bear' by CW2 Jethro Fread, is depicted on US military JOG Air chart, scaled at 1:250,000. The actual terrain is darker than the surrounding soil. Imagine the bear's snout is pointed to the West, with a front paw and lake for an eye. (*Courtesy of CIA, Public Domain*)

2003 – CW4 Alan Mack leans on his MH-47E air refueling probe. The beginning of his duty cycle began at dusk. Pre-flight inspection before the sunset is crucial to rapid target prosecution after dark. Note the dull brown sky in the background. The suspended dust erases the horizon making night flight a challenge. (*Photo provided by Alan Mack, 160th SOAR*)

Service in the 160th is a calling. CW5 Alan Mack stands with his son and fellow Night Stalker, SPC Andrew Mack, in front of an MH–47G. (*Photo provided by Alan Mack, 160th SOAR*)

CW4 Alan Mack attends Ensign Stephen Mack's Officer Candidate School graduation in Rhode Island. Stephen's career path led him to the cockpit of an F–18F as a Weapons Systems Operator (WSO). (*Photo provided by Alan Mack, 160th SOAR*)

CW5 Alan Mack enjoys time with his sons Sgt Andrew Mack and LTJG Stephen Mack after assuming command of West Point's flight organization, 2nd Aviation detachment. Though a much different mission than the previous decade of war, the eclectic mission of his small unit would prove to be an emotional recovery. (*Photo provided by Alan Mack, 2nd AV DET, USMA*)

Above left: A young SP4 Linda VanAssen, the future wife of Alan Mack, heads to work at William Beaumont Army Medical Center (WBAMC) in El Paso, Texas.

Above right: Patti Mack married Alan Mack in 2015 in New York. He credits her love and support for his emotional recovery and subsequent happiness after leaving the 160th SOAR following his late wife Linda's passing. (*Photo provided by Alan Mack*)

'Scooter' looks ready to play. A mixed-breed dog combining Jack Russell Terrier and Beagle, known as a 'Jackabee', is a high-energy bundle of joy and fun. Alan's companion for many years helped him endure his wife's addictions and troubles. (*Photo provided by Alan Mack*)

Above left: CW5 Alan Mack gives up his command of 2nd Aviation Detachment, the culmination of an Army career spanning nearly thirty-six years. Once the Guidon is passed to his successor, he retires and remains in the local community. (*Photo provided by Alan Mack*)

Above right: This is the official distinguishing unit insignia (DUI), also known as the unit crest, which shows an armed flying centaur with a moon in the background. The 160th SOAR primarily fights at night. They live by the motto, Night Stalkers Don't Quit (NSDQ)! (*Photo from the Army Heraldry Institute*)

"I want you to convert eighty knots true airspeed to calibrated speed and give me the answer."

Joe Gorst watched quizzically from the jump seat as I talked Jethro through the conversion. He didn't understand why I would have Jethro running numbers on his slide rule.

Joe just sat there, puzzled. Hypoxia was taking hold of him and everyone else not on O_2. I wanted to keep Jethro's hands busy so he wouldn't touch the controls again. I didn't have time to explain.

"Jethro, put -25 degrees Celsius over the twenty thousand foot mark and read along the inner scale till you see eighty knots true airspeed."

I let him spin the wheels for a second.

He stopped.

"Jethro, what is the calibrated airspeed?"

"Forty-four knots," he said with confidence.

I slowed from one hundred knots to forty-four; and up we went. The vertical speed needle showed about one thousand feet per minute. I couldn't keep up with Dal in the climb, but once we leveled off, I caught him.

We flew across the terrain at fifty feet above the ground, but roughly twenty-one thousand feet above sea level.

We were going to make the mission happen, even with more than half my crew drunk with hypoxia.

Navigating the terrain and weather of Northern Afghanistan was a challenge none of us had experienced up until that time. Arlo tried, the Air Force tried, now I was encountering problem after problem. Altitude sickness might kill the sick man if I couldn't get to him – I couldn't quit.

Our determination paid off as I descended into the valley below. An IR strobe marked the landing zone and flashed brilliantly in my NVGs. Dust was almost nonexistent as we set down adjacent to a small stream. The gravel covered landing zone had a pleasant aroma almost like fresh linen. We'd made it over the Hindu Kush, now we had to get back across the mountain. Our patient needed sophisticated care medical care. I thought that maybe we could sit in the HLZ for a bit to recover from our hypoxic trip over the hills. But we were still around ten thousand feet, too high to make a difference. We needed to get moving.

The upside to sitting in the HLZ was a continued fuel burn, making us significantly lighter for the return trip. We easily climbed out of the Panjshir and made it effortlessly back to our side of the gigantic mountain range. I was entertained listening to my previously incapacitated crewmates become lucid. It would be funny if the ramifications weren't so serious. The conversations crossing the northern dunes toward Dushanbe reminded me of the morning hangover after a huge house party. Not many of them remembered what we'd done for the last two hours. A couple thought we still had to get to the CASEVAC site until our medic pointed to the new passenger on the stretcher.

We burned fuel making us lighter, but there was a tradeoff. To get back to friendly territory, and especially to medical facilities, we desperately needed to refuel.

Our tankers weren't cleared to operate in Tajikistan, so I was supposed to meet my MC-130 in Uzbekistan.

It was painfully obvious we weren't going to make it to the refueling track. I called our tanker in desperation. "Dude, I'm on fumes. I need you now."

I needed to get my patient to K-2 for medical care, but my priority was safety of all the helicopter occupants. We might need to land here in the middle of the mountains – not ideal by any means. *"Wow,"* I thought, *"look at the TACAN."* My tanker was closing faster than I'd ever seen. He must have been doing over three hundred knots – these guys could fly. Their biggest challenge was dissipating excessive speed in the turn around my backside.

Crew coordination calls calmly sounded in my helmet:

"Tanker at eight o'clock, four miles, coming around fast."

"Tanker at four o'clock and two miles."

"Tanker at three, approaching two o'clock."

The MC-130P virtually stopped at our two o'clock, allowing Jethro to ease up to their left wingtip for refuel. I completed the observation checklist as Jethro descended toward the pre-contact position. He never paused, continuing to move toward the drogue. You always stop for reasons that were about to become painfully obvious.

The fuel gauge indicated two hundred and fifty pounds of JP-8; maybe another two minutes of flight. If Jethro missed the drogue, we had to land immediately or risk a dual engine flameout.

He was dead on, center-punching the coupler. He hit fast and hard. The hose sine wave rippled as he pushed-in – up and left, toward the refueling position. Without pausing in the pre-contact position, he gave himself severe vertigo, maybe Coriolis illusion. "Contact... Al, I'm moving to refuel position. Oh crap... I feel like I'm spinning end over end and to the left – take the controls!"

"I have the controls."

"Thanks, Al. I think I'm gonna puke."

I started describing my moves to keep the crew calm. "We're in the refuel position. My cues are good... Dump tube, Bat Ears, and the hose is middle-range."

The helicopter was now ready to accept fuel, and if we didn't get at least a squirt soon, we were going down.

My flight engineer worked the fuel panel. He checked his switches and lights, then allowed the flow. "Sir, we're taking fuel – one thousand pounds so far."

He kept counting up as the tank filled to comfortable levels. I think the collective sigh of relief could be heard over the sound of our still-running engines. God, that was too close for comfort. I didn't like running on fumes.

Jethro started feeling better after sipping from his camelback canteen. Still groggy from hypoxia, he asked me to fly the remaining route home. I was happy to oblige. K-2, maybe forty-five minutes away, would be a welcome sight as we crossed 'The Bear.' Upon arrival, the cockpit was silent, as was becoming our ritual. We reflected on our efforts and luck as we were towed back to our parking spot. My lower back ached, and my left ear still hadn't cleared from our extreme altitude. I was starting to feel my age but smiled in anticipation of enjoying our newly-installed showers. Hot water and soap would be a nice end to the night. I watched with satisfaction as our patient's stretcher was loaded into an ambulance. He'd be OK, and so were we. Life was good.

+++

US forces were all over northern Afghanistan, and with Kabul firmly in Northern Alliance hands, we moved into another phase of operations. It was time to chase Usama Bin Laden. Intelligence sources felt he was hiding in the Tora Bora mountains. The Taliban no longer blocked our access to him, making him potentially accessible

Bagram, a former Soviet Airbase, just north of Kabul, would serve as our new Forward Operating Base (FOB). Arlo and Gold Team packed their three-day rucks for a quick overnight mission to support 5th Group and another Army SOF troop as they pursued Bin Laden. They'd work around the kinetic strikes and check caves in and around Tora Bora. Arlo was excited and, for a change, I was happy for him. Earlier in the deployment, I'd have been jealous, but I'd stay busy at K-2 supporting SF teams in the field.

Chapter 15

QRF

The cold November air made for pleasant flying. A light fleece and long underwear were fine for even the highest flights. Scheduled missions were standard by this point of our deployment. It seems that if we stuck to our established norms, missions were predictable and boring. Occasionally, the enemy voted different than us. Which was usually not much of a problem because we'd anticipate their likely and most deadly reactions. Most plans had a backup course of action or contingency in place. That didn't mean the enemy couldn't surprise us. Emergency response missions like CASEVAC and Quick Reaction Force (QRF) are on standby just in case. They are the riskiest endeavors we can undertake. Some events are more dangerous than others, and sometimes things don't go our way. Usually, we come out on top through skill or overwhelming firepower. Some would claim we get lucky. I'd like to think we make our own luck. I have to believe that, because if someone gets in trouble, we're never going to say no. Night Stalkers don't quit!

+++

Soldiers' families get the impression that their loved one is fighting for their life 24 hours a day while overseas. Those of us who have served know that life in a combat zone can be routine and boring. Even soldiers manning remote outposts in hostile territory aren't getting attacked every moment of the day. But you must be prepared to fight for your life at any moment.

Surprise. You're on the toilet when incoming mortars fall nearby. Ready or not, you're in the fight.

Sleeping and off-the-clock? Someone is in distress. You're going, no matter the hour. Get moving because there's no one else.

Personal equipment, weapons, and aircraft are ready at all times for a rapid launch. The passenger load varies based on who is best suited or maybe just who is available. Either way, details of where you're headed are usually sketchy at best. Flexibility and persistence almost always lend themselves to an adventurous reinforcement or rescue.

Qala-i-Janghi Prisoner Uprising

After capturing Mazār-i-Sharīf, General Dostum's immediate move on the Afghan capital was bold and successful. American military forces now unexpectedly occupied Bagram airbase, just north of Kabul and the former US Embassy in Kabul. Dostum's mere presence and cult of personality in Mazār-i-Sharīf were enough to intimidate enemy combatants and prisoners keeping them in check. Once it was obvious he was going to remain in the capital, things took an ugly turn.

I glanced up at the blazing sun as I was running to the TOC. Arlo was close behind.

In Dostum's absence, prisoners of war being held at the fortress of Qala-i-Janghi had rioted. Northern Alliance, American soldiers, and Agency interrogators were vastly outnumbered and needed reinforcement. I cringed at the thought of a daytime flight. We blasted out of K-2 with a flight of four MH-47Es, two MH-60L DAPs, and one MC-130P tanker. We loaded as many SF and infantrymen from the 10th Mountain Division as we could carry.

There was no time for a briefing, but we were well practiced and standardized by this point. The control tower cleared us immediately, and we went as fast as our MH-60s could go. The DAPs had rockets, Hellfire missiles, and a 30mm chain-gun on wing stores which, when in a fight, were desirable, but when trying to get somewhere quickly, the aerodynamic drag limited us to around one hundred and twenty knots, best case. I hadn't flown across 'The Bear' in daylight, and when I wasn't punching numbers into the IAS, I looked around to take in the scenery I'd been missing. Not much to see in that part of Uzbekistan.

Our tanker was waiting 'on track,' I had the 60s take fuel from the left wing while Chinook Chalks Two-through-Four got their gas on the right. As soon as the Blackhawks were full, they dropped off and dove away from the flight, accelerating ahead to meet us at the fortress. Then I moved onto their now vacant hose and refueled. By the time I finished 'tanking,' the other three 47s were done and beginning to cross back to the left to join on me. I thanked the tanker crew and sped up to around one hundred fifty knots.

No sandstorm. The sun high in the sky. We could see everything. Sounds good? It means the enemy could see us too.

The prisoners had regained their weapons, to include RPGs and heavy machine guns. Our rules of engagement were adjusted to allow us to engage anything not deemed friendly. I wasn't really sure what we were going to do when we got there. I'd seen the area before, but only in the dark, and just in passing. There were plenty of places to land between buildings, which would provide cover while we were unloading. Of course, during the approach to landing, we'd be vulnerable to ground fire.

Even with their head start, we caught the 60s before arriving at the fortress. They were already talking to the ground controller asking for a SITREP. And about ten minutes out we received our first situation update. At least one American had been killed in the initial uprising. No known living friendlies were within the walls of the fortress. Combat Air Support (CAS) assets were starting to fill 'the stack' overhead. With no friendlies in the target area, the JDAMs began to fall into the central yard of Qala-i-Janghi. The precision-guided airbursts gave our guys a chance to re-enter the fortress under supporting fire. And with the enemy heads down, we were able to land and reinforce unopposed.

After successfully retaking the Fort and with no CASEVACs to perform, we returned to K-2. We hadn't taken any friendly military losses or injuries; unfortunately, Mike Spann, a CIA officer, was killed while interviewing prisoners. I was grateful that we didn't have to fight, and I think we would have taken heavy losses without the overhead CAS. My luck was running out. I figured it was only a matter of time before I put my helicopter in a situation that I couldn't escape.

That night I lay in bed trying to flush the day's thoughts from my head, but my mind raced. How many close calls had I already encountered? They were piling up. Statistically, I figured, the more I was exposed to danger, the more likely that my luck would eventually run out. But as I liked to say, "miss by an inch or miss by a mile – a miss is a miss."

Cobra 22 Evades (Dec 2001)

An SF team near Pol-e-Khomri was caught between two quarreling Northern Alliance factions, a situation referred to as Green on Green fighting. And they had to evacuate in a hurry. They entered a mission profile known as E/E. Escape and Evasion was something everyone planned for but hoped not to do. The ODA, escaping in two SUVs, drove south along a winding dirt road. And since I knew their destination, I could make an educated guess at how they'd get there.

My co-pilot Craig and I had no communication with the fleeing team, so we sent an AC-130 gunship ahead to gain line-of-sight contact. I took off expecting to find the team and bring them home. A 'hot exfil' was likely, so our DAPs came along as armed escorts. We raced across the Amu Darya into Afghanistan, holding back on speed to allow the 60s to keep up.

An RPG flew past my cockpit, just off the nose.

A second RPG missed, passing my tail by a few feet.

"Razor 03, Sponge 01, you had two RPGs fired at you. It looks like they originated from along that East-West running road."

"Sponge 01, Razor 03, Roger. We saw them. One led us too much, and the other not enough."

"Razor, Sponge copies all. Listen... it looks like the way ahead is blocked with fog or clouds. The mountains are obscured. There's no way we're following you over the top. BREAK... So, we're going to stay right here trolling for those RPG gunners. I'll try to draw them out and see if they'll shoot at me. Then I can kill them."

"Sponge 01, Razor 03, copy all. Good hunting... I'm going to accelerate. BREAK... Razor 04, I'm speeding up to one hundred and forty knots... activate TF, three hundred-foot clearance altitude. Pick up two miles separation... execute in 3,2,1."

The DAPS slowed back and trolled around tempting the enemy gunners. If the bad guys took the bait, they'd get a face full of 2.75-inch rockets and 30mm HEDP; I left them to do their business.

In the meantime, the fog-shrouded mountains lay ahead. The Multi-Mode Radar (MMR) was going to pay dividends again as it generated a climb command penetrating the fog bank. Craig was on the cue, and I studied the digital map. I figured I could steer well south, let down into the valley, and turn back to the north for an intercept.

Over the ridgeline and in descent, the clouds parted. And once in the clear, I was faced with a choice. Two roads led to the north.

I made an educated guess and pointed to our left, indicating my preferred route. "Craig, turn slightly left and follow that road, it's about a three-four-zero heading."

"Roger. Turning left to approximately 340°."

"Craig – Tracer fire incoming, two o'clock."

"Got it, evading – looks like 23mm."

Several large tracer bursts snaked across the sky to our front, then over the top of us. If even one of the hundreds of rounds hit us, we'd be in trouble. Craig climbed slightly and banked gently away from the life-threatening projectiles. As soon as he had a chance to terrain mask, he banked hard to the left with a decisive drop behind a small hill. That's all it took, and we were out of the enemy field of fire. The AC-130 overhead didn't engage the AAA piece because there was still a layer of clouds between us. I was concerned that the ZPU 23-2's range was about 2,500 meters, which was beyond our 1,500-meter range for my Miniguns. He could hit us, but I couldn't reach him. Hiding and escape was our only option. This close-call confirmed Afghanistan was still a dangerous place. In just two months, I'd had more enemy ordnance fired at me than I cared to count. I was becoming immune to fear; something that would bite me later at Takur Ghar.

My left gunner worked at clearing a malfunction of the left Minigun. It jammed during our ingress test fire. We'd need all guns operational before reaching the team. The butterflies in my stomach were getting worse in anticipation of a firefight short one gun.

No one spoke for several minutes.

That is until my crew chief broke the silence. "Sir, Left Gun, I've got it fixed. I swapped the feeder de-linker and re-routed the ammunition chute. She'll fire now."

"Okay. Left Gun, clear to test fire."

The M-134 came to life with a familiar roar. And bright red tracers highlighted the thick stream of bullets impacting a nearby hill; sparks flew where the 7.62 mm rounds impacted rock.

"Bill, why does that gun have daylight tracers instead of low-light?"

"Sir, this aircraft was scheduled for the air gunnery range in the morning. We weren't expecting to fly tonight, and I forgot to swap the belts... Sorry."

"Okay. No problem. It just caught me by surprise."

The UHF radio crackled in my headset as I turned up the volume. Our AC-130 established comms with the evading team's radio operator, callsign Cobra 22. They had no injuries but couldn't return to their FOB due to the Green on Green fighting. The team was pursued initially but broke contact as they pushed to the south. Now with their actual coordinates, I could link up and exfil before the sun came up.

Craig saw them first. "Look – there at ten o'clock, about three miles – two white SUVs."

Sure enough, two vehicles with IR strobes taped to the roof sped along a dirt road, dust billowing behind them. We coordinated a pickup, and landed beside the lead vehicle, leaving plenty of room for Chalk Two to land behind us.

Once loaded, we recrossed the mountains and met our waiting MH-60 DAPS. They were where we left them an hour before. Pulling that SF Team out of harm's way was a gratifying feeling. I felt like I was born for this life.

SEAL Rescue

Chuck Grant and I sat on the front steps of our burned-out OPs building. We joked about the new sign next to the door. *Motel Six, we'll keep the light on.* The sun was setting at our backs and illuminated the snow-covered mountains over East River Range in the Bagram valley. I was pleased that my cigar was burning evenly and observed the gentle wisp of white smoke curl ever upward. The quiet moment enjoying the tiniest of pleasures was about to be interrupted.

Steve Reich rounded the corner at a trot. He was out of breath. I'm not sure if it were how fast he'd run or the elevation of Bagram itself.

A SEAL reconnaissance team had been ambushed. The vehicle, an armored SUV, had been disabled by heavy machine gunfire, with one man wounded. The SEALs moved from their disabled vehicle and hunkered down in a nearby grove of trees and were slowly being surrounded. Our SOF Troop commander, let's call him Tom, came to fill us in. He didn't have any more details than we already knew. I grabbed my M-4, jumped into the back of a Hilux pickup, and went to our helicopters. The incident was in the Jalalabad valley, maybe twenty minutes away if we flew as fast as we could. The longer it took to get there, the more chance enemy reinforcements would arrive and not only outnumber the SEALS but our QRF. Chuck took lead with a small force of British Special Boat Service (SBS) troops. I followed close behind as his wingman carrying Tom and the boys from SOF.

The sun continued to set, and I flipped my NVGs into position. They displayed a clear, bright video. At least the weather was good.

We arrived on scene, but I couldn't identify friend or foe. The occasional tracer flew past as Chuck started a hard-left orbit around the palm grove. There, in the trees, I saw an infrared strobe – friendlies.

The tracer fire stopped, most likely due to our presence.

Chuck described a small clearing along a dirt road for landing and instructed me to pick up the team. He'd provide overhead security.

In my entire career, I can name three of the best landings I've ever made – all in Afghanistan, and this was one.

I could tell the ground was dusty, and the landing area was going to be tight among the palm trees. Telephone lines ran along the east/west running dirt road, and a small clay building to the south created a tight HLZ. In just one orbit, I knew exactly how I wanted to land. Pushing my fingers deeper into my flight gloves, I selected MFD hover symbology and began a steep approach. "Alright guys, this is a 'bravo' approach to the ground. Expect heavy dust."

My crew chief on the right ramp started his calls. "Heavy dust at the ramp. Continue approach... Aft gear off 40 feet...20..."

Craig was calling out groundspeed and confirming or correcting the altitude calls. 20 knots – 40 feet, 10 knots – 20 feet.

The crew coordination calls came faster than usual.

"Dust mid-cabin, now at the cabin door."

"Aft gear 5, 4, 3, 2, 1, contact, forward gear down. Ground contact lights illuminated. Ramp clear down?"

"Roger, ramp clear down. I looked up from the MFD, where I'd been focused on the hover symbology vectors. The dust cloud was so dense, I still couldn't see the obstacles around us.

I let Chuck know I was safe on the ground. "Razor 01, Razor 03, safe on the ground. Deploying QRF."

"Roger, I'm in a left-hand orbit around you. Give me a heads up before pitch-pull."

"Roger."

The dust cloud was so dense, Chuck never saw more than my rotor sparkle, otherwise known as the dust halo. The SEALs and my team were onboard in less than a minute. I needed to come straight up until we cleared the dust and obstacles to avoid becoming twisted metal, fire, and blood.

"Razor 01, Razor 03, Pitch-pull in five seconds."

I held the brakes to avoid rolling as I added power. Coming straight up, we cleared the trees, telephone wires and dust without a rotor strike before accelerating away. I consider this mission a death-cheater to this day. Christmas was near, and I didn't want to ruin my kids' holiday by dying.

Chapter 16

Tora Bora and the Hunt for Bin Laden
(Dec 2001)

Usama Bin Laden was hiding in Tora Bora, near the Pakistan border. A bombing campaign began in earnest, trying to kill him. His cave complex withstood Soviet attacks of the 1980s and would likely shelter him successfully again. That's where our MH-47s came in. We'd shuttle US soldiers and Afghan troops to the openings of bombed caves so they could be explored and exploited. So many bombs were dropped, the mountains glowed even without looking through NVGs.

The operation lasted longer than the expected two to three days, so after about a week, Joe Gorst called for my team of two MH-47s to replace Arlo's. The man I brought to swap with Joe was a young captain, straight out of the 160th training platoon, known as 'green platoon.' Captain Bart Jenkins looked like he was twelve years old. Young looking, but smart, he was a good fit to command my Silver Team at Bagram. I still remember the SOF Troop Commander's face when Bart introduced himself. "Hi, Bart Jenkins, damn glad to meet you." There was a short pause, and I thought that was all he'd say, but Bart added, "I just got out of Green Platoon."

"What? I'm sorry, did you just say you just graduated from training?"

Joe Gorst stepped in. "Don't worry, Tom. Bart is sharp. You'll be happy to have him; besides, you have Al, here. He's one of the most senior MH-47 pilots in the Regiment. Trust me. You're in good hands."

I don't know if he bought it, but he really didn't have a choice. Gold Team was heading back to K-2 for a reset. If the Tora Bora campaign went on for much longer, we'd exchange positions again with a Relief-In-Place (RIP). Because we arrived better supplied, we could stay longer than the first group. I suggested that we do three-week rotations, which seemed agreeable to everyone.

Bagram, as a camp, was run by the 5th Special Forces Group, and I enjoyed the relaxed atmosphere around the base. We were encouraged to grow beards and were told to wear civilian clothing whenever possible. Not to blend in as Afghans, but to mask who we were. It made it more difficult for non-military folks to figure out who was whom.

One of the highlights of camp was a newly-erected shower tent near our building. The only downside was that we couldn't control the temperature. It had one setting – scalding hot. I think it burned the dirt and grime from our skin.

We had no dining facility, so we heated Army T-Rations on our pot belly heaters. Packages from home would occasionally arrive full of Hickory Farms summer sausage or cans of SPAM. A quick spin in a hot skillet with some Texas Pete hot sauce or teriyaki marinade made for a tasty meal. Good food was a luxury we didn't often get to enjoy. However, I do remember our First Sergeant sending a pallet of fresh tomatoes from K-2 via C-130. We cut the tasty veggie-fruit into quarters, added salt and pepper, and enjoyed a feast fit for a king. I can't look at a tomato to this day without remembering those days in Bagram.

Ironically, life back at K-2 started to suck again. A new command element from the Air Force assumed control of Stronghold Freedom. With the new leaders came new rules – stupid rules. These folks had just arrived in theater and had no idea what everyone had endured in the early days. Arlo and his team were miserable there. He called and told me that Bagram didn't seem so bad in hindsight. I had to agree. My team and I were happy sleeping in the burned out 'motel six.' Sure, it was dirty, but no one messed with us. On the lighter side, the enemy harassed us a bit near the edge of camp. We had to urinate in 'piss tubes' near the camp perimeter. Concertina wire surrounding our camp was the only barrier between us and bad guys. No one wanted to pee during the day for fear of being shot by snipers. At night you could go with impunity. Albeit you'd get a flashy show of tracer fire to the west as you stood doing your business.

+++

The terrain in Afghanistan varied from desert plains, dunes, hills, to mountains. Flights to Tora Bora crossed several mountain ranges, some large and others were small. One night I was asked to take a newsman along. He was going to deplane and stay with the SF teams searching the caves. When we were about thirty minutes out from landing, he politely asked a question. I wasn't particularly busy, so we talked a bit.

"I'm John, by the way."

"Hi John, I'm Al. You're flying on Razor 03. What's your question?"

"Why are we flying so high in the mountains? I thought for sure you'd be flying fast and low through the valleys and draws?"

"Well, John," I said in a matter of fact tone. "I'm not down there for a couple of reasons. First is that what you just described is what's being broadcast on news programs every day. I'm not about to do what anyone expects. I'm about as predictably unpredictable as they come when missions are involved." I wondered which news organization he was with but didn't ask. I didn't have a very high opinion of news reporters at the time, but he was nice, so I kept talking.

"Look, the threat to us is MANPADS, small arms fire, and the occasional AAA piece. All require that the shooter see us to engage. If bad guys are down there in the valley waiting for me, their missile seeker heads won't get a good 'lock' up here due to background clutter. We've had several fired at us in the last couple of months, and our flares have decoyed the missiles. About three quarters of the way up the ridge is called the military crest. We fly up here because the remaining twenty-five percent of terrain above us provides the background clutter I mentioned to help spoof heat-seeking missiles. If I'm fired at, I can simply ease back on the stick to trade speed for altitude without increasing power and by association, my heat signature. Once we reach the crest of the ridge, I can descend on the opposite side, achieving cover from any potential follow-on shots – the same goes for AAA fire."

"Son of a gun. Who would have thought," he said, almost embarrassed – I liked him. It turns out he was John McWethy of ABC News. Ironically, he was one of my favorite on-air personalities before the war. I tried to look him up several years later, only to hear that he was killed in a tragic skiing accident.

+++

Cave complex missions in Tora Bora became more frequent as the bombing diminished. An interesting twist in cave exploitation presented itself when a robotics team with a novel approach came to assist. I volunteered to test infil the futuristic hardware; we lowered a tracked robot with multiple cameras from our helicopter near a cave opening. The robots weighed nearly thirty pounds but were easily lowered using '550 cord' from a hundred-foot hover. The robot operator had a small laptop console with a couple of joysticks to control the device. If I kept my ramp oriented toward the cave, we had about a two-mile range. We never used them again from the air after December, so I don't know how effective they were.

+++

'Motel 6,' as we called it, was a bombed-out Soviet era barracks. The numerous rooms had the smell of an old charcoal grill. The interior walls were cracked and scorched. Our electrical power came from a bank of generators tucked away in the corner of the camp. Cables fed through a hole in plywood window covers. My cot was not as comfortable as a bed, but I slept well. The lighting was limited to one bare lightbulb per room except for the common area, which doubled as a place to plan missions. Everything we did revolved around plans, and this place was no different. About this time of the deployment, our battalion added a crew and Chinook from Alpha company. That brought our tiny force at Bagram up to three helicopters, leaving two in Uzbekistan. Our DAPs were being pulled back to the

States for potential follow-on missions. I didn't want to see them go, though there wasn't much they could do in our AO anyway.

Christmas approached, and I told Arlo that he could stay at K-2 if he wanted. My entire team was glad to live at Bagram. As it turned out, the next time Gold Team came back to Bagram, we'd all stay. Bin Laden had somehow escaped into Pakistan during a cease-fire. But that didn't mean we wouldn't go after him if he were sighted again. TF Dagger was going to close down operations, leaving us attached to Task Force, TF-11.

Chapter 17

Bagram Liberation Medal (Dec 2001)

Winter was in full swing, and the mountains were covered with several feet of snow. The climate was freezing at night, but comfortable during the day when the sun was out. Our Battalion SIP, Chuck Grant, joined our team and brought a box of cigars to share. He and I would sit on the front steps of the 'motel 6,' and look at the beautiful snowcapped mountains as we went through his cigars.

We passed the time talking about our families, though we weren't really up to date on how they were doing. We didn't have a morale-phone at this location yet, so we relied on writing letters home.

In many ways, our tiny enclave was kind of fun, if not a little dangerous. The area was heavily mined, and it was smart to stay on the beaten path when walking around. A Jordanian mine-clearing-unit chewed up the ground around the airfield and living areas, with a 'flail' machine. The rotating spool in front of an armored tractor spun, beat the ground, setting off unexploded ordnance, and planted mines. We got used to hearing unexpected explosions as the Jordanians did their business. The only time we went out of our way to check on surprise booms or bangs was if the 'Jordos' were not active. We occasionally had soldiers or local citizens trip a device and require immediate medical care.

+++

Life around Bagram evolved into a comfortable cadence. Along with our Air Mission Commander, we needed someone to be responsible for running our camp. Captain Steve Reich shared the role off and on with Captain Marty Keiser. They were both well suited to the task and a pleasure to work with. I think Steve did the most time at Bagram in those early days. He often said he felt like he was the warden of a prison farm or work camp. So, we nicknamed him 'the warden.'

Steve created a mock award for living at Bagram, called the 'BLM.' The Bagram Liberation Medal was meant to remind those of us that lived there, of the adventurous days before concrete and restaurants took over the base. Unfortunately, Steve was killed in action several years later with the Quick Reaction Force during Operation Redwings.

The Bagram Liberation Medal
Chief Warrant Officer Three Alan Mack

Be it thus forever known, CW3 Mack demonstrated exceptional endurance, diligence, and competence in securing and preserving the freedom of the sprawling, metropolitan center of Bagram. As the decisive moment of the campaign, this individual's actions personified in every aspect those ideals associated with living, breathing, and being the 'Tip of the Spear.' Continuously operating under the threat of celebratory fire, low crawling from the tent to the outhouse, and always looking forward to the next stovetop dinner, the above-mentioned individual ensured the history of Bagram will forever be linked to the men of the Dark Horse. May you remain every vigilant. Beware the Darkhorse.

+++

Embassies around the world are little gems, demonstrating to all who can see that a commitment has been made through diplomatic means. The doors of the US embassy in Kabul were closed in 1989 with the Soviet Occupation. And on the 17th of December 2001, it re-opened for business. The significance of that event required high-level recognition. So, I was assigned the job of flying the CENTCOM commander, General Tommy Franks, and his entourage to the embassy for the high-profile opening day ceremonies.

They wanted to fly during the day, which I felt would expose the VIPs to potential enemy fire. I suggested they drive, but the risk for driving was considered more dangerous. I warned the CENTCOM staff of the danger. They assured me the country was secure now; the Taliban had fallen. I tried to convey that we received enemy fire every flight. And but for the grace of God, luck, or skill, we never got hit, but Afghanistan was still a dangerous place to fly.

It seemed to me the folks at CENTCOM were a little out of touch with reality. Their lack of knowledge regarding the threat, outweighed their desire to celebrate the significance of regaining our embassy. Not only did I carry the Commander, but he brought along his wife, and the Afghanistan commander, General Harrel. The executive entourage climbed aboard my MH-47E for the short twenty-minute flight to Kabul. The sun was high in the clear sky and no wind to speak of. The flight to the embassy should have been enjoyable, but as we often say, 'the enemy gets a vote.' That's a saying that can ruin any day.

About fifteen miles out, our infrared missile countermeasure system automatically deployed flares. A MANPAD homed toward the decoys, missing both Chinooks. I suspected an inadvertent flare launch but was informed that a missile flew between our wingman and us.

No proximity fuse – no direct hit – no damage. I wasn't about to tempt fate or wait for a second shot, as I descended to about ten feet and accelerated to one hundred and seventy knots, which is approximately two hundred miles per hour. The low altitude allowed me to use even the smallest hills and swales as cover from the most likely missile launch points. Our passengers were wearing headsets and heard the cockpit conversations. They sensed no danger due to the conversational tone of our voices. Many of the combat movies I see, portray the crew freaking out when shot at. As I mentioned earlier, we'd been shot at nearly every flight; we were as cool as cucumbers.

Routine or not, I had two Generals and a spouse to deliver safely. The slowdown for landing took some effort. About a half-mile out, I started my aggressive approach and dropped into the courtyard as soon as the helicopter cleared the embassy walls. No reception party was waiting. We'd surprised them. No one even heard us coming. The passengers deplaned and we were on our way.

"Razor 04, this is Razor 03 on FM... expect an aggressive departure – Pitch–Pull in five seconds."

CW3 Willie Martinez, my wingman, was right behind me. As soon as I cleared the embassy courtyard, I 'nosed' the aircraft into an extreme acceleration. Surprise of all surprises – kites everywhere! The Taliban had banned kite flying, during their rule, but now they were everywhere over Kabul.

Who knew?

At my low altitude, I felt like I was dodging barrage balloons from a Second World War beachhead. I weaved, I swerved and avoided every kite I could. I probably chopped a few strings at two hundred miles per hour.

Kites were forgotten quickly, because another MANPAD headed my way only to chase another set of countermeasure flares.

Willie clued me into what I already knew. "Razor 03, you just had a missile fired from about three o'clock."

"Roger, 04. I see it. I'm going to keep my speed up to minimize our exposure – try to keep up."

We flew as fast as our aircraft could go to get into the next valley, which I hoped was out of the engagement zone.

We arrived back at Bagram with no more incidents. I knew we shouldn't go back for pick up until dark. My adrenaline was starting to return to normal about the time my main rotors coasted to a stop. My back ached as I climbed out of the helicopter and tried a few stretches. Willie headed my way with a purpose. The next conversation was gonna be a hoot. I already had an funny idea to wind him up for laughs.

A couple of nights earlier, we'd watched a movie – *Flight of the Intruder* by Stephen Coonts. The protagonist, Jake Grafton, and his bombardier make an unauthorized bomb run on Hanoi during the Vietnam war. Missiles, rockets, and AAA narrowly miss them as they fly through what was known as 'SAM city.'

Their bombs don't deploy, and their target is not destroyed. The whole mission was a waste without destruction of the Surface to Air missiles. The pilots turn to each other, and one says something like, "I guess we should go back; they'd never expect us twice."

Willie Martinez was from Puerto Rico, and he often played up his thick accent for laughs, but this time, he wasn't kidding. He was animated and agitated. 'Holy Shit, Al! Did you see that shit? Missiles and fuckin' kites. Oh, man, that was craaazy."

"Willie, you realize we've gotta go back to bring them home."

His arms flailed. "What? No fuckin' way."

"Willie, think about it… They'd never expect us to go there twice."

The look on his face was priceless.

I can't list the expletives he uttered; most were in Spanish anyway. He couldn't understand why I was smiling. I was able to calm him down after pointing out the movie reference. Then I talked to our operations folks and let them know what occurred and that if the VIPs wanted a safe return trip, they should wait until after dark or drive – they drove.

MANPADS had been fired at everyone but me up until that point, and so far, nobody had been hit. The smoke trail from the first missile fired at us appeared to be a SA-7. A nearby SF team recovered the expended Grip stock from the second missile belonging to an HN-5. Throughout the days and weeks, the only face I showed to anyone was a cool, calm professional. No fear. Later that night, I sat in the dark, sipping bottled water, struggling to calm my mind. I thought about my family, and wondered how my wife and sons were holding up. I missed them and wanted to see them again, but our missions were bound to get harder. I had to believe the enemy was going to adapt and learn from our actions. The pessimistic thoughts were strong – *"there's no way I'm going to survive this deployment,"* I thought as I downed the last of my water.

The following day, I stopped by General Harrell's office to see if he had anything to say. He told me he didn't have any idea we'd been fired at as we approached the embassy. He thought the wild ride as I evaded the missile, was me showing off. The passengers were never concerned.

That was okay with me.

Chapter 18

Christmas at Bagram (Dec 2001)

Nobody wants to be deployed during the holidays. It's no fun being away from your family. Most guys compensate by decorating their bunk area with Christmas lights or holiday bobbles; quite frankly, I just tried to ignore it. In my opinion, Christmas was for home. Linda always went overboard decorating. She and the boys would festoon our Clarksville home with plenty of holiday cheer. I, on the other hand, was living in that same burned-out building at Bagram Airfield. Decorations couldn't hide our scorched walls, but at night, our single bare lightbulb hanging from the ceiling wouldn't throw enough light to see the damaged plaster anyway.

I'd been outside, getting some fresh air, and shivered as I entered the planning area. The damp air added some chill to our already frigid night. Fog was forming in the low areas and around water sources. Several guys were lounging around watching one of our few VHS tapes, while others read or wrote letters. The Christmas spirit was nowhere to be seen, except for a small two-foot-tall tree with ornaments sitting in the corner. 'The Warden' had just returned from a meeting with 5th SFG. They asked for a resupply mission to one of their isolated ODAs. It was Christmas Eve, and Steve gave me the option to go or not. I asked my crew if they wanted to go and got a unanimous, yes.

The weather was 'iffy,' but I saw a window of opportunity in the forecast.

We sat waiting at our Chinook, ready to go when a pickup truck full of cargo rolled up behind us. A couple of SF ODB guys downloaded a large-screen television, a VHS VCR, and a box of tapes. Our C-130 unit made an effort to bring supplies on Christmas, so who was I to say no. "Fuck it," I said. "Merry Christmas – Let's go."

Once everything was tied down, we cranked and departed to the south toward Gardez. I know the night is supposed to be dark, but the fog and low clouds obscured the stars, and whatever cultural lighting existed. We didn't have Rudolph's nose to light the way, but we did have a Multi-Mode Radar.

Chalk Two picked up a two-mile separation, and off we went.

The MMR's terrain-following hadn't let me down yet, and this night would be no different. In less than an hour, we were unloading our precious cargo into a Hilux pickup truck on top of a large sand dune. The SF guys were happy.

Who risks death flying through crappy weather to deliver non-essential gifts on Christmas eve? The Night Stalkers.

The look on those battle-hardened SF soldiers reminded me about the meaning of Christmas. Giving to others was the key for me. Not the gift itself, but the time, energy, and attitude that made the effort special.

I felt blessed for the opportunity to make someone's day. We weren't performing a lifesaving CASEVAC, we didn't kill an Al Qaeda leader, but we softened the hearts of soldiers, reminding us all to remember that all-important humanity that can be lost in times of war. As good as giving felt, I have to admit, being on the receiving end can be just as nice. While we were out playing Santa, the same C-130 that brought in the gear for the SF ODAs, brought supplies and goodies for us too. I couldn't believe my eyes as I walked into our sleeping area to drop my gear. My cot was stacked with shoeboxes with my name written all over them. Tears welled up in my eyes. The timing couldn't have been better. Linda's Christmas spirit reached me thousands of miles from home when I needed it most.

Those boxes could have come on a later flight, a day or two later, but thanks to the C-130's crew and our First Sergeant, Christmas in Afghanistan wasn't so bad. I couldn't wait to share my holiday bounty with my roommates. The boxes were stuffed with snacks, goodies, small presents, and photos to remind me of home. All six pilots and 'the warden' sat under that miserable bare lightbulb with a quartz heater nearby. We talked about the night's activities and wondered how many generations of soldiers spent their Christmas in similar circumstances or worse.

Summer sausages, crackers, cheese, tortilla chips, and salsa tasted heavenly as we feasted in our bombed-out barracks. To this day, Christmas 2001 in Afghanistan ranks as one of my most memorable and fond memories. What made the evening so special was not the events, but the people. I'd do anything for the guys I was flying with and those I supported. Our unit motto Night Stalkers Don't Quit, wasn't just a set of words – we lived by it.

I closed my eyes and thought about how easy that night's mission unfolded. Just a couple of months earlier, a TF flight in the mountains of Afghanistan would be considered high risk and maybe even undoable. Yet there we were zipping over and around the terrain in limited visibility to deliver Christmas goodies. How the heck did we manage that?

Chapter 19

The Tanker and the Mountain (Feb 2002)

A hot cup of coffee brewed on the pot belly stove started my day. We'd moved out of the 'motel 6' into a cluster of tents. They were cleaner and probably had less of a chance of giving us hepatitis. But I sort of missed the burned-out building that we'd called home for so long. Our tents were surrounded by an eight-foot dirt berm, topped with concertina wire. I'd say our living conditions had improved. We even had our own morale phone for calling home – No lines.

You could call just about any time of day, but you still had the same OPSEC restrictions.

I didn't use the phone often, but Linda and the boys were doing well, her spirits were up, and the boys were behaving. I couldn't ask for more.

I relooked my mission packet I'd just put together. We were preparing for another Bin Laden raid. The SEALS were convinced that he had slipped back into the Barmal Valley of Afghanistan near Shkin. We dragged everything we owned from K-2 to Bagram, never to go back. I was the overall Flight Lead to kill or capture the leader of Al Qaeda, and I put together a plan involving three AC-130s, seven MH-47s, and five MH-53s. We briefed, rehearsed, and stood ready before the mission was put on hold. The Intelligence Community couldn't agree if he was really there. I was disappointed that we wouldn't have a chance to kill him. But the next-best-thing was about to come our way – Mullah Mohammed Omar. The one-eyed protector of Bin Laden was found. He was just out of our unrefueled range, but doable with tanker support. Unfortunately, when TF Dagger dissolved, our MC-130Ps moved into Pakistan and no longer supported us directly. We'd need to pull them from their regular duties to give us the extra 'legs' for our mission. My responsibility was to deliver a SEAL team deep into central Afghanistan, where they'd link up with a reception team and the Northern Alliance. Terrain elevation was going to be a problem. The plateaus and flat areas were around fourteen thousand feet surrounded by even higher mountains. I searched the map for a lower area to air refuel – found one – nine thousand feet.

The Afghans would lead the SEALS to Omar so they could kill him. The timing was crucial; we needed to get there fast. Of course, the SEALS were already on a mission in Bamiyan, making it impossible to coordinate with them before departing Bagram. We'd have to talk en route.

I was flying in Razor 01 instead of my usual Razor 03, with an experienced co-pilot, Razor 02 was also crewed with an experienced pair of pilots. Our weak point was our third crew led by a new FMQ from Alpha Company and a newly graduated pilot from Green Platoon. There really was nothing complicated about our mission. Fly to Bamiyan airstrip, put SEALS in Razors 01 and 02. Razor 03 had Airforce PJs for CSAR and medical coverage. The 23rd STS PJs, like us, had new people filtering-in to augment the guys we'd been working with since the beginning.

We had a mix of men who'd been in Afghanistan dealing with the limitations of aircraft power, experience with weather in the mountains, and aeromedical issues like hypoxia. The lessons we learned in the early days were only as good as memory and the ability to pass along essential tips. I think we may have missed the mark in some respects.

Leaving Bagram at night was easy. Though air traffic was increasing at the airfield, not many units other than us, flew at night. Weaving our way through the mountain passes to Bamiyan was not tricky but landing on the dirt strip was. Even though the runway was packed and stable, the billowing dust clouds produced by our rotor wash, made landing a challenge.

Not long after touchdown, the SEALS began to load. I gave the team leader a hard time about taking too long to load, but it wasn't their fault. The Afghan truck drivers had an English-speaking deficit, which slowed things down a bit. Every minute they delayed shortened our fuel range, to the point we might not even be able to take enough from our tanker. I know they'd have loaded up quicker if we'd had an opportunity to talk beforehand, but we didn't, and here we were, burning fuel.

'Slab,' the team leader, was rushing from group to group trying to get things moving. In the meantime, our MC-130P hadn't been told a time that we'd arrive for gas, so they set up for refueling as soon as it got dark. They were running up and down the track at our proposed refueling altitude of 9,500 feet. The altitude is a crucial component of this vignette. A military aircrew may fly between 10,000 feet MSL for an hour, and up to 14,000 MSL for thirty minutes without the use of supplemental oxygen. From 14,000 feet MSL and above everyone onboard must use oxygen. According to their altimeter, the crew of Ditka 03 was at 9,500 feet for well over two hours. Their weather forecaster gave them a different altimeter setting than ours. As near as I can tell, they were actually several hundred feet higher than their instruments indicated, causing a slow onset of hypoxic hypoxia without supplemental oxygen. Remember my experience rescuing the SF soldier from ODA 555 back in November? They were unintentionally flying impaired, almost drunk-like. Decision-making and flying skills affected.

We were wearing oxygen masks, so weren't affected by our altitude. Their hypoxia didn't seem to affect our rendezvous, and I had no reason to suspect they were not at their peak performance. I stayed on the left wing with Razor 02. Razor 03 crossed over to grab his fuel from the Right-wing. 'JT,' my copilot, was flawless. He moved to contact and slid up and left to assume the refuel position.

The turbulence wasn't as bad as, we'd seen lately, but the visibility was affected by a gray haze. The surrounding mountains, capped in snow, blended into the neutral background. Avoiding optical illusions was going to be a trick until we got off the tanker. Razor 02 exchanged places with us and took his fuel. And once done, he assumed a staggered left formation behind me. Now, we were just waiting on Razor 03. He'd been having trouble 'plugging' into the right hose. Right-side refueling is harder than the left, so I offered the left hose. Craig, the pilot-in-command, snapped at me on the radio. He had the new copilot, so I figured he had his hands full. I'd leave them alone as long as they didn't become an issue. He 'plugged' and fell off, he missed above the drogue, then below the drogue. The new guy didn't have the benefit of several months of Operations Desert Thunder and Fox.

I looked at my MFD. We were nearing the end of the track and would have to move on.

No more delay. I needed Craig to make the plug, his copilot's feelings be damned.

He snapped at me again.

I snapped back and demanded his fuel total.

He only needed another five minutes on the hose and accepted my offer to cross over to the left wing. I could tell another pilot was flying now.

I didn't find out until the AAR that Craig was the original pilot. He was nasty with me on the radio because he was frustrated with HIS performance. Lucky for him, his brand-new copilot had no problems at all.

We passed the end of the track and could have turned around to buy more time, but we needed to get going. A minor turn to the left got us heading in the right direction, so I asked the tanker to drag us along our course and try to maintain altitude until Razor 03 finished. I took my radar out of standby as we banked to the left. It immediately showed terrain ahead. My NVGs couldn't differentiate between the hazy background and the snow-covered ridgeline to our front. And I wondered aloud if the tanker pilots saw the obstacle in our path.

Razor 03 fell off the hose again. I considered sending them back to Bagram. They just didn't have the talent this night. I was relieved to see Ditka 03 start a gentle climb to clear the terrain ahead. But the C-130P stopped climbing and began to descend.

I called to warn them as they pitched up dramatically. We broke to the left and climbed, as a wall of stone appeared from the haze. The C-130 couldn't have hit at a better angle as they 'pancaked' into the snow-covered slope.

"Holy Shit, guys. The tanker just hit the mountain," I said to my crew as I took the controls from 'JT.' "I'm coming around to the left to check for survivors." "Razor flight, this is Razor 01... Ditka 03 has impacted the terrain. Pick up a left orbit and look for survivors."

The snow cloud from the impact was clearing with a slight breeze. There sat the tanker, upright, and broken in half about mid-ship. A large circular life raft deployed on its own, looking like a humongous rolled condom from our overhead view.

What should I do? We'd briefed that if an aircraft went down, we'd continue our mission and report the location for someone else to recover. I reached down to my CDU to store their coordinates when I saw a man crawl out from the crack in the top of the airplane. "Guys, there's at least one survivor. Look at the top of the plane. I'm going to land in the snow."

I've landed on all kinds of terrain in my career. This was going to be tricky. This was to be the second-most memorable landing in my career. I figured my best chance for success was to make my approach to the ground – a modified 'Bravo.'

'JT' started calling out altitude and airspeed. I flexed my fingers and pulled my flight gloves tight. We were either going to crash miserably in a cloud of snow, or this would be a fantastic feat of airmanship – okay, maybe just lucky. The helicopter attitude for deceleration matched the slope of the mountain. I would describe the final phase of the approach, as just flying into the ground. It worked, and we landed smoothly. I like to joke that the only thing holding us in place on the mountain slope was the V-shaped VOR antenna on the belly of the helicopter. It's fiberglass, so it's not really possible to act as a grappling hook. But heck... you explain it.

'Slab' and his team didn't wait. They moved uphill to the stricken Air Force crew. Once at the MC-130, they sent the ambulatory crew members downhill to us. The forward rotor blades had to be no higher than three feet from the ground; just the right height to cut a man in half. I thought it was about to happen as the first of the tanker crew approached. It was dark, and he was walking toward the sound of our engines and rotors; the same rotors that would be his end if he didn't go around. It's not like I could beep a horn, but I desperately needed to get his attention. The white, Air Refueling light might work. I fumbled for the switch. My God, this was going to be close...

The bright light mounted high up on the forward pylon flipped on, illuminating the rotor tips. The first survivor was just outside the disk – he stopped short – inches to spare. He circumnavigated the airframe to safety. The other crewmembers followed suite. Eventually all but one was aboard my helicopter. The SEALS were struggling to free the remaining man lodged in the wreckage. Craig carried the CSAR team. His PJs wanted him to land near the wreck so they could do their job. I was pissed that he couldn't get on the tanker in the first place, and I didn't think he could perform the same landing I'd just done. But his PJs were pestering him to get into the fray. They had equipment that could dislodge the trapped crewman. It was against my better judgment, but I allowed him to land. Jethro, in Razor 02, reminded me that he had enough gas to make it home if I released him right then. That would also leave enough fuel in the spare MC-130 for us to complete the rescue and get everyone to safety.

The PJs extracted the injured man and moved him to their Chinook. While they loaded and prepared to depart, I passed coordinates for an F-14 that had shown up, to destroy the aircraft.

The rescue delayed us long enough that we no longer had enough fuel to complete our mission to snatch Omar. We aborted and headed back to Bagram. Luckily, Ditka 02, the spare tanker, had enough fuel to pull us to Bagram. I wondered if Craig would be able to 'plug' this time – he did, and we headed home.

As we closed in on Bagram, Razor 03 requested to push ahead of us, so he could land at the hospital helipad; his patient was critical, and mine were all ambulatory – I agreed. In hindsight, that was a poor choice. You see, Craig took the most direct route toward his landing area without regard for what lay between... A line of GP medium tents full of sleeping soldiers lined the taxiway near the helipad.

Not one tent stood up to his rotor wash, each erupting in flames as they collapsed onto the pot belly heaters – luckily, nobody was injured. Although after landing, I walked back to our TOC, passing a couple of clusters of army cots sitting among canvas ash. I didn't know if any of the pissed off tent occupants knew I was the leader of the flight that almost killed them. So, I moved away with a purpose.

Our AAR was brutal that night. We didn't get Omar, we lost a tanker, and we embarrassed our organization by almost injuring three tent loads of 101st soldiers. We needed to do better.

The upside of the event was that all the C-130P crew lived. The Ditka 03 Aircraft commander wrote me a very heartfelt email to thank us for picking them up. Years later, we ran into each other, and he gave me a large bottle of whiskey.

I want to place the importance of removing them from the mountain in perspective. About one year later, a Casa cargo airplane operated by a contractor took off from Bamiyan airstrip, heading west during a hazy dark night. They encountered similar conditions as Ditka 03, crashing onto a high plateau of deep snow. All crew and passengers survived the crash sequence; setting off their Emergency Locator Transmitter (ELT), they waited to be picked up, but no helicopters came until the following day. The crew and passengers survived only to freeze to death waiting for help that never came. Exposure to the elements killed them, as it would have done to the Ditka crew if we hadn't landed to pull them off the mountain – I'm so glad we picked them up.

Chapter 20

Lejay – SEALs vs. 160ᵗʰ SOAR
(February 2002)

I was sitting around the planning tent a couple of days after the Tanker rescue and over a cup of hot cocoa, we discussed strengths and limits of our operation. The group concluded that one of the SOF's strengths is quality people and habitual relationships. Realistic training was a distant second. The special operations community trains and works together a lot. All that time spent together, seeing the same faces over and over builds friendship and trust.

I learned during the Tora Bora Campaign with the CAG Operators that since they didn't know me, they really didn't know if I could be trusted to do things the way they were used to. The SEALS had the same problem. I was still trying to prove myself and gain their trust when a strategic reconnaissance mission popped up near the small village of Lejay.

We were still chasing Omar and Bin Laden, and intelligence operatives indicated one or both might be holed up in the area. We needed to put eyes-on as soon as possible. So, after dark, I took a flight of two Chinooks and the same SEALS from the C-130 crash, to a ridgeline overlooking the area of interest. The Recce team would stay in place for a couple of days observing a local village to discern Pattern of Life (POL). If a High-Value Targeted (HVT) individual were present, there'd be indications. I hoped they wouldn't stay too long; a weather front was moving in from the west. Jethro and I were set aside to exfil the SEALS if they needed assistance.

The SEALS had been busy as I slept through the day. 'Slab,' the team leader, was being asked to bring a local man back to base for questioning. The only objection to the proposed 'snatch' was from our commander, LTC Jake Brass. He knew the weather was going to turn bad in the next several hours, making helicopter extraction risky. The SEALs, never subtle in their confidence in our ability to support, executed the operation regardless. Time for an immediate exfil.

Joe Gorst nudged my shoulder. "Al, wake up. You've got a mission."

I leaped out of my sleeping bag and quickly started to dress.

"Al, slow down. The mission isn't urgent. The SEALS in Lejay snatched a guy, and they want exfil before the villagers figure out what they've done. They should be able to hold their position for quite some time, and the weather is turning to shit."

"How bad is the weather?" I asked.

"Low clouds, obscuring the mountains, snow, fog in low lying areas. I don't think you can get to them tonight."

"That sounds like easy weather to TF through. I shouldn't have any trouble with that."

Joe had a couple of close calls flying with Arlo in this same type of weather. He'd decided that we'd pushed our luck too often and were due for an incident. His new conservative views weren't popular with everyone, especially the SEALS. "I don't want you to TF. Those fuckers were told not to snatch that guy; now they can sit out there and think about it,"

I couldn't believe what he was saying. There's no way I was going to leave them hanging.

Joe was convinced the SEALS would be okay until the weather cleared, but I wasn't so sure. I looked hard at how I could sneak through the passes visually. A quick map recon convinced me that a purely visual run was not possible. "Look, Sir, I think it's a waste of time trying to get them without the Radar. Let me TF. I can get them."

Joe was steadfast. He wanted me to go sit in my MH-47E on auxiliary power, ready to go, if the weather forecaster changed his mind about deteriorating conditions. CDR Gishmont, the SEAL squadron commander, decided he'd like a front-row seat to what was unfolding. So 'Gish,' as he was called, showed up at my helicopter, asking to go along for a ride. He'd watch everything we did and listen to every comment from my crew.

We sat for several minutes, ready to go in a moment's notice, but I knew the forecaster wasn't going to cave in. I figured we'd sit until the duty day ended – then, the SATCOM came alive...

"Mako Control, Mako 30 on SAT."

The SEALs in Lejay were about to make life more interesting.

"Go ahead, Mako 30, send your traffic," came the reply from the JOC.

"When is Razor coming to get us?"

A long pause ensued... I pictured an argument in the JOC, the SEAL commanders wanting their men back at base, and our commanders raising hell that they advised not to conduct the 'snatch.'

'Slab' was pissed. "What the fuck is going on? Get the Razor guys off their asses and get them out here."

I couldn't believe my ears. He had to know I was monitoring the same radio.

Gorst dug his heels in and wouldn't approve my launch. It just got better from there.

"Mako Control, Mako 30, I suppose the pilots don't like the fucking weather, but I'll tell you this, the fucking weather is clear here. I see stars and no fucking clouds in the sky. I must reiterate, the weather is fine here. Get them moving."

I sat there as the weather slowly got worse, not better. I thought it better to keep my mouth shut and let things play out. But it was awkward listening to the SEALs insult us with their commander onboard.

A colorful reply formed in my head. *"Fuck you asshole. Walk home."* I never verbalized my thought. I hoped my crew would take my cue and remain professional – 'Gish' stayed quiet as well.

I don't know what transpired in the JOC, but my launch was approved, with a caveat that I not go in the clouds. This was going to be a waste of time without the radar, but we cranked and headed south of Kabul. I was trying to get into one of the many mountain passes that might give me access to the interior valleys. I desperately needed lower elevations to stay visual. I ran into one dead end after another. the trip was impossible. I circumnavigated clouds, skidded over fog banks, and hugged mountains. I pushed and pushed until every opening I tried proved undoable. I wanted to just activate TF and push through the weather. I couldn't quit. There had to be a way past the clouds.

While I was cheating death to pull my buddies from their circumstance, I learned 'buddy' is just half a word. I tried one more pass before fuel became an issue, and I had to turn back. I called the JOC with the news. "Mako Control, Razor 03 and flight are turning back. There is no way through the mountains visually. I made it to within fifty miles before I could go no further. I want to return to Bagram, hot-refuel, and go back. For the next run, I estimate about ten minutes of TF."

Before I received an answer, 'Slab' chimed in. "What the fuck! If they couldn't make it through the first time, why do they think they can get through. Razor is just stalling."

'Buddy fucker!' I really should have told him to walk. But instead, I kept quiet and worked my way back to Bagram. When I got close enough to call our TOC on the line-of-sight radio, I asked again. "Eagle 99, Razor 03, I can get through the weather with the radar. Let me do this."

Joe and Jake Brass must have already discussed the situation and immediately granted my request. "Razor 03, Eagle 99, your mission is approved, but you will recover to Kandahar instead of Bagram. We're packing your sleeping bags and will deliver them to the FARP. Good luck, and don't take any unwarranted chances. How copy?"

I acknowledged the orders, got fuel, and tried again. This time I had a better idea of where to go, and when confronted with the fog, clouds, and snow, I had Razor 04 pick up two miles of separation and activated Terrain Following. Sure enough, we pushed through the weather in a measly fifteen minutes, and it was beautiful on the other side.

I hadn't heard Mako 30 on the radio, I guess he ran out of insults.

Before I knew it, I was on short final to his HLZ. There wasn't much to land on. 'Slab or John Chapman, his CCT was standing in the only possible landing spot waving me in. My wheels just barely fit on the snowy pinnacle. The aircraft nose hung out over nothing. I looked down several thousand feet through my chin bubble. I called Jethro to let him know I was safe on the ground and passed along a few tips to get into this spot without tumbling down the mountain. I lifted off, and Jethro mimicked my actions, allowing a quick exfil. Triumphant, we turned south and headed for Kandahar.

A group of Rangers met us at the airfield and took us to their small compound. They'd prepared a heated tent for us with comfy army cots. Regardless of how the SEALS viewed us, we knew what we'd accomplished. Exahusted, we unpacked our sleeping bags. I heard a thump on the plywood floor. All within earshot turned to look. A forbidden bottle of Jack Daniels Whiskey hidden in a sleeping bag now lay at our feet. Satisfied with our efforts, we passed the bottle around and slept soundly...

+++

The SEALs were already heading back to Bagram on a C-130 by the time I woke. I wouldn't have to deal with them. I didn't want to sit through an awkward apology that surely must come. If I could avoid them for a day or two and pretend this night never happened, maybe we could ignore 'Slab's' comments on the SATCOM. I could not have been more wrong.

At the end of the three-hour flight to Bagram, I just wanted to jump in the shower and slip into some sweatpants and relax. It was not in the cards. Joe Gorst was waiting for me as I entered our Operations tent. I hoped he wasn't mad at me for pushing so hard to get the SEALs. To the contrary, he complimented me. "Good job, Al. Do me a favor and grab Jethro - be at the planning table in five minutes."

This seemed a bit odd, but Jethro and I did as we were told. We had no idea what was coming, until 'Slab' and John Chapman entered the tent. Silent and stern, they sat across the table from us. Something was amiss, and I didn't like it. Joe and the SEAL squadron commander stood to the side; arms crossed. Serious facial expressions set the tone. "*Oh shit, tell me it doesn't get more awkward,*" I thought – it did.

'Gish' started the ball rolling. "Slab, what have you got to say?"

Just like parents forcing their kids to shake hands after a scuffle on the playground, the conversation I tried to avoid was happening.

Embarrassed, 'Slab' spoke with his eyes averted. "Al, I'm sorry about what we said on the radio. You guys are the best pilots I've ever flown with."

"*There he said it.*" I forgave him immediately.

We weren't done.

'Gish' prompted 'Slab' for more words. "AND?"

"And – I behaved poorly, and you still came to get us. Thank you." 'Slab' glanced at 'Gish' to see if that was enough. It wasn't. The process continued for about ten minutes, repeating itself over and over.

"Holy shit give me a chance to speak," I thought. But eventually, the apologetic ass-kissing was over.

All eyes were on me. "Thank you for the kind words, but there's really no need. I'll do whatever I can to support you guys, no matter what. Remember that please. Let's move on. Okay?" I slid my chair back from the table while extending my hand to shake.

Nope, not over...

Joe had patiently waited. The dam of pent up anger let loose like a hand grenade wrapped in firecrackers. I can't write the expletives he hurled. Suffice it to say, he didn't like his guys being disparaged. If it ever happened again, Joe would deliver an ass-kicking for the ages.

'Gish' must have really been mad at 'Slab,' because he remained quiet while his guys got their asses handed to them. To this day, both Joe and 'Slab' are friends of mine, so I won't even hint who I think would prevail in a fight.

By the way, both 'Slab,' and John would later go on to each earn the Congressional Medal of Honor – not a bad couple of guys to mix it up with.

Chapter 21

Operation Anaconda (March 2002)

Our time in Afghanistan was nearing its end. We were going to change places with Alpha Company. A Relief-In-Place can be as smooth or as bumpy as the personalities involved. I was ready to hand over everything I knew. And decided Alpha Company could do business any way they wanted. But, before the RIP, we had to finish up with an Operation being lined up by the 101st. Once done, we could go back to the States and leave OEF to Alpha Company, Second Battalion. Our Third battalion was already filtering into Kandahar with their older MH-47Ds.

Our group was emotionally and physically exhausted; we'd hit the ground running just weeks after 9/11, and now we were hoping for a break.

Captain Marty Keiser called all the pilots together to explain Operation Anaconda. The 101st was going to conduct a vast air assault into the Shah-i- Kot valley, near Gardez. Intelligence sources felt that Al Qaeda and a significant Taliban element were present fomenting dissent and violence. The 101st planned to clear and secure the valley. Our job was to help set the conditions for the operation. Coalition Special Forces would be placed in strtegic locations on key ridgelines and hilltops. These Observation Posts (OPs) would get eyes-on avenues of escape and call for fire on any enemy troops. This was the proverbial anvil. The hammer would be the conventional forces in cooperation with General Zia's formidable Afghan Militia.

My role was to attack any identified High-Value Targets (HVTs) like Bin Laden or Omar. Chuck, after his infils, would stand up a Quick Reaction Force. His QRF would come to the aid of anyone needing reinforcements, CASEVAC, or rescue. Operation Anaconda was only a week away. And we were anxious to get it underway.

The best-laid plans must still get past the weather. A front moved through our area with a snow and ice mix delaying the operation. Not to waste time available, someone unofficially allowed the Non-Governmental Agencies, like the Red Crescent, the UN, and USAID to be notified about the large American Military Operation about to commence, and they should get their workers out of the AO. Draw your own conclusions, but by the time Anaconda kicked off, the enemy was dug in and well prepared. The element of surprise was non-existent.

+++

Just because we were delayed didn't mean preparations halted. The 'Anvil' needed to be created. Arlo worked with our coalition partners to devise an infil plan for the Observation Points. Arlo had a mix of Americans, Canadians, Australians, Germans, Dutch, among others. Satellite imagery available in those days was ridiculous by today's standards and the best maps with terrain relief were old Soviet charts. Foliage, rocks, and trees couldn't be discerned using the tools at hand. The old-fashioned PACE LZ selection was necessary for each team. So, Arlo had to sit down with each group to identify possible infil sites. The laborious task of identifying a Primary, Alternate, Contingency, and Emergency HLZ proved to be time-consuming.

The teams arrived every day at the beginning of Arlo's duty cycle. We jokingly referred to our planning tent as the coalition cafe. We'd make small talk with them over coffee, waiting for Arlo to wake up. Everyone spoke fluent English, though with a robust national accent. They were always professional and by-all-means funny. For the purposes of this description, let's say the German Team Leader's name is Klaus, and the Aussie is Harry – their accents are stereotypically thick.

Klaus pours his coffee while greeting Harry. "Guten Morgen, Harry. Alles Gut?"

"Good morning, mate. How's the Java?"

Klaus selected a Styrofoam cup from a stack on the table and filled it for the Australian captain. "Here is a cup of black coffee, just how you like it. I think Arlo is coming soon. I have coffee with creamer prepared for him... I think he will like it."

Arlo shuffled into the tent, interrupting the conversation. "What the fuck are you guys doing here so early. We aren't supposed to get together for another hour."

Klaus wasn't intimidated by Arlo's attitude. "Guten Morgen Arlo. Here is your coffee, just the way you like it." Arlo accepted the cup of hot coffee, while Klaus turned to the room and announced the obvious: "Arlo is grumpy this morning. Don't worry, he will return to 'nice-Arlo' before you know it."

Arlo smiled and got down to business. The fact the Germans knew how Arlo liked his morning coffee, shows how much time they spent together. The collaboration was worth the effort. Arlo was able to insert each and every team in at least one of their HLZs. The difficulty in obtaining quality satellite imagery would go on for another year or so until we obtained better access to newer products. His hard work paid off. The OPs were all in place.

The 'anvil' was ready to smash the enemy.

+++

With improving weather, a new date was set for Anaconda – March 2nd, 2002.

B-52, B-1, and B-2 Bombers prepped Objectives Remington and Ginger. Air assaults with 101ˢᵗ and 10ᵗʰ Mountain soldiers began at dawn. The enemy fighting positions, covered in rock, held up to the barrage of bombs that fell impressively on top of them. It was time for the 'hammer,' General Zia's force of roughly 500 Afghans, to fall on the "Anvil."

SF Warrant Officer Stanley Harriman led the convoy that represented the main effort, only to be misidentified by an AC-130. The deadly Gunship was as accurate as anyone could ever ask for; unfortunately, they targeted Harriman. He was killed when the AC-130's 40mm peppered his SUV. Without their American leader, Zia's forces withdrew. No, they ran.

Anaconda's main effort had stalled. The 'hammer' never fell, at least not in the strength required to destroy the enemy. Taliban and Al Qaeda forces held firm. Friendly forces maintained a tentative foothold but couldn't advance without regaining momentum. Inserting a Recce unit on top of the most prominent mountain in the AO would allow accurate Aerial Bombardment calls-for-fire and laser designation of targets. All available units capable of such a task were engaged, all except our SEALS. I dropped them off the night before in case they were needed. Now they had to go to the top of Takur Ghar.

+++

Razor 01 piloted by CW4 Chuck Grant was on his way back to Bagram. He'd successfully repositioned the last coalition team as I was headed south. We passed each other, heading in opposite directions. I was leading a flight of two MH-47Es to FOB Gardez. I was flying aircraft tail number 499 with 'JT' as my co-pilot. Jethro followed about a quarter of a mile back in aircraft tail number 469 with copilot CW3 Jamey Felix.

As usual, we cleared the built-up areas and test fired. "Razor 04, Razor 03, on 'Fox Mike,' conduct test-fire and report."

"Razor 03, Razor 04 WILCO."

The deafening roar of my Miniguns broke the silence. Sometimes you can hear fluctuations in the feed motors indicating an impending jam – these sounded good. "Razor 04, Razor 03, all guns operational."

"Razor 03, Razor 04, all guns operational."

Now, all we had to do was avoid known enemy emplacements and stay out of the line-of-friendly-fire. The concept of our mission was straightforward. We'd proceed to the AFO safe house, Gardez (Gavin DZ), to pick up two SEAL teams. We'd depart Gardez as a flight of two, then proceed to the respective HLZs. Jethro's passengers, callsign Mako 21, was a northern HLZ located in the lower-valley wadi. Mako 30 riding with me would infil approximately 6 km to the south- southeast of Mako 21 at the base of Takur Ghar mountain. They'd move from there under cover of darkness to the peak to set up an OP.

I'd overfly the northern HLZ with Razor 04 who'd drop-off and infil Mako 21. Then I'd continue to the southeast to Mako 30's landing area. After infil, Jethro and I would join in the air over a checkpoint, then return to Bagram again as a flight of two. We had a dedicated AC–130, Nail 21.

No plan survives the first contact with the enemy.

We were 6 minutes from landing when Nail 21 called to inform us that he could not put 'eyes-on' our target or HLZs because of B–52s inbound, forcing him to clear the target area until the strike was complete. We didn't have fuel to waste, so we returned to Gavin DZ to ground laager.

I wanted Nail 21 to get over our objective and verify that no enemy troops were present.

I'd have to wait.

Even sitting on the ground, our fuel burn was excessive. We tried some conservation tricks but eventually had to shut down the engines. Nail 21 had the same problem and had to leave before the strike was complete, so he'd pass our HLZ details to his replacement, Nail 22.

Eagle 99 called on the SATCOM to inform us that another 101st Air assault was inbound, extending our delay. Fuel conservation was imperative, leaving us no choice but to shut down or we wouldn't have enough fuel to get back to Bagram.

+++

I was still strapped into the left seat of 499. Mako 21, let's call him Mick, came over from Jethro's bird to inquire about timing. He was getting concerned with the delay. He'd be okay in the northern HLZ, but Mako 30 would not be able to climb to the top of Takur Ghar before sunrise. "Al, can you take the Recce team to the top of Takur Ghar instead of the bottom?"

"I don't know. I haven't seen imagery for the top of the hill – I don't know if there's even a place to land at the top."

Mick made his sell; "I've seen imagery. You won't have any problems with landing up there."

I considered his request but declined. We'd stick with the original plan. We just had to wait for the 101st air assault to clear the area.

+++

Airspace over Objective Remington was finally clear. We began to 'crank' our helicopters. During the start sequence, my number 2 engine 'ran away' with what's known as a 'high side' malfunction and had to be shut down. My aircraft was non-mission capable. The aircraft was repairable, but I wouldn't be allowed to fly it. It'd have to be flown back to Bagram by a maintenance test pilot.

My only other choice – call for a spare aircraft to be flown to our location with a maintenance pilot to recover 499.

Mako 21 expressed his concern about the approaching daylight. His team would definitely not have enough time to move from their primary HLZ to their OP in darkness.

He asked me again if I could take them directly to their OP.

This time, I was willing to try.

I was concerned that I hadn't seen imagery. I wanted to support the SEALs' request, but I couldn't guarantee a successful infil on the hilltop. Mako 30 recommended a 24-hour bump. He knew things weren't going to work out. I relayed the request, but he was told that the OP was critical to the overall situation and that he should reconsider using the current cycle of darkness. The urgency of their infil was apparent, so I said I would try – no promises.

To make the infil happen, I needed the incoming spare helicopter to depart Bagram with a specific fuel quantity. Anymore and we'd be too heavy – any less and we wouldn't have enough to get home. Razor 01 and 02 arrived at the Bagram FARP and were refueling; it wasn't long before they were headed our way.

My crew chiefs suggested swapping only the pilots to save time. I moved my stuff to tail number 476 and Jethro got tail number 468. Aircraft 499 and 469 were now out of the mission and would return to Bagram. I'd never flown with my new enlisted crew from Alpha company. I'm embarrassed to say I didn't even know their names. Nevertheless, I briefed them on the mission.

We took off before 2200Z. Sgt Mike Murtah, the Flight Engineer, told me they had a problem with the guns during the earlier flight and requested another test fire en route. Unfortunately for us, an unintended consequence resulting from the fratricide that killed Chief Warrant Officer Harriman was that our weapons-control status changed from 'TIGHT,' to a more restrictive 'HOLD.' There were so many Afghan allies scattered around the battle, and we didn't want to risk more fratricide.

We'd need to be fired at before we could engage anyone not identified as friendly. It sounds chivalrous to let someone shoot at you first, but the reality is that if someone shoots at you from point-blank range, you risk dying before you can return fire.

Captain Tim Danning, sitting in my jump seat, tried to confirm coordinates for our landings with Nail 22. We expected the AC-130 sensor operator to visually sweep the landing areas and the immediate surroundings. There was a discrepancy with the coordinates, so Tim corrected them and asked Nail to conduct a new sensor sweep. It wasn't long before we got an all-clear from the AC-130. He also let us know he was breaking station for another tasking – Troops-In-Contact (TIC).

Since our HLZs were deemed to have no enemy presence, the TIC took precedence, and we were left alone.

The moon was up, illuminating everything, to include us. 'JT' banked left, and we began a climb to 10,200 feet. The snow-covered HLZ on Takur Ghar was easy to spot. Our north to south approach gave us excellent visibility of the landing area. I didn't see any movement on the large, mostly convex, but occasionally flat top of the pinnacle. On short 'final,' I noticed a string of footprints in the deep snow. People walking in the highest mountains was not out of the ordinary, so we continued inbound, just more wary. Considering the raging fight in the valley below, the mountain was quiet.

Or was it?

'JT' noticed a 14.5mm machine gun sitting unmanned to our right front. "Guys, DSHK on a tripod at one o'clock."

"Roger that, Sir – look to the right. There's a donkey tied to a tree at three o'clock."

Obviously, we weren't' alone. But were we in danger?

"Sir – 'left gun,' I just saw a man duck behind a berm at our nine to ten o'clock."

If the ROE hadn't become more restrictive, we'd have killed him without question.

"Do you still see him?" I asked.

"No, I don't."

"If he pops up again, that's hostile intent – Kill him," I ordered.

Before my gunner could answer, I caught sight of a Rocket Propelled Grenade flying at us. I swear time slowed down as the RPG, sparks flying from its tail, approached and struck the side of the helicopter somewhere just behind my seat. The explosion was loud and warm. My MFDs went blank. The cockpit went quiet as the fans quit working in all of our control panels and black boxes. I had no way of knowing the status of any equipment, and the engines sounded funny. I couldn't be sure they were running at their full potential. Apparently, our main generators were offline, which also meant our M-134s had no power – the AC powered Gatling guns sat useless on their mounts.

The crew chief on the ramp was yelling over the noise of the aircraft, "fire in the cabin, go, go, go," I could hear the thud, tink, tink of bullets hitting us. My mind raced to assess the situation. *Where were the SEALs? Are they still on board? If so, I can lift off and escape. If they're on the ground, do they want back on? Should I get out of their way and let them fight?* More machine gun rounds impacted our airframe. Tink, tink, thud, tink... The worst-case scenario is having half the team on the LZ and the other half onboard. My front gunners were quiet. I wasn't sure if they died from the RPG blast or were just incapacitated. But since I was being yelled at to take off, I could only assume we were ready to go – one way or the other.

I jerked the thrust to get off the ground and surprise the enemy. A gentle lift-off would be easy to detect, allowing gunners to easily lead me with their fire.

The engines, without normal electrical power, were operating in a Reversionary Mode. I could hear and feel the droop in RPM as we left the ground, leading me to believe we'd lost an engine. We didn't have sufficient power to stay aloft with only one engine, and I might lose the other. I nosed the aircraft down the slope toward the valley floor below. I pushed the thrust to the floor stops to take the load off the blades and regain rotor RPM. The crew let me know both engines were running. I eased-in the power to prevent further descent – I was rewarded with level flight.

My two forward gunners, stunned by the blast regained their senses as fresh, cold air poured into the cabin. 'PD,' the ramp gunner, had been ripped from the aircraft holding on to a falling SEAL. Neil Roberts dropped about twelve feet from the ramp to the snow-covered hilltop below. Dan, the Right Ramp gunner, climbed hand-over-hand as he pulled himself from the floor. He thought another RPG had hit us from behind; he was wrong. He'd been shot in the head. The bullet lodged in the Styrofoam insert of his flight helmet; that one-inch foam would allow us to cheat death for the night. Dan pulled on the gunner's harness leading from the floor to somewhere outside the aircraft, where our fallen gunner hung. After dragging him aboard, he heard me comment about a hydraulic leak, and that I couldn't move the flight controls.

Dan could hardly keep his footing as the bullet ridden aft transmission spewed oil and hydraulic fluid everywhere on the slippery floor. He knew what he had to do – three spare cans of hydraulic fluid were stashed with a can opener in the framework of the cargo ramp. He poured the first can into a fill port and began to work a small hand pump to pressurize the flight controls. Within seconds, I had control of the helicopter again, though it flew poorly. The aircraft was lurching and bouncing like a washing machine out of balance due to a foot-wide hole in one of the blades, and chunks missing from several others.

I could see key terrain features below and knew exactly where I was even without a GPS... I banked to the north to find a landing area away from the battle below.

As if the situation wasn't bad enough, my crew let me know about our missing passenger... I still didn't know we'd lost Neil Roberts. My ramp gunner tried to grab him but was unable to overcome the momentum of the falling SEAL; he was still on the LZ. My mind raced through probabilities vs. risk. I couldn't leave him behind. "Guys, we're going back to get the SEAL."

"Yes Sir, but our guns don't work without electricity."

"I know, use your M-4s. We may have surprise on our side. They'd never expect us to come back. *(sound familiar?)*"

As soon as I started turning to the right, the controls became more difficult to move, then they stopped. We'd lost our hydraulic fluid in less than a minute. We were going to die in the next minute or so if I couldn't control the helicopter – Neil would be on his own.

"Guys, I'm sorry," I said.

The idea that there was nothing I could do was somehow calming... there was nothing left to do but die. Then without notice, the cyclic stick moved, and I regained control. Dan poured another can of hydraulic fluid into the servicing reservoir – one more chance to save Neil Roberts.

"Guys, I've got control. Let's get back to the HLZ."

But as soon as I rolled out of my turn, the controls became heavy and stopped again. Dan refilled the system with our last can of fluid. I had one chance to save everyone on board. We had to get on the ground, and only had about a minute before the reservoir was empty again. This time, I banked away from the mountain, setup a descent, and slowed to around seventy knots. I hoped that we'd get to the ground in time, but if not, maybe we'd crash going straight ahead with survivable speed and glide path.

At approximately 10 feet above the ground, I could no longer move the cyclic stick. We had flown about 7 km from the HLZ, and the hydraulics were running out again. The helicopter started an uncommanded slide to the right that I couldn't arrest without cyclic control. There's a saying in aviation circles: "Never stop flying the airplane." The cyclic was dead but I figured I had at least one more movement of the thrust and pedals. I stomped on my right yaw pedal to straighten the nose in the direction of travel. I felt the landing gear brushing the scrub-covered slope, so pushed down on the thrust, allowing the aircraft to settle softly on a 15-degree upslope and approximately 10 degrees of right-side-high cross-slope.

'JT' pulled the engine condition levers to stop, shutting down both engines, then applied the rotor brake stopping the spin of both rotors.

"*Fuck! We're alive*," I thought. How about that, a shootdown just like Joe made us train for. I couldn't help but smile, and mutter under my breath, "Not another Gorst Game."

I 'zeroed' the mission computers and COMSEC while the crew further disabled and sterilized the aircraft. I jettisoned my cockpit door, collected my maps, and climbed out and onto Afghan soil. An aviator on the ground, no matter how well trained, is not a professional shooter – I think I was in a mild state of shock.

I went to the rear of the helicopter to link up with my crew. The SEALs had already begun setting up security and a portable SATCOM. My portable GPS initialized, and I plotted our position on a map. As near as I could tell, we were on the northern edge of Objective Remington, just outside the main battle. I moved from person to person, checking on everyone's condition. I was meeting my crew face-to-face for the first time. I was more than a little embarrassed that I hadn't taken the time to get to know them before this.

I ended up next to Combat Controller John Chapman, who was working the radio call to HQ.

"Dude, I'm sorry I crashed," I said.

Chapman looked up from his radio. "You call that a crash? I've had harder parachute landings. You fuckin' rock."

I don't know why it was important to hear that, but it helped.

Chapman went back to work and I looked for the SEAL team leader. I was out of breath – a combination of altitude, shock, and adrenalin. I looked around, still struggling to breathe as I noticed Mako 30 standing uphill from me. I didn't recognize him with his snow gators, body armor, NVGs, and Pro-tech helmet. "What's your name?" I asked.

He chuckled. "It's 'Slab.'"

I still didn't place who he was. "Who?"

"It's me... you know, the asshole from Lejay."

"Got it," I said. "I'm sorry I crashed."

"Dude, we're fucking alive..." He noticed I was still out of breath. He knelt down till we were face-to-face. "Breathe!" He paused then repeated himself. "Breathe – just breathe normally... Look up. See the AC-130? He's pulling security for us, and he's passed our location to Razor 04, who should be here shortly. We're in good shape."

Jethro had done as briefed. He arrived at our rendezvous point, waited fifteen minutes for me to arrive, then started a radio search. A new AC-130, Grimm 33 showed up and relayed our situation to him.

'Slab' asked if we could remain in place while Razor 04 took them back to Takur Ghar to help their man. I looked around at our surroundings and asked if he could leave one of his guys with us. A flush of embarrassment hit me, and I instantly regretted the question. We could take care of ourselves. "Never mind," I said. "We'll be good – go get your guy."

Chapman had been talking to HQ and handed me the mic to answer a question for the AFO commander. I explained our plan to rescue Roberts with Razor 04, with my crew holding up near our helicopter. But Grimm 33 reported enemy troops headed our way and suggested we move as soon as possible. That ruled out us staying. Instead, Jethro would pick us up, reposition all of us at Gardez, where 'Slab's' Team could re-group and head back to the fight.

Roughly forty-five minutes after hitting the ground, Razor 04 could be heard approaching from the north – what an impressive sound. I watched him through the phosphorescent glow of my NVGs. The thick dust cloud, common with most dust landings, engulfed me as he landed not far from my helicopter. Small pebbles propelled by the heavy rotor wash hurt like little pinpricks all over my body.

The SEALS and my crew headed toward the rescue bird. I surveyed the area to make sure we hadn't left anything valuable behind, especially men. I took one last look at my crippled Chinook and ran toward Jethro's ramp. The sandy ground made it hard to gain traction, and I struggled to breathe in the thin air. As if in a dream, my boots were heavier than they should be – I couldn't run any faster.

I could feel my heartbeat in my head as it pounded like a morning hangover. Was I running in slow motion? With each step closer to the waiting bird, my chances of getting shot grew exponentially in my imagination.

If this were a movie, the crew chief is waving for me to hurry.

Just as I get within speaking distance, I get shot, struggling to make the final distance only to...

Then – thud – the air expelled from my lungs as my torso hit the ground. It wasn't immediately replaced. I'd knocked the wind out of myself falling just short of the ramp.

Had I been shot after all? No, but I nevertheless hit the ground like a sack of potatoes.

I'd tripped over who knows what.

The timing was perfect. All who saw, assumed I'd been shot. And just like the imaginary movie playing in my mind, I struggled to get up, body armor weighing me down.

The ramp came up behind me as I moved forward to the companionway between the cockpit and the cargo compartment. The flight engineer handed me a headset. I spit out a quick description of what happened on top of the mountain. I described how and where to land. Then I suggested that I replace Jethro's copilot. But both pilots looked back at me and said "no" in unison. They made a good crew mix and told me that I sounded like I was in shock – I probably was.

+++

Gardez Firebase looked like the Alamo to me. The clay walls stood roughly twenty-five feet tall with distinct firing points on each corner. I found the front door and worked my way to the main operations room to call Bagram. LTC Brass answered the phone on the first ring. I explained the night's events and detailed how things were playing out.

Brass told me to hang tight. It was going to be a while before they could send a helicopter for us. So, we settled in, trying to pass the time. Most of the FOB residents had repositioned with the British CH-47s to get ready in case the SEALs needed reinforcements.

The Gardez base was left guarded with General Zia's militia, one engineer from the 10th mountain division, one Air Force weather forecaster, two communications guys, and one SEAL, named Hal.

Hal gave me a tour. The only entry and exit were two large steel doors facing the main road. The compound walls surrounded a rectangular courtyard with a dirt floor. In one corner was a tarp-covered three-foot-deep ditch filled with ammunition. Each corner of the upper walls had a parapet connected by a walkway permitting riflemen to fire over the top. One of the communications analysts came to let Hal know they'd had an electronic intercept indicating we'd be attacked before noon.

Enemy forces observing our compound knew that all of the 'shooters' had left the base relatively undefended. A Taliban convoy intended to take advantage of our lack of fighters. The Taliban still had to get through over four hundred Afghan militia to get close enough to engage us directly. But I wasn't so sure of everyone's allegiance – Hal agreed. As we sorted through our options, the sound of a Chinook filled the air. Razor 04 was back, landing at Gavin DZ.

The rotors coasted to a stop as I walked up the ramp into the empty cargo compartment. I headed straight for the cockpit to find out how Jethro's infil had gone. About halfway to the front, I started noticing bullet holes here-and-there; Razor 04 had taken a terrible beating.

+++

Jethro's crew had been through a harrowing experience putting the SEALs back in play. He'd approached the mountain from the North at low-level to avoid visual detection. They'd hear him, but with the rotor noise reverberating off the canyon walls, he knew they'd have trouble figuring his approach direction. He arranged pre-assault fires to keep the enemy heads down while he approached and landed. Nail 22 agreed to lay down fire on the now known fighting positions.

As they got close to the base of the mountain, he eased back on the cyclic to rapidly climb and slowdown on the way to the top. Once in line-of-sight of the enemy positions, the enemy machine guns opened fire, hitting Jethro's helicopter on the first burst. Jethro pointed out the enemy fire to the AC-130, expecting them to neutralize the DHSK, spitting death in their direction. Rules of Engagement allowed the 'AC' to rain hell from above, but they didn't.

Razor 04 continued inbound. The DHSK gunner continued to find his mark – steel hit sheet metal and plastic. Voice Warning alerts filled their ears as large-caliber rounds tore through his airframe. Jethro's gunners couldn't get an angle on the guns to return fire, so they had a choice, abort and try another angle or continue and hope for the best.

The incoming fire let up... the enemy gunners had poured so much fire into his helicopter, they needed to reload. That opportunity was all Razor 04 needed to land, unload, and dive down the mountainside to avoid more enemy fire – the SEALs were in.

Razor 04 raced back to Gardez with an aircraft full of holes and very little fuel. Upon touchdown, the aircraft fuel total indicated zero. He'd run out of gas, so he was now stuck at the firebase with us. My guys went out to help strip Razor 04 of machine guns, sensitive items, and zero the COMSEC. Both crews moved inside the walls to help us reinforce the 'Alamo.'

Hal gathered us to discuss base defense. If the incoming enemy convoy got past Zia's checkpoints, we'd have to defend ourselves.

We took inventory of our assets.

Between my two crews and Hal's equipment, we had four M-60 machine guns with several thousand rounds of 7.62mm ammunition. My fourteen aircrew were all armed with M-4 rifles with at least five magazines apiece. Each helicopter had an ammo ruck full of twenty magazines and six M-67 hand grenades. Best of all, each Chinook was equipped with two AT-4 anti-tank weapons; we'd be able to mount a formidable defense.

Even so, Hal didn't think we'd be able to hold out until reinforcements arrived. So, he directed our 10th mountain engineer to rig the back wall of the compound with explosives enabling a hasty exit. My responsibility in the escape plan was to crawl into the ammunition pit and arm a satchel charge to blow-in-place any additional explosives. Hal positioned three SUVs in the main courtyard, pointed toward the back wall. This dramatic setup turned out to be unnecessary. The convoy eventually got too close, and an AC-130 was cleared to engage, turning the convoy around with some well-placed rounds. Now we just had to wait for our friends on Takur Ghar to get rescued. The QRF was on the way. Razor 01 and 02 were just minutes out.

+++

My friend Randy Olsan, flying Razor 02, arrived unannounced in Gavin DZ, shutting down to his Auxiliary Power Unit to conserve his ever-precious fuel. Chuck Grant, in Razor 01, wanted only one aircraft at a time over Takur Ghar, so he sent Randy to ground laager until called forward. He was not on the ground for long when Razor 01 attempted to land where I'd been ambushed. ISR platforms circling overhead recorded the withering machine gun and RPG fire that poured into his Chinook. Jethro and I escaped a fate that Chuck would not...

Razor 01 was down on the top of Takur Ghar after losing an engine. The next several hours, the survivors on the hill would fight for their lives, outgunned and overmatched. Air Force Tech Sergeant John Chapman and Navy SEAL Britt Slabinski would each be awarded the Medal of Honor for their actions that day.

Once Razor 01 was shot down, making a total of three MH-47s down from enemy fire, any daylight rescue was out of the question, but that didn't mean Randy couldn't help. He cranked and repositioned Razor 02 to a lower portion of Takur Ghar, out of the line of fire. There he let off a squad of Rangers and Mako 21. They'd claw their way up the mountain to reinforce the survivors of Razor 01 and the SEAL recce team.

After infil, Randy returned to Bagram in preparation for an after-dark rescue.

+++

The phone rang in the Gardez TOC. It was Colonel Brass. H-hour for a nighttime rescue was set. He told me to be in PZ posture at Gavin DZ no later than thirty minutes after wheels down on the mountain. As darkness approached, we loaded our crew-served weapons and sensitive items into a Hilux pickup truck for a ride to Gavin DZ to meet our ride home. We obviously had an idea of when the helicopters would land, but had to be prepared for a short or no-notice arrival.

Timing is everything – minutes before the flight of MH-47s touched down on the mountain, an unrelated event near us began...

Our Air Force weather forecaster ran into the TOC out of breath, and excited. "Sir, a car full of journalists, just pulled up to the front door! They stopped at a fake checkpoint. Some bad guys shot into their car then tossed a hand grenade in. The lady in the back; she's..."

I waited for him to finish, but he just stood there, trying to regain his composure.

I used 'Slab's' technique from my earlier panic. "Breathe!" I ordered. "Just breathe normally... Go grab our medic and see what he can do for her."

"Yes, Sir, but there's blood everywhere."

"Okay. That doesn't necessarily mean it's a problem. Especially if we treat her quickly. Get Doc 'Z'."

I wasn't sure where this situation was leading us. If we left without stabilizing her, she'd definitely die tonight in Gardez. My medic was good. If she could be saved, he'd keep her alive. *"This is getting complicated,"* I thought.

He might need to stay behind, in which case, I'd stay with him. I must admit, I wanted to get back to our base.

Every time I got an update on our pickup time, I'd check with 'Z.' "How's it going?"

"Workin' it," he'd say.

"Okay. As near as I can tell, you have ten minutes. If we can't stabilize her, you and I will stay."

He never looked up from his task. "No problem. I'll let you know."

Ten minutes changed to six, then three, and of course, the eventual arrival of our ride. 'Z' walked away from the woman, pronouncing her stable and likely to survive – and she did.

+++

Takur Ghar held no more Americans as two of the rescue Chinooks landed a few hundred meters away from the 'Alamo.' It took longer than expected to get to the waiting helicopters. It was too dark to drive fast as we navigated the minefield protecting Gaven DZ. Our Afghan driver, familiar with the explosive-laden area, weaved and swerved as he negotiated the known mines, pulling up to the ramps of the running helicopters. Fuel, always an issue, was now a critical component of the trip home.

While we loaded, Dave Gross, the Pilot in Command, coordinated the use of a 101st FARP to get enough jet fuel to make it to Bagram. Getting onboard his aircraft had its own challenges and delays. Unknown to us, all of the Americans killed on Takur Ghar were lying on the floor. That is until my Flight Engineer tripped and fell on top of one of the bodies. Freaked out by the shock of seeing his deceased friend, he stood up and snapped his vest into a nearby railing and would move no further. No amount of yelling or cajoling would push him forward to allow room for the rest of us. We had to go now, or we wouldn't make it home.

I loaded the last piece of our equipment and slumped onto the floor among the dead.

As we flew toward the Refueling Point, I looked around the cabin; the smell of death and blood saturated the air. The dead bodies were laid out as respectful as possible.

I was thigh to thigh with Neil Roberts. We started this journey together and would now finish together.

Fatigue, stress, and emotions played on my mind. The luminescent markings of Neil's watch glowed in the dark, bouncing with the rhythmic vibrations of the helicopter. *"Was he moving under his own power?"* I imagined he was trying to tell me something. But no – he was there in body only.

I don't know how long we flew, but with three missed approaches into the FARP, I knew the dust had to be bad. I also knew we were going to run out of fuel soon.

Finally, I felt the aft landing gear touch the ground, and we screeched to a halt as the forward gear came down. I could hear the squeal of the brakes as the pilot frantically stopped at the fuel point. Not a moment too soon; the number one engine along with the Auxiliary Power Unit (APU), sputtered, coughed and suddenly grew silent. Both turbines fed from the left main tank, which had to be empty for them both to quit. Number two was still running and would provide electrical power while we refilled the left tank.

Fuel pressure at the point must have been good. It wasn't long before the APU, then number one restarted. If we'd run out any earlier, we'd have crashed in the desert. *"Holy Crap. Does it get any worse?"*

Maybe not, the cargo ramp closed, and I could feel the aircraft coming light on the landing gear, then we abruptly lurched into the air and began accelerating.

The forty-five-minute flight seemed like hours. Then we arrived. I didn't know where, but we started to four-wheel taxi. Our trip terminated at the base of a control tower I'd never seen before. The glow from decorative landscape lighting was unfamiliar. I was totally disoriented: *"Where the heck am I?"*

We were ushered off the helicopter to make way for the deceased men. I thought maybe we were in Kabul.

Nope. We were at Bagram. None of us had ever seen the lights on before.

Only the dead got a ride. No one was waiting for us. So, we grabbed our gear and began the trek down 'Disney highway' toward our compound. The dirt road was full of ruts and mud puddles that needed to be avoided. The walk was surreal, and the disorientation overwhelming. I thought I was going to vomit. But I wanted to set an example for my crew, so I held it in.

I passed through security and pushed aside the tent flap leading into our headquarters. Captain Marty Keiser greeted me with a hug. I could feel everyone's eyes on me. I needed a hot shower, a cup of soup, and a warm sleeping bag.

+++

The next day came quickly. Excitement permeated the air as Joe kicked my cot. "Al, get up. We might have Bin Laden."

I didn't say anything as I jumped out of bed. Arlo was going to lead an intercept flight targeting a small convoy. Intelligence sources felt strongly that Usama Bin Laden was among the SUVs.

Arlo wanted more firepower, which meant me. Joe looked my way. "Al, how do you feel? Can you fly?"

"Me fly?" I thought. I'd just been shot down, could I not have some time to work through my emotions?

My hesitation was obvious. Joe quickly rescinded his offer to let me go on the mission.

Embarrassed at my slow response, I tried to convince him I was ready to go. "No, I'm good. I can fly!"

Too late. I was relegated to the bench while Arlo rushed out the door with the others. I stayed behind with Randy Olsan. We would hang around as the QRF, only flying if necessary.

Arlo and the guys hunted the speeding convoy directed from an overhead ISR platform. The drivers couldn't evade the vengeful fleet of powerful helicopters. The vehicle interdiction ended poorly for the bad guys. They died in a hail of M-134 daylight tracers. Bin Laden was not one of the occupants, but equipment from Chuck's Chinook on Takur Ghar was present.

+++

That evening I got another chance to fly. A winter storm was brewing and heading toward our Special Forces Observation Posts in the mountains surrounding Shah-i-kot. If they didn't get pulled from their perches high above the valley, the coming blizzard would probably kill them. There was no reasonable way to get down from those hills except by helicopter.

Arlo's team had already flown the VI, leaving two of the Third Battalion crews and one from my team. I looked around the room for volunteers and found none.

I stood in the center of our tent. I looked into the eyes of each man. They were all still a little shaken from Anaconda. Nobody wanted to go back out into the mountains.

I knew for sure who'd join me – Randy.

I pulled back the flap to his tent and poked my head in. "Randy. Want to go with me to pull the coalition troops off the mountains with Third Battalion?"

"Fuck yeah, let's go."

"We're not leaving for about two hours. We're waiting for an AC-130 to cover us."

While I waited to launch, I disassembled my rifle and pistol for cleaning. You could hear a pin drop in our tent as I reassembled my weapons. The metallic sound of my M-4 bolt ramming forward as I released it for a function check got everyone's attention. Memories of March 3rd and 4th were fresh in everyone's minds as I left our tent. I really did not want to fly, but someone had to get the SF teams before the storm arrived. I guess it was gonna be me.

One of my unit's most often used quotations is from the Bible's Isaiah 6:8 – *Then I heard the voice of the Lord saying, "Whom shall I send? And who will go for us?' And I said, 'Here am I. Send me!'*

I was ready to go again.

Activity in the center of the planning tent caught my attention. The last team scheduled to come out of the mountains were the Germans. And they'd just reported enemy presence outside their perimeter; a concern in and of itself. To compound the problem, the enemy troops were reported to be armed with RPGs.

"Just kill them," I said calmly.

I had everyone's attention.

"It's simple. Unidentified men outside the German perimeter are armed with weapons that can bring down an exfil helicopter. ROE permits the use of pre-emptive deadly force. Tell the team to mark their position with IR strobes and glint tape and the AC-130 will engage anything outside the perimeter within 200 meters."

I was correct in my interpretation of the Rules of Engagement, but the Air Force Liaison, still raw about the Harriman Fratricide, wasn't willing to commit to pre-assault fires – I flipped out. My calmness evaporated in a hot second; I called the Air Force the worst words I could muster.

To his credit, the Air Force Colonel kept his calm and reasoned that the AC-130 would be watching closely. If we were fired at, they'd take action immediately.

"That sounds just like the conditions that took me out to the sky," I said.

Joe came from across the room to create distance between the LNO and me. He and I exchanged some choice words. *"Fuck it."* Whatever happened, happened.

I asked Randy to sit in the left seat and run the flight. He'd make all the big decisions; I just wanted to pilot the helicopter as Chalk Three.

Third Battalion's Flight Lead took us to a Release Point, where our three helicopters parted ways, each of us picking up team after team. As the night went on, we just kept cramming them into our crowded cargo compartment.

Only the Germans remained. The two Third Battalion Chinooks waited in a holding pattern.

Six minutes and we'd be out of harm's way or in the thick of it.

Randy called for a sensor update, but the AC-130 told him they were leaving the area for home. They didn't want to be in the air after sunrise. *"You've got to be fucking kidding me,"* I thought.

The only HLZ with the likelihood of enemy contact and the AC was going to leave a minute before my arrival. They had to be joking, but they weren't. Randy did the impossible, he shamed them into hanging out for just a few more minutes.

I landed on a snow-covered mountain surrounded by thick evergreen trees. The Germans were ready and loaded fast. Two minutes later, we were in the air and out of enemy small arms range. Randy released the gunship, and we joined our flight to return to Bagram – Anaconda was officially over. It was time to go home.

Section IV

"Let me not then die ingloriously and without a struggle, but let me first do some great thing that shall be told among men hereafter."

– Homer, The Iliad

Chapter 22

Recovery from First Deployment
summer 2002

Homecoming from Afghanistan was nothing like my Desert Storm arrival. No band, no news reporters, and no VIP treatment. Linda had no beer or pizza waiting, as a matter of fact, she was pissed. Don't get me wrong; she was happy to have me home, but she was mad at me. She found out that I had a chance to call on a Satellite phone before the news broke about two of our aircraft being shot down; now, there was hell to pay.

When the story broke on CNN, the news reported that two MH-47s from the 160th SOAR had been shot down, losing a total of eight men. Do the math from Linda's perspective. We had four 47s as far as our families knew, and with two flight leads, there was a better than fifty percent chance I was dead.

Our wives got together at Joe's house to compare notes and glean any information they could from open-source news outlets. Sharing in the tragedy made it easier for our wives to pass the time until that faithful unwanted death notification.

Linda never let me forget that she believed I was dead – she never let it go. I had trouble letting go too. My dreams replayed the RPG running hot, its sparks leaving a slight smoke trail as it exploded just behind my armored seat. Two feet more to the front, and I would be a 'crispy critter.' My body would deform and shrivel as the aircraft burned on the HLZ. Two feet further to the rear and the main fuel tank would have blown to smithereens – same result – dead and burned. More and more scenarios, each ending with my demise entered my dreams night after night. No matter what mindset I took to bed, nightmares ended with me burning to death on the mountain. Survivor's guilt and a cold sweat were the order of the day. "*How did I survive? Why did I survive?*" I saw myself still strapped into my seat, blackened and shrunken? It freaked me out. The only way I could remain asleep was with the help of whiskey. I drank it first with coke, and when I ran low on soda, I poured it over the rocks.

If I tried to go light on alcohol, I'd meet Neil Roberts sitting next to me on the floor of our exfil Chinook. He sat there only an arms distance away, looking at me. He never said anything, but I'm sure he wanted to know, why didn't I come get him while he lived. I could have crashed on Takur Ghar instead of the valley below. At least he wouldn't have died alone.

My nights were hell without booze, but my days were better. I'd compartmentalized my emotions and memories. Only my subconscious knew how messed up I was. Linda was no help, though she did suggest I go speak to someone; I chose the Regimental Psychologist. I'd made small talk with him several times before Anaconda. Though I knew him, I was afraid he'd pull me off flight status, which I didn't want to happen. I was the Battalion SIP – the chief MH-47 pilot. I needed to be reliable, steadfast, and ready to get back in the fight. In reality, I was ready to collapse and cry if I let my guard down.

I explained my feelings, dreams, and sleep problems. The doctor listened. I was sure his notes said something about me being nuts. I asked him about my psychological profile from assessment. Did I perform as expected, or did their tests fail to identify my flaws?

The doctor pored over my records. "Hmm..." He tapped his pen on his notebook. "I think you're normal," he said.

+++

I've always kept my feelings close hold – they're mine. No one else needs to know what I'm thinking or how I feel, but talking to the Psychologist helped. My nightmares stopped almost immediately. The doctor told me that I'd already taken the first step in dealing with my emotions. My coming forward showed him that I knew I had a problem. The feelings and memories are still with me today, but they don't bother me the same way.

+++

With my emotions under control, Linda and I tried desperately to reconnect. We made sure to spend as much time together as possible. No matter what we did, we did it together. Results were quick – we found our groove and rekindled our loving relationship. I wanted to get away from work. As a couple, our happy place was the beach – any beach. We'd spent a lot of time on the Gulf Coast during our times at Fort Rucker, Alabama. Linda spent hours surfing the internet looking for the ideal waterfront condo. We'd stayed several times near Panama City, Destin, and Pensacola. That summer, we tried Alabama, near Gulf Shores.

I still love the ocean, but there is something special about the Gulf of Mexico. The emerald-colored water and powder-white sand make an ideal combination. Linda and I could sit for hours with our feet in the water and listening to the waves. But with two sons, I couldn't just sit and tan. The water was so clear, we needed to go swimming. A quick trip to a local surf shop for masks with snorkels was all we needed to get going. We spent our days on the emerald coast with no internet, no television, and no stress.

Jet skis were a highlight of our trip. Stephen and Andrew were capable of riding their own watercraft, so I rented three machines. We ran up and down the Old River inlet, north of the Gulf. The boys and I raced, chased, and jumped each other's wakes. As much fun as riding the jet skis was, it kicked our butts. Our arms and thighs were sore from the wild activity; what an amazing feeling. We spent the rest of our time snorkeling and building sandcastles, even at our age.

All-in-all, our week on the coast was a great recharge for all four of us.

+++

Rest and recuperation were going to prove more important for me than I knew. The summer of 2002 wasn't the time for an expected withdrawal from Afghanistan. On the contrary, most of the forces of Operation Enduring Freedom would remain in place. Additional forces staged in preparation for an invasion of Iraq.

In the meantime, mainstream news commentators questioned the wisdom using Chinooks as assault platforms in combat. The MH-47 was described as a slow lumbering beast with no business in any role but cargo movement. USASOC had a potential PR disaster on its hands, so invitations went out to news organizations to come to visit the 160th SOAR compound on Fort Campbell. They'd be allowed unfettered access to commanders, aircrews, and mechanics. The culmination of a series of briefings and question and answer sessions was a tactical profile ride in an MH-47E. Newsweek, US News & World Report, along with a list of other prestigious organizations, took us up on the offer. Keep in mind, the 160th is a secretive unit that does not typically interface with the Press at all. So, imagine the awkward scene as the briefing presenter welcomes the reporters, then runs through an unclassified slide deck. The reporters' appetite had been whetted. Here's the first series of questions and answers:

"Thanks for having us. How many men in a Battalion?" asked a reporter.

"I'm sorry I can't discuss that number."

"Okay, how many men in a typical line-company?"

The briefer was in his resistance posture. No matter how much he wanted to cooperate. His instincts were kicking in. "I'm sorry, that number is sensitive."

"But not classified?"

"No, but I can't share that information with you."

The reporters shifted uncomfortably in their seats. This was going to get ugly fast if we didn't share some of the facts.

Finally, another reporter tried to break the ice. "Look, you asked us here. You promised access and an open atmosphere. What's it gonna be?"

The briefer was skittish but realized what he needed to do. It was like a switch flipped and turned on the fountain of 'gab.' Questions and answers flowed back and forth in a way I'd never seen.

Next was a tour of our compound, the hangar, and, more specifically, an MH-47E. I'd volunteered to escort the visitors and was rewarded with some great conversations along the way. I'd been cleared to answer any question they had.

The reporters climbed into the cockpit, toyed with the M-134 Miniguns, grabbed Fast Ropes, and looked through windows and openings. The whole time they're examining the airframe, I'd spout some useful factoid of Chinook trivia or operational capacity. "The aircraft has a maximum speed of one hundred and seventy knots," I'd say.

"How fast is that in Miles Per Hour?"

"About one hundred and ninety-six." I'd answer. "The center cargo hook is rated to carry twenty-six thousand pounds. We have seats for thirty-three troops, but with a seats-out waiver, we often carry forty to fifty, though I've seen as many as ninety crammed in during an emergency."

We were getting along great. The reporters wanted information, and I was in a talkative mood. So, they invited me to join them for lunch while the MH-47E for our demonstration flight was prepared. I stuffed a chunk of ham sandwich into my mouth as the conversation took on a more personal tone.

I now had a group of friendly and curious reporters ready for a ride in the mighty MH-47. Even I was excited about the demo flight to the Fort Campbell training area. Our entire group had been crammed into a fifteen-passenger van for the ride to lunch and back. Our driver pulled up to the ramp of our Chinook, and we piled into the helicopter. Our Flight Engineer gathered everyone for a passenger briefing and safety orientation. I used the opportunity to tell our pilots what we were expecting.

The pilot-in-command, Juergen Stark, was a 'plank holder' in the 160th, meaning he'd been around since the unit's inception. He was infamous for his adventurous flying skills and famous for using a Chinook to steal a Soviet MI-24 gunship from Libya in 1988. This day, his flying skills were what we were interested in. Keep in mind, the reporters were invited to see a big, ungainly, sluggish cargo aircraft act as an assault platform. The ride should be fun.

I worked my way to the cockpit past the reporters to have a word with Juergen. "Hey, boss, what's up?" he asked.

"Our passengers are here to see you put 'this baby' through its paces. Take us to Range 29 and drop us off. We'll watch you make a couple of passes, banks, and combat style approaches, then come pick us up and bring us back here."

"Okay," he said. "No problem. We'll take the Blue route to the range."

I'd flown with Juergen many times. He'd give us an exciting ride; I was sure of it.

I sat toward the front of the cargo compartment. I raised my visor so everyone could see my smiling face. There were a few nervous looks, but I reassured everyone we were in good hands. In no time, we were in the air flying along at tree-top levels, running about one hundred and twenty knots. The low-level flight stuck with the contours of the terrain and foliage. Sitting on the left side, directly opposite from the open cabin door, I had a spectacular view of the tree branches zooming past. *"Holy shit! Juergen, what are you trying to do?"*

I thought I flew aggressively at low altitude; I had nothing on him.

He made me nervous, but I didn't want to show my concern to the passengers.

The reporters seemed happy as we downloaded everyone at Range 29; smiles on all faces.

"Okay, everyone," I said as Juergen lifted off, leaving me a quiet landing zone. "Our Demo Pilot is going to make a few runs past us. He's going to start from behind that ridge over there and fly past us in several profiles." I had everyone's attention until Juergen appeared unexpectedly out of nowhere. I could hear the comments.

"I never even heard him. How did he do that?"

"Look at that thing go."

"I didn't know something that large could be so nimble."

Then I swear we played out a scene from a movie... Juergen ran at us at about one hundred and fifty knots, just below our elevated position. He banked ever so slightly toward us and climbed to what looked like our level. It looked like he'd hit us in a second...

Everyone dropped to the ground. I stood alone on the elevated pad, hands on my hips, watching Juergen pass by about twenty feet above us. I could hear embarrassed laughter from the ground around me as the startled reporters realized their mistake. I seized the opportunity – "Ladies and Gentlemen, imagine that aircraft, or better yet, a group of three to five are coming at you, guns blazing, rockets from support aircraft keeping your head down. Do you still believe the MH-47 is unsuitable as an assault aircraft?" My new friends dusted themselves off in preparation for our return flight.

I consider the time spent answering questions candidly, sharing my opinions, and war stories set the tone for a fabulous demonstration flight. To my knowledge, not a single negative article appeared in the press again regarding the MH-47's capabilities in combat.

+++

The rest of my summer was relatively uneventful. Linda and I installed an above ground pool in our backyard, giving us something useful to do until the rest of our unit came home. We had some crazy notion that we'd have everyone home before Christmas of 2002. I shared the belief that our unit wasn't designed for long-term deployments. We'd already gone longer than anyone in the organization expected. So, it was a surprise when, not only did we leave helicopters in Afghanistan, but we sent more. The increase in airframes meant there needed to be a corresponding increase in crewmembers – which meant me.

Linda wasn't ready for me to return to a combat zone. She felt she'd sacrificed enough and wanted me to stay home. I had a different outlook. We were going to give A-2 a much-needed break before they participated in the soon-to-happen Iraq invasion. The southern provinces near Kandahar were being covered by Blackhawks and Chinooks assigned to our third Battalion from Savannah, Georgia. Everyone needed to share the load. My family wasn't going to be spared from the same fate of many others – deployment after deployment.

I'd come to grips with my post-Anaconda emotions, but Linda had not. This was going to be a problem. We just didn't know it yet.

Chapter 23

OEF– Back in the saddle
(August – September 2002)

A wedding ring is a traditional symbol of joining two lovers in a lifelong relationship. The deaths of my friends during Operation Anaconda taught me a valuable lesson about wearing that beautiful token in combat. Though it's fantastic to remind yourself you've got someone at home missing you, simply by looking at the ring on your finger, there is a downside. Depending on how you die in combat, that ring becomes more of a treasure to the surviving spouse than most other physical items on the planet.

During Anaconda, one of the men killed, lay in an open field, his wedding ring visible to the surviving members of the crew. Knowing he'd want his wife to have his wedding band, my friend CW5 Don Tabron crawled through and under enemy machine-gun fire to retrieve the tiny circle of love. Don made the journey, all the while knowing he could die for a piece of jewelry, but for him, it needed to be done.

Later in their ordeal, when the survivors of Razor 01 knew their rescue was imminent and that the injured would be sent away to Germany, they collected all the personal effects of the deceased and placed them in a locked ammunition can for safekeeping but subsequently misplaced. A week or so later, the widow of the deceased ring owner asked about his wedding band. She wanted it back. The misplaced can, had actually been secured by a well-intentioned person. If she couldn't have her husband, she wanted his ring. Things got nasty for a bit as accusations of thievery flew. After a time, the box of personal belongings was found locked in a unit safe, and the contents returned.

I never wanted my ring to be the subject of such an event. I made sure not to carry anything that anyone should risk their life for – no ring, no jewelry, no pictures.

Before every deployment, I'd slip my ring to Linda and ask her to take care of it until I came home. Every time I placed it into her palm, she cried. I hated seeing the waterworks as she realized what I'd given her. But I felt it was better than her dealing with a missing wedding band. One of the happiest and symbolic moments of any deployment was when she handed it back, meaning I was safe at home with her.

The summer passed quickly, and August 2002 was upon us in a blink of an eye. It was time for me to go back overseas. My first deployment seemed like it ended just a week ago, but in reality, it had been five months. In hindsight, Linda needed more time to get ready for our next separation. I was committed to the fight, and she played along, but neither one of us had any illusions that I'd make it home this time.

+++

My C-17 landed at Bagram as the sun was rising over the east river ridgeline. Even though we were in the tail end of summer, the still snowcapped ridges stood out in contrast with a clear blue sky. Afghanistan has some of the most beautiful scenery I've ever seen. I don't know how many times I've thought about peace in the Hindu Kush. No fighting could mean tourism, resorts, and business; but that's not what the Afghans want. As near as I can tell, they just want to be left alone. Without our presence the Taliban or Haqqani would terrorize the citizens. At least with us there, they could live in relative quiet.

Infrastructure at Bagram had improved since I left in March. Our compound, surrounded by a ten-foot dirt berm, had grown since my departure. The tents had been replaced with nicer wooden 'B–huts,' with temperature control and improved lighting. There was even a mess hall, improving the food and dining experience. The gym was nicer than most in the States. Best of all, a bank of morale phones and internet-capable computers popped up, improving communications with our families. The bandwidth wasn't great, but we could talk almost every day. These incremental improvements were a sign of things to come. We were going to be in Afghanistan for a long time.

+++

Missions still revolved around Usama Bin Laden and the Taliban. Occasionally other terror groups such as the IMU got our attention. Since Tora Bora, HUMINT sources were plentiful but often unreliable, forcing us to shake things up and gather our own intel. SF Teams began Special Reconnaissance missions in earnest. Helicopter insertions were still the best mode of transportation into areas of interest. Luckily, the weather was mild, and the teams could stay in place longer without resupply as they observed patterns-of-life around the country. The teams were embedded with outside support entities providing services not typically organic to ODAs. Communications specialists, engineers, linguists, and interpreters, known affectionately as TERPs added to the skilled workforce. The need for these specialists eclipsed the fact that they weren't trained in Fast Rope Insertions.

Fast Roping is similar to a firehouse pole. The ropes themselves vary in length from twenty-five to one hundred feet long; they're thick and fat, making them easy to grip. There is a learning curve to descend a Fast Rope without burning through the leather gloves usually worn. The new support folks hadn't been taught yet, so we were limited in how we could land. The benefit of a Fast Rope capable team is that I could come to a stationary hover over a small clearing no larger than the bed of a pickup truck and allow them to slide from the helicopter to the ground from as high as one hundred feet. Without the ropes, I'd need to get at least two landing gear on the ground to unload passengers. At night, with no moon among the rotor wash induced dust cloud, maintaining a two-wheel landing, akin to performing a 'wheelie' was difficult at best.

My first mission since returning to Afghanistan included a lengthy two-wheel landing. We'd set the team in the middle of a saddle, high up in the mountains overlooking a valley of suspected Taliban. I was a little bit nervous for my first flight. My copilot, Rob wasn't the best mountain flyer I'd ever seen, yet he was on the controls.

Only two minutes from landing, I finished the Before Landing Checks and set our brakes. My four crew chiefs scanned the area surrounding us looking for threats, but none showed themselves. Rob's approach angle was slightly higher than the line of demarcation. He looked good. His rate of closure was just above effective translational lift until slowed to a hover.

The cabin-door crew chief picked up the required calls to put our aft landing gear just on the lee side of the ten-foot-wide ridge saddle. "Landing area in sight – continue forward forty feet."

Rob complied. This wasn't going to be bad, after all. I switched on the infrared searchlight. There was only a slight dust cloud, the landing area was mostly rock and scrub. My only concern was the walls of rock on either side of us. I couldn't tell exactly how much room we had, but it was close; we couldn't afford to drift at all.

The aft right gunner started talking as the aft gear approached the ridge. "Hold your left, you're drifting slightly, slide right two, and continue forward ten." The crew calls came quickly now.

"Aft gear off three. Hold your forward and come down slowly...three, two, one, contact – ground contact lights on."

We were in position; Rob just had to relax on the controls and maintain the landing attitude with the thrust.

"Ramp clear down," I said.

"Roger, ramp clear down. Unloading passengers at this time."

Rob started to tense up, and the brakes slipped, allowing us to roll forward over the ridge lip and down the other side. The aft rotors would be awfully close to the terrain. The only choice now would be to come up to a hover and backup, which was not something I wanted to do. We didn't have a lot of visual references to begin with, and now Rob was stressing the crew. The calls came faster and more confusing as he tried to listen and perform.

"Hold your left – you're drifting."

"Hold your down."

"Come back ten and slide right five."

"Hold your back, climb five, climb... climb, climb, climb!"

My first flight since Anaconda and I have a partial team on the ground, my copilot is going damage the aircraft if he doesn't calm down, and the crew is now feeding off the tense vibes. *"It can only get worse,"* I thought. My head began to spin, and my chest tightened, making it difficult to breathe. I was going to throw up. The situation felt out of control. *"What if the guys on the ground came under fire while we still had the rest of the team on board?"* I wondered.

The confusing and now conflicting instructions from the crew snapped me out of my self-imposed anxiety attack. I slid my feet toward the yaw pedals. *"Should I... Yes!"*

"I have the controls," I announced. "I'm going around." I climbed around the left peak, while Rob reset the brakes. I settled in on a comfortable approach angle. The crew's calls became steadier and more reliable as I placed the aft landing gear on the ridge. I was rock steady, maybe one of the best two-wheel landings I'd done in some time; I was running on automatic.

"Last man on the ramp. Aft ready, clear to come up."

"Forward ready, clear for flight."

The infil was done. The one moment of panic had come and gone. And as we made our final preparations to land at Bagram, I thought about how I'd almost failed, but with men already on the ground, I couldn't quit. I was going to be okay.

The rest of my rotation passed quickly, but my challenge was no longer the enemy, terrain, or weather – it was Linda.

+++

Linda and I had been talking often by email. She was depressed and not sleeping but assured me she was okay. She'd also been talking to her mother a lot, which worried me. I'd say about seventy-five percent of their conversations resulted in Linda crying. The remaining twenty-five percent could be divided as pleasant or indifferent. Linda was convinced that ratio was improving, but I couldn't understand why she'd take the chance of a demoralizing call with her abusive mother while I was away. If she was going to try and repair that dysfunctional relationship, she should wait until she had my support. It was almost like she wanted the drama.

I had no idea how bad things were at home until my Battalion Commander called. With a couple of days left in my deployment, he explained that Linda was in the hospital, but stable. She'd been cutting herself, lost several pounds from bulimia, and was suicidal. The only good news was that she'd reached out to our Battalion Chaplain before she went through with a suicidal plan. My replacement was already on the way. I'd get home as soon as possible. In the meantime, our Battalion Chaplain was helping Linda as she waited for my return.

In no time, I was on a C-17, homeward bound. Twenty or so hours later, I touched down at Campbell Army Airfield and went straight to the hospital. Linda was in dire straits as I walked in the door. The staff had sedated and restrained her. She looked pathetic with big tears rolling down her face.

I was pissed. How was my wife going to get better strapped to a bed? I found the head nurse and let her have it. I unloaded my frustration and fatigue on the staff. I didn't see them as caring medical professionals, but as unsympathetic bullies. I even overheard some of them complaining that Linda should be reminded that sick people need their help, and she occupied their time and a bed that could be used for someone with real health problems. I understood their feelings, but this was my wife. Do your job professionally, or don't do it at all.

I signed her out against medical advice. *"Probably not a good idea,"* I thought, as we headed into the parking lot. She tucked her pain meds into her pocket and clung to my arm. She was in my care, and I would get her to a follow-on appointment. Now we needed a good therapist. Linda was grateful; she promised this time we'd get things right.

Once again, I'd come to Linda's rescue, for better or worse.

Chapter 24

A Kandahar Christmas and follow-on deployments (2002-2003)

Linda's new psychiatrist didn't like me; I never knew why. But he was working to understand her depression and control issues. She'd battled anorexia a few years earlier, and she gained about twenty pounds since. I thought that was behind us; not only was it back, but she was cutting herself again.

I made her an offer. I'd stay home and work a job in operations. No more deployments.

But Linda played the "I'll be a failure if you don't go" card. She turned my desire to stay home into a detriment to her emotional growth. I wonder, in hindsight, what would have happened if I just ignored her and did what I thought was right.

Regardless of what I wanted to do, I agreed to continue my work abroad, as long as she continued to improve. We set some additional safety nets before I deployed. Dan Lay, our church's youth pastor, needed help with several of the fall and winter programs, so Linda volunteered. He promised to let me know if she got into trouble or struggled while I was away.

I had an upcoming trip that would serve as a good test. I'd be embarked on the USS *Kearsarge* (LHD-3), a Navy helicopter carrier, for about two weeks. I wouldn't have phone communications with Linda for about seven days. Quite frankly, that was enough time for her to fall apart if she was still not well. I was nervous about leaving town but figured Dan could keep her in check – and he did.

He kept her working on church projects and ensured she got plenty of positive reinforcement.

I came home to find a happy and healthy wife.

Maybe I didn't have to quit after all.

+++

Never a dull moment in Special Operations; preparations for invading Iraq were ramping up. I'd have no part in those early missions; instead, I'd stay in Afghanistan. That was okay with me. I was comfortable with the terrain, weather, and enemy situation in Enduring Freedom. Though we were about to experience a slight change. We, meaning B Company, 2nd BN, were going to add a small presence at Kandahar airfield. Six MH-47Es and two flight leads would support

Special Forces Teams conducting Special Reconnaissance and Direct-Action raids in Taliban-controlled areas that had previously been ignored.

The terrain in South-Central Afghanistan was different than where we'd been operating up North. Kandahar and South consisted of vast rolling sand dunes, and areas just to the North consisted of foothills and mountains. Elevations were lower than we were used to – the terrain less jagged than the Hindu Kush. Engine power availability wasn't a problem. Our biggest issue was suspended dust in the air, limiting visibility, more often than not.

Our intel folks considered Kandahar more Taliban friendly than other places we'd been operating. And the enemy early-warning-network was robust and persistent. So, any flight that required surprise to succeed needed an element of deception. If I'd learned anything from my earlier deployments, I wanted to be predictably unpredictable.

This deployment was going to be a long one, beginning just after Thanksgiving and running through February. Then I'd have a short thirty days at home, returning to Afghanistan in February through June. I was going to feel the chill of fall, the cold of winter, and the warming of spring.

I planned to call home and e-mail much more often to keep tabs on Linda. I considered my sons to be my eyes and ears in the house. If the boys wanted me home, I'd be on the first plane returning to the States. But no intervention was necessary. Linda behaved outstandingly.

Life was good.

+++

Linda was holding up emotionally but did have some pain to deal with. Her general practitioner, Doctor Parker was taking good care of her. My back was killing me, and I needed large doses of Motrin, but Linda used Vioxx for non-narcotic pain relief.

I can mark the month and year that Linda's opioid addiction began. It was when the FDA took Vioxx off the market.

September 2004 started Linda's need for opioids. None of the replacement medicines prescribed by her doctor could relieve her back, knee, and shoulder pain. They tried Fentanyl, oxycodone, and eventually settled on methadone.

Ignorant of potential problems down the road, I was just happy she found relief. Pain kept her from sleeping, no sleep resulted in poor decisions, and that led to unfortunate choices.

+++

With Dan in place and Linda in therapy, I compartmentalized her issues and focused on staying alive in Afghanistan. Though the deployment was long, and busy, only two missions are worth highlighting. The first is a five-ship mission to the village of Tizni, where we assaulted a series of compounds with a Battalion of Special Forces ODAs. The mission lasted so long, we required three separate air refueling tracks. No friendlies were injured, and we caught our targeted individuals – a success by any standard. The second involved an SF soldier falling down a well and breaking his pelvis. The weather was so bad, ordinary Medivac helicopters couldn't fly. We even had to turn around once to wait out an ice storm. But once it passed, Arlo Standish and I each flew an MH-47E utilizing TF Radar as we dove into thick valley fog and passed through low clouds obscuring mountain tops. The Multi-Mode Radar proved its worth again as we forged onward to ultimately break-out of the clouds about four hundred meters from the injured soldier. The capabilities of our helicopters allowed us to do missions no one else would try. I'm sure our peers in conventional units thought we were crazy cowboys, but they had no idea what tools we had at our disposal. And we flew every night regardless of darkness, visibility, or threat. We stayed busy, which helped pass the time... but the holidays were still difficult.

+++

Christmas in Kandahar wasn't as epic as my 2001 experience at Bagram, but it did have its own appeal. Our commander, Captain Ken Kellog, gathered everyone in our briefing tent. Bless his heart, he was trying to cheer everyone up. He read a deployed soldier's letter home from a war long past, thinking he'd associate our sacrifice with World Wars One and Two as if the historical similarities would make our time away from family easier to take. But his holiday pep talk fell on closed ears. No one wanted to listen. From my location in the back of the tent, I could see heads hung low. Kellog's efforts had fallen short – something needed to be done – I knew just how to motivate this bunch.

I made sure I was behind everyone with an easy escape path. Pew-like bench seats occupied most of the tent, leaving very little room to move from front to back. Now was the time.

I addressed the group. "Hey!" I paused for effect, but lethargy still gripped the men. "I said, hey! What the fuck is wrong with you sad individuals?"

Now I had their attention.

"It's Christmas, and you guys are grumpy and sad... oh, poor you..." I shifted my weight to my outboard foot, ready to run. The guys shifted restlessly, but I needed one more taunt to get them moving. "Let's go, you sad fucks. Catch me if you can!"

That did it. Benches, tables, and chairs tipped over as the men jumped up and tried to rush me.

"Get him!" they yelled in unison.

Arlo, Dave, and Jethro intervened and blocked the aisle while I ran out of the tent. The night was dark, with no visible moon. Heavy cloud cover made it difficult for me to tiptoe through the maze of rebar tent stakes and lines that littered the area. I was moving fast but cautiously, trying not to slip in the cold mud between the tent and our planning building. I scampered up three wooden steps to the door leading to safety and freedom. A stubborn combination lock slowed my progress. I hastily entered the combo, but the door wouldn't budge. I tried again, then a third time. Too late. The pilots couldn't hold back twenty-five charging crew chiefs. I was hoisted above their heads like a body surfing rock star. I looked down as I passed over the rebar tent stakes – one slip and I might end up impaled. But I found myself gently placed into the cold mud as twenty or more crewmembers piled on top of me, forcing me deep into the muck.

The combination of laughter, screaming insults, and the weight of the 'dogpile' made breathing almost impossible. My vision started to fade as I neared blackout. The cost of getting a rise out of these guys was going to be my lungs squeezed through my nose if I didn't get out from under the pile. Someone with Christmas spirit grabbed my ankles and pulled until I emerged from under the pile, muddy and out of breath.

We had a good laugh and moved into the now unlocked planning building for hot chocolate and snacks – another Christmas in Afghanistan...

+++

Linda was always on my mind. Her episodic depression could really take a bite out of our lives. She was managing her pain and held up emotionally. She deserved a reward – a trip to the mountains – and she had a plan. A week of skiing at Cataloochee Valley, North Carolina was in order. She rented a cabin expecting me to return within a day or so of her non-refundable reservations.

An MH-47E was coming home on the next C-17 for phased maintenance. I would be on that flight. The Chinook swap had to happen, so I'd definitely have a ride home. She set a date with a wide buffer to allow for weather, maintenance problems, and the occasional Air Force crew rest problems. She would not be denied her due. Only two things that could derail our vacation. I could miss the C-17 for whatever reason. If I missed that ride, I'd have to wait at least two more weeks for the next. Linda's plan could absorb roughly eight days, so a missed seat would constitute mission failure. The only other way I might miss the C-17, would be if I died. From Linda's perspective, if I missed the plane, I'd better be dead, because she'd kill me herself.

Daylight exfils of the assault force are the exception rather than the rule, but they stay on target until it's all secure and sensitive site exploitation complete. Look closely at the M134 'Miniguns'. Their long fabric-covered dump tubes expel expended brass casings overboard at a rate of 4,000 rounds per minute. (*Photo provided by 160th SOAR community pool*)

A crucial facet of the 160th SOAR's mission is deployability. Although the MH–47 has an expansive range of operations with extended range fuel tanks and air refueling, sometimes a ride on a C–17 is needed to get to the far reaches of the globe. Experienced and motivated mechanics/maintainers skilled at their trade can build up or tear down an MH–47 within hours. (*Photo provided by Dave Gross, 160th SOAR*)

2001 – CW3 Alan Mack stands outside his burned-out barracks nicknamed 'Motel 6' at Bagram Airbase during the Tora Bora campaign to kill or capture Usama Bin Laden. Relaxed grooming standards and a dirty flight suit are a way of life. (*Photo provided by Alan Mack, 160th SOAR*)

2001 – Karshi Khanabad airbase, Uzbekistan (K2). Task Force Dagger Forward Staging Base (FSB), nicknamed Stronghold Freedom, in its early stages of improvement. A dirt berm surrounds the newly erected encampment of tents. MH-60 DAPS and MH-47E Chinooks are visible in front of the hardened aircraft shelters (HAS). (*Photo provided by Alan Mack, 160th SOAR*)

CW5 Alan Mack observes an MH-47E landing on an LHD from the comfort of the ship's tower, known as 'Primary Control,' or 'Pri Fly.' Whenever Army aircrews practice their currency, a liaison supports the 'Airboss' as he controls the 'bounces' and cycles the aircraft around the 'Charlie Pattern'. The 'Tower Flower', as he is known, coordinates the unit's goals and intent with the ship's normal operating parameters. (*Photo provided by CW5 Alan Mack, 160th SOAR*)

Somewhere off the coast of Africa – helicopter Air Refueling viewed from the left-wing refueling position. The MH47G on the Right-wing is moving to contact with the para-drogue. Once in contact, they will slide up and right to take on fuel. Simultaneous receivers are routine, and movements on and off the tanker of subsequent aircraft are coordinated without radio communication and use of light signals. (*Photo provided by CW5 Alan Mack*)

Training is constant in the 160th SOAR. Here an assaulter descends the forward Fast Rope of an MH-47G. The normal FRIES operation is conducted from the Aft mounts. The procedure shown here is only used when necessary. One downside is the temporary loss of the right M134 'Minigun.' (*Photo provided by Dave Ritchie*)

Left: A view of an MH-47E looking over an M-240 machine gun mounted in an early design prototype. Note the round window instead of the large gunner's port. (*Photo provided by David Burnett, 160th SOAR*)

Below: Ripples in the hose are captured at the moment of probe to drouge contact. Air refueling from an MC-130 can be challenging at times and can actually be defined as fun when conditions warrant. Either way, refueling on the right-wing is always a little trickier due to airframe aerodynamics. (*Photo provided by CW5 Alan Mack, 160th SOAR*)

I wasn't too worried. After my days deployed, nothing was going to keep me from rewarding Linda's good behavior. Not only did she deserve it, but if I wanted her to repeat this again and again, I needed her to know she mattered. She needed to know I would prioritize her and put my overseas work on the back burner for her. Besides, I needed a break too. A ski trip was just the thing.

I tore another day from my *Far Side* calendar. Departure day was closing in. I'm not sure who was more excited, me or Linda. Our mission schedule had lightened somewhat, as it always did in the winter. So, short of Bin Laden being found, I should have no trouble getting home in time.

A four-ship offset vehicle infil popped up on the schedule for the day after I was to leave. Captain Kellog insisted that I stay for the flight. He was firm. I needed to stay regardless of my plans with Linda.

He had to know her troubled history. How could he not? I jumped on the phone to gauge her reaction, and it wasn't good. She was not bending on this vacation. It was non-refundable, the snow conditions were excellent, and she'd been on her best behavior knowing that we'd get this chance to recharge with each other.

I had to fight for this. I understood Kellog's position, but I had to make mine clear. If he made me miss my wife's vacation because of a simple infil mission, I was done.

"Sir," I implored. "I've never asked for anything. Nothing. I've done everything expected of me and more. I've got to go home on the C-17."

The young Captain looked at me as if I hadn't heard his decision. "Al, I want you to stay. We need you for the 'four shipper.'"

"Sir, if you don't let me go, and my wife melts-down, I'm done – I mean done." My threat was sincere, but to be honest, I don't know what I meant. I guess I thought that Linda would make my ability to deploy impossible if I didn't work with her on this. She'd done her part, now I needed to do mine. I'd put the unit before my family every time before. This time the choice was clear. I demanded to put my family first – just this once.

Arlo came to my aid with what we hoped would be an acceptable replacement for me. He proposed that our maintenance pilot could fly the mission. After all, it was an offset vehicle infil. They were going to fly from our base in Kandahar and land at a desert landing strip (DLS) an hour away. The target was a three-day drive for the SF team. We wouldn't even be exposed to enemy troops. He didn't buy it at first, but after dinner, he gave in.

The C-17 arrived at Kandahar on time, allowing our maintenance team to download the incoming replacement and exchange places with a torn down MH-47E for the trip home. I was nervous the whole time expecting to be pulled off the flight at the last minute. Even as the large cargo airplane raced down the runway and rotated into the air, I thought Kellog would ask them to turn around and drop me off. An hour into the flight I knew things were going to be fine. I looked around the red-lit cabin. Everyone else was already on the uncomfortable floor sleeping. I unrolled my sleeping bag and joined them.

It turns out the offset infil went smoothly without me and I got home with plenty of time to spare.

+++

Linda had the minivan loaded before I got home. She packed my bags, had my skis serviced, and purchased whiskey and wine. She was ready. We were going to have a good time or die trying. I took a shower, donned my jeans, and we headed east to our rented cabin at the base of the Cataloochee ski resort. I'd never skied there, and it was awesome. Located on the backside of a natural mountain bowl, the snow is protected from the sun in a way that allows large quantities of manmade snow to create a deep base while even more significant amounts of natural snow accumulate there every winter. We had a blast skiing from opening till dark. At dusk, we'd throw our clothes into the dryer then head back out for a quick bout of night skiing.

When the kids went to bed exhausted, we stayed up drinking and rekindling romance.

All-in-all, that trip was everything we needed it to be. And Linda, true to her word, allowed me to return to Afghanistan three weeks later for another four-month-deployment. I was convinced we'd turned the corner on her demons. Life was good. And it looked like I wouldn't need to quit after all. Not that I could; the Army instituted a 'Stop Loss' in November.

The approaching fight in Iraq and the unfinished war in Afghanistan was going to require as many soldiers as the Army could place on the field of battle. Men and women that had completed their service obligations were involuntarily extended until further notice. We were in for the long haul, but since Linda was doing surprisingly well, I had no worries. I'd keep flying in support of the Global War on Terror.

+++

The invasion of Iraq and the subsequent campaign had priority over Afghanistan, taking most of our overhead assets and intelligence gathering resources. The Taliban didn't come out to fight in the Spring like they usually do. Intelligence sources indicated the Taliban and Haqqani eased up on their attacks, hoping that we might pull out of Afghanistan if they left us alone. Even they knew we were taxed fighting in two countries at once.

I wondered if our leaders could see we were tired. Nothing eventful occurred for us in Afghanistan through my spring deployment, nor later for my 2004 summer deployment at Bagram. The guys in Iraq were having a hell of a time. Unlike the 1993 invasion, where the Iraqis surrendered in droves, the military dropped their uniforms and melted into the civilian population, creating an armed insurgency problem for the US military.

I still kept my focus on Afghanistan, even with numerous Stateside training trips to Texas, Albuquerque, Florida, and Korea. Linda's only problem was a bum knee needing MCL surgery. I asked her if she could hold off until November 2004. I'd be home for Thanksgiving and Christmas. She agreed to wait.

Chapter 25

V22 Simulator

Not every military story has a life-or-death struggle. Service rivalries can be just as fun. And a story too good to pass up is our visit to Albuquerque in 2004. My good friend 'PJ,' a former MH-47 pilot, transferred to the Air Force to fly MH-53s. As fortune would have it, the Air Force decided to withdraw from rotary-wing special operations, retiring their helicopters. 'PJ' would have the benefit of joining the folks on the ground floor of the V-22 Osprey fielding. The tiltrotor technology had been around since the early sixties but was just now being implemented with the Air Force and Marines.

The Army, feeling the V-22 was more of a spiral technology demonstrator than an actual warfighter, stayed away from the program. Interestingly the cockpit at the time was based on the IBM design used by the MH-47E. The MFDs and Integrated Avionics System were almost the same.

The Air Force V-22 training program was situated at Kirtland AFB in Albuquerque, NM. While I was there conducting Green Platoon desert and mountain training, we met 'PJ' for drinks. He bragged about how fabulous the V-22 was, and it was going to put helicopters out of business. I had my doubts but figured it had a niche. I asked 'PJ' to get us a flight in the simulator.

The next afternoon we met at the Osprey simulator building. We had the privilege of receiving our demo flight with the Air Force's lead V-22 instructor. He seemed grumpy showing a bunch of Army Warrant Officers his new ride. My impression was that he thought he was better than us and just a little bit snotty – maybe rude is a better description.

We climbed the ladder to the cockpit. To me, it looked just like an MH-47E. The only difference was that in place of a Thrust lever, there was a fixed-wing-style throttle. Instead of moving up and down, it moved forward and back. Our instructor let's call him 'Colonel Demo,' explained how the MFDs displayed information and flight data. The aircraft was simple to fly. Many of the functions were automated or assisted, and easy to manipulate with just a thumb or finger push – I liked it.

Our maintenance pilot climbed into the pilot's seat first. I listened to the instruction and explanations he received. 'Colonel Demo' was an excellent instructor, but he was definitely condescending. Yes, he was a dick. But he talked each of us through a series of maneuvers, each one becoming more complex as we went along. The next pilot had been paying attention and performed everything asked of him with no difficulty. From our perspective, the thing flew like a

Chinook, but with the tandem rotors side-by-side instead of front and back. Then it was my turn.

'Colonel Demo' was surprised that the first two pilots had no trouble with his maneuvers. He considered the V-22 too challenging to learn in just one flight. Something was wrong with us... Was 'PJ' setting him up for a joke?

He decided to put me through the wringer. "All right, Alan, go ahead and pickup to a hover."

I did as he asked. The Osprey hovered like a Chinook.

"I want you to take off, climb to five thousand feet, and level off."

I'd watched the other pilots closely; it didn't look hard. I just needed to tilt the engine nacelles with my thumb while adjusting pitch and power. "Like this?"

"Yes, now turn around and land as quickly as possible on the dirt road below. Expect a brownout."

I decreased power, slowed back, and transitioned from fixed-wing mode to helicopter in a rapid descent. 'Colonel Demo' was concerned with my rate of descent, which was approaching conditions for settling with power. I banked hard to the right, tightening my turn. The angle of bank allowed me to see the landing area more clearly. A 'Sink Rate Warning' displayed in little red boxes on the MFDs. 'Bitchin' Betty,' the voice warning system started nagging, and 'Colonel Demo' got nervous. He didn't want to crash the simulator, but I knew what I was doing. I wasn't going to add power to get out of trouble. At this point it would make the sink rate worse. As I saw it, I really only had one option – increase my rate of descent. So, I adjusted the controls to enter the autorotative aerodynamic condition; in other words, outrunning my rotor vortices. The Colonel was upset. In his mind, I'd made things worse, but I'd dealt with tandem rotor settling with power in real life. This was too easy.

I adjusted my speed and bank to flare into a landing attitude. Dense dust enveloped us almost instantly. No problem – I transitioned to the hover symbology displayed on the outboard MFD, softly plopping my landing gear smack dab in the center of the road.

"Yes," I whispered.

'Colonel Demo' was pissed. We couldn't be just some guys off the street. None of his students could handle the machine the way the three of us did. He smacked his palm on the yellow mushroom-shaped freeze button. "Who are you guys?" He was genuinely astonished. "Nobody, and I mean nobody just gets in this thing and flies like you guys just did."

I wasn't sure where he was going with his line of questioning. "We're MH-47E pilots from the 160th SOAR. This aircraft is similar to ours in many ways." I smiled. "Thanks for the fun. This thing is much easier to fly than I expected."

He kicked us out, feeling stupid for assuming that Army pilots couldn't handle his machine. I guess we showed him, never underestimate your enemy. And for us, the encounter was fun and not bad for our egos.

Chapter 26

C-17 ride and a tale of Desert Storm (Mid 2004)

Linda and my sons were doing well, Iraq was in the hands of the United States, and I was heading back in Bagram. I was looking forward to that particular deployment because the intelligence on Usama Bin Laden looked promising, and I wanted to be present for whatever mission rolled down the pipe. I was happy as a clam to be headed back to the familiar area of operations, but multiple deployments were starting to take a physical toll. My back was acting up. Nothing terrible, but a nagging ache that seemed to never go away. Occasionally I'd end up with painful spasms – this was one of those trips.

The day I was leaving, a muscle in my mid-left back spasmed so hard, I could barely move. Anyone who has 'thrown out' their back knows how painful every movement can be. But I needed to get to Bagram to relieve my counterpart and maybe go after Al Qaeda's leader once and for all. The flight surgeon was a phone call away. I hoped for pain relief. He had me come to the aid station for a quick treatment. Upon arrival, he and an orthopedic doctor were waiting for me, ushering me inside the clinic. They got me onto a treatment table and injected the offending muscle with what I'll describe as a Steroid-Novocain mix. They gave me a handful of Valiums and sent me on my way.

+++

The C-17 Flight was long and boring as usual. To pass the time, I read a book while music played in noise-canceling headphones. One of our new pilots plopped down in the seat next to me "What's up, Tom," I asked.

"Not much. I'm bored. Got a couple of minutes to talk?"

"Sure," I said. "What are you thinking about?"

"You were in Desert Storm, right?"

"Yup. Why?"

"How do you compare then to now?"

I had to think about that one. "That's a tough question to answer. A lot has changed, and it may be tough to place events in context."

"Well Enduring Freedom is about getting back at Al Qaeda and preventing another attack in America. We're pretty much on the offensive, he said."

"Well. Okay. We've got a long flight. Let me spin a quick yarn for ya. Operation Desert Shield was about staging military forces in Saudi Arabia to keep Iraq from invading Saudi Arabia. Our presence was supposed to be enough to defend the kingdom, and it was. But we weren't going to just sit around and look scary for a year or two. Ground units kept pouring into the country and dispersed. You might say this is the biggest difference from then till now. It took months to build up sufficient force to attack Iraq and it took us a couple of weeks to take Afghanistan."

My hands were cold, so I slipped into a pair of Nomex flight gloves. I turned my attention back to Tom. "Once we got into country, we used our Chinooks to deliver supplies of fuel, food, and parts to armored units in the field. As a WO1 I needed flight experience and the older guys were happy to give it to me. 'Desert Express' came into being. Equipment flown into King Fahd Airport would be met by us as soon as it arrived. Within minutes of landing, we'd be on our way to whatever Forward Operating Base or logistics facility awaited our cargo. As the junior pilot, I was on the schedule every day.

A typical mission began around 16:00 hours (4:00pm). The day was cooling off, and we'd be able to lift more weight or take more gas to fly further. We wanted to land at our destination while still light out. Landing a heavy Chinook in the dust without hover symbology was tricky enough, and we preferred not to unload in the dark. Conversely, the flight home would be at night using Night Vision Goggles."

Tom looked perplexed.

I had to put what I was saying into context. "I know, hard to believe by today's standards, but many of the senior pilots hated flying with NVGs – considered them too dangerous. I couldn't understand their fears. We were at a turning point in Army Aviation. NVGs, GPS navigation, and aircraft with improved systems were just making their debut, and the older guys didn't like what they were seeing. Each new item provided a new capability, but as with any new technology, there are growing pains. Learning how to exploit strengths and avoid limitations of equipment was and is a challenge that the next generation of pilots would capitalize on. I was fortunate to be part of this evolution in night fighting capabilities."

"As a matter of fact," I said. "The Army was in for a nasty surprise as we began flying missions in and around Saudi Arabia. The first and most important lesson I can share is that all deserts are not alike. Sand is sand, you might say, but desert terrain is not the same. We always trained at the National Training Center (NTC). Much like JRTC, it's a great place to practice, but relying on the Mohave desert as a realistic training ground may have lulled our pilots into a false sense of security about how good they were in the desert."

Tom got up to use the facilities and came back with an apple. "They were giving these out, up front. Want it?"

The tart apple juice was refreshing, and of course I wasn't going to pass up the chance to tell more stories. I picked up where I left off.

"You know how the ground at the NTC is rock infested sand with scrub-like vegetation? Well that terrain relief helps with depth perception more than you can imagine. Saudi Arabia has vast rolling dunes, looking more like piles of a pudding than terrain. Guys flying low level were unintentionally scraping the tops of dunes they didn't see until they were dragging their landing gear across the sand. We didn't have voice warning systems to alert us about low attitude. To fill that technology gap, the command put a rule in place. We could fly no lower than one hundred fifty feet and we had a safety pilot in the jump seat to fly at night. His job – to monitor the radar altimeter and speak up if the crew descended below their imaginary 'hard deck.' It worked. Nobody else ran into dunes for the rest of Desert Shield.

Of course, now we just set 'Bitchin' Betty' and she sounds off if you get too low."

+++

Tom's attention was drawn to his backpack. Some electronic device was beeping due to low battery power. While he attended to his power issue, I stopped talking and thought about the famous left hook of 1991.

The pace that Desert Shield and Storm began with was snail-like compared to the lightning fast deployment for Enduring Freedom. On January 17th, 1991, our unit disbursed into the desert, trading our heliport in Dharan for an unpopulated expanse of the desert – Desert Storm and the liberation of Kuwait had begun.

We spent two nights sleeping in our helicopters parked on an unused highway cloverleaf waiting for instructions – we were to stay put until called forward.

Wild camels roamed around, curiously sticking their heads inside our aircraft. Other than the fact we were now at war, they were the only memorable things to happen in our desert laager area. I was glad to get the word to move back to Dharan to prepare for movement to our final site. In the meantime, we returned to our compound; our beds were comfortable, we had showers and good food, but now we were exposed to Iraq's missile attacks.

The first sign that a SCUD missile was inbound was the sonic boom of a Patriot anti-aircraft missile leaving its tube to meet its incoming counterpart. The noise was enough to make me drop to the floor and look around the room. It wasn't long before it was clear; we hadn't been hit. We tuned our TV to CNN as reporters Charles Jaco and Carl Rochelle smelled an unexpected odor and donned a protective gas mask and helmet. It was slightly humorous as we watched the two reporters stumbling in protective gear, live on-air. To their credit, even though visibly shaken, they stood on camera and described the Patriot missile-to-SCUD intercept. It took about two minutes before someone out of view informed them that no nerve agent was detected. What they smelled on their rooftop perch was merely rocket exhaust.

No direct hit on our compound, but that didn't mean the SCUD didn't carry a chemical warhead. *"Crap,"* I thought. This was going to suck. Someone loudly announced the call to don our NBC gear, "GAS, GAS, GAS,".

Gas masks, gloves, and charcoal suits made up our ensemble. Can you imagine how it felt? I was sitting on a sofa watching CNN in full chemical protective gear, my head tilted ever-so-slightly to the side to get a good view of the program through the plexiglass eyeholes in my gas mask.

Within thirty minutes, we got the "All Clear," allowing us to remove our uncomfortable suits. It wasn't long when a second Patriot launched, causing us to repeat the entire process. I would say that we were never really in danger from the SCUDs, but they did hit a nearby barracks, killing twenty-eight soldiers in their sleep. The missile threat would not last long, because we would trade our posh compound for tents in the middle of the desert. We moved several hundred miles to our northwest as part of the now famous 'left hook.' Our new home, in Assembly Area Palm, was not bad, as far as tent-cities go. Engineers surrounded our tents with a four-foot-high protective dirt berm. Someone had seen photographs of helicopters parked in revetments in Vietnam and thought we should do the same.

An engineer unit placed U-shaped berms; six feet high around each of our aircraft parking spots. We needed to land inside them engulfed in a total brownout. The rotor wash induced dust clouds were so dense that we couldn't see out our windows to land. Every day the return to base included several seconds of terror as we touched down just short of our parking area and rolled to a stop just short of the dirt wall to our front and sides. To this day, I think about those revetments every time I land in the dust with MH-47 hover page.

+++

Another difference between life in AA Palm and my schedule in OEF, was the Operational Tempo (OPTEMPO). Afghanistan was busy and we flew almost every night, facing either poor weather conditions or enemy fire. Saudi Arabia was quiet and mostly boring since we were the first elements to move north and west in preparation for the big assault into Iraq. Convoy after convoy drove past us on the 'tap line' road. We could see we were gonna be part of something big, though we hadn't been 'read on' yet.

So, how were we going to spend our time? I had to share this with Tom.

"Tom, I've got to tell you a funny story about Desert Storm."

"Alright, go ahead."

"Ok." I paused for effect...

"If necessity is the mother of invention, I propose that boredom is the father of mischief. Back in those days, cigarette smoking was the norm. Most soldiers survived on coffee and cigarettes, and I lived in a tent full of smokers. The non-smokers occupied the tent next to ours, providing an environment for the 'war of the tents.'

I don't know how 'hostilities' began, but the battle was fun, giving us something to do. You could say we fired the first shots as we captured Barry, one of the non-smoking pilots at night while he peed on the nearby dirt berm – a definite no-no. His laziness could get us sick, so we took matters into our own hands. We 'hogtied' him with rope and dragged him back to our tent and set him on an unused cot. The noise of a Polaroid picture capturing history broke the silence of the night– *snap, grrrr, phip*. A still-drying photo was entrusted to me to hand-deliver to the senior ranking officer in the non-smoker's tent (NST).

At first, the NST played hardball. They did not want to negotiate and demanded they be allowed to visit per the Geneva Convention. We agreed that they could visit, and we'd let him write a letter to his beloved non-smokers. I thought we were more than fair in allowing them into our tent. Imagine our surprise when three of the non-smokers entered our tent and brandished cans of Coca-Cola. A vigorous shake, and they presented them as if they were hand grenades.

"Okay, nobody moves. Keep calm," the leader said.

We were in deep shit. If the non-smokers pulled the tabs on the warm shaken coke cans, our sleeping bags and other personal items in the tent would become coated with the sticky fluid."

Tom knew how miserable that could be for us. Chemical Warfare he said with a smile.

I nodded in agreement and continued. "What do you want?" we asked.

"Give us Barry and give us free passage back to our tent, and we'll forget this ever happened." Our tent commander decided he wasn't worth holding on to. We'd achieved our fun for the night. No need to let our stuff get wet with soda.

"Fine, you may have this criminal, but don't let him pee on the berm anymore," we said.

His tent mates carried him back to the NST and dumped him on his cot. The funny thing is they left him tied for several more minutes.

The next morning at our daily accountability formation, one pilot stepped out of formation and took his place addressing everyone with a mock press briefing. Guys in the crowd acted like reporters.

"So, were there any casualties in last night's raid on the smoker's tent?"

"No serious injuries were reported by either side," the briefer said.

"Is it true, chemical weapons were used during the rescue of the non-smoking pilot?"

The briefing officer shuffled his papers as if to search for the answer. "No chemical weapons were released. Although the friendly forces of the non-smokers did threaten the use of non-lethal 'cola grenades.' The smokers surrendered the prisoner without further violence, destruction, or discomfort."

We had our laughs as the briefing went on. The pranks went on for days until one day we didn't show up at formation. The NST gang placed large sheets of plywood in front of our tent entrances, then wrapped the tent with nylon straps, trapping us inside. We'd have been happy to stay in our tent all day except the dirty rats disconnected the fuel source for our pot belly heater, effectively freezing us in our sleeping bags. Our platoon leader eventually rescued us when she came to find out why we missed formation."

Now the story turns darker. My behavior in the cockpit is still influenced by the next story.

"The day we had been waiting for had finally come. We were going north of the Saudi border into Iraq and Kuwait. Our job was to fly artillery, fuel, ammunition, and food, thus establishing Forward Operating Base Cobra. Looking back, I can tell you this operation was a logistical masterpiece. Over one hundred CH-47D helicopters, operating as lifts of five, arrived in FOB Cobra every fifteen minutes for several days. As far as missions go, it wasn't flashy, but it was effective.

Each flight of five Chinooks started in a Forward Arming and Refueling Point (FARP). The Heavy FARP, as it was known, had twenty-five pads next to each other in a long line. It is the biggest hot refueling setup I've ever seen.

We'd land as a flight into the FARP, plug in the fuel hoses, top off with jet fuel, and wait for the pickup zone coordinator to pass our assignment... The radio call sounded something like this, "Silver flight, PZ control, prepare to copy."

I was fortunate to be the copilot of our flight's lead aircraft, callsign Silver 01. I was the pilot on the controls, and my PIC, Captain Will Sutherland answered: "PZ control, Silver 01, go ahead."

"Silver 01, your load goes to Helicopter Landing Zone fifteen, Silver 02, your load goes to HLZ seventeen, Silver 03's load goes to HLZ zero-three," and so on. We already had the coordinates for all the HLZs in Cobra. PZ control gave us about five minutes to put our individual destinations into our navigation systems, then moved us to the 'heavy pad' to hook up and depart."

It really was quite a feat to grab our cargo and get moving. Each load weighed eighteen thousand pounds in a tandem sling configuration. The five of us hovered from refuel pads to load pickup. The impressive 'hookup guys' were some of the most aggressive I've ever encountered. They stood on top of each load, and as we passed slowly over their heads, they'd slap the sling clevis onto the forward and aft cargo hooks – the CH-47D had three. I listened carefully to my flight engineer as he directed me over the load.

"Sir, the load is in sight, come forward thirty feet, slide left five feet. Maintain altitude and continue forward – Left three, two, one – hold your left – Come up one foot, continue forward twenty."

I made very smooth adjustments to comply with my crew chief's calls.

"Slow your forward, come right one, five, four, three, two, one, hold your forward, maintain position," he said.

I was trying to stay over the load without moving. My hand was going numb, and I was afraid I was going to drift in the dusty cloud. All five of our aircraft were close to each other, and our rotor wash generated unwanted turbulence.

"Sir, the forward hook is hooked, aft hook is hooked, left two, and clear up ten feet."

All five Chinooks used their maximum power for our takeoff run. I don't think we were over the 'heavy pad' for more than a minute or two, and we were off to the races. We repeated this grueling but exciting process several times for the next couple of days. This was my first time into Iraq and my first actual combat mission.

"Once we got away from the 'Heavy Pad,' the flight into Iraq was over flat terrain with virtually no identifying features for back up navigation – no GPS back then. Lucky for us, the 160th Special Operations Aviation Regiment placed several 'pathfinders' along the route with tactical navigation beacons to guide our way."

In my mind, the biggest difference in Operations was the controlled chaos upon arriving at Objective Cobra. I had to let Tom know how insane the airspace was. "Dude, when our flight crossed the release point, and we each went to our individual Helicopter Landing Zones, helicopters were zooming in all directions. How we didn't have a midair collision is beyond me." I suppose that's why we only flew these support missions to Cobra during the day. Now with the equipment, experience and training of the 160th, we could have done this mission at night without any near misses.

"Hostilities ended in less than one hundred hours as Iraqi soldiers surrendered in droves. Holding areas for Prisoners of War (POW) sprouted up around Iraq. The POWs needed to be taken to facilities in Saudi Arabia until they were repatriated to Iraq. The job of moving them fell upon us."

Tom was yawning. Maybe he'd had enough.

"Tom? You awake?" He was not.

With no one to share my story I reminisced about the worst part of that mission: March 3rd, 1994 started early. My Pilot-In-Command, Will Sutherland, woke me from a sound sleep. We were part of a five-ship flight to pick up POWs, and we needed to take off at first light. Not everyone in my tent was going to fly, so I quietly got dressed using a flashlight. Then I slipped out to my helicopter without waking the others and began a pre-flight check.

We were third in line to depart. Chief Pilot and Standardization Instructor, CW3 Bob Hughes, and our Commander, Major Marie Rossi, flew as lead. Within an hour we'd arrived in the middle of nowhere. Iraqi PoWs were corralled inside a concertina wire enclosure. There had to be over one hundred fifty Iraqi soldiers that needed transport to more permanent facilities. None of the POWs were secured with zip ties or handcuffs. Looking back, it's hard to believe that we carried thirty to forty enemy combatants unsecured in the back of our aircraft, with no additional security. We were armed with .38 caliber revolvers. Lucky for us, the prisoners were happy to get a helicopter ride away from Saddam Hussein. To show they were not hostile, one of the POWs used hand gestures to ask for a cigarette. Dave, my crew chief, pulled a pack from his pocket, lit one, and handed it to the nicotine craving prisoner. What caught us all by surprise, is he then passed the cigarette along to the man next to him, who took a puff and passed it on as well. Thirty or forty POW lips later, it made its way back to Dave. The Iraqis gestured for him to finish the now soggy 'butt,' and he did it. The POWs erupted with cheers of support for Dave's gesture. The proverbial peace pipe had been passed, and the rest of the flight to Saudi Arabia was uneventful.

+++

The long day was nearing its end, as we landed at a Saudi prison. The light was fading as dusk approached. And Major Rossi, our commander, told us to depart for home, with five-minute intervals and return to base 'single ship,' and not in formation. Believe it or not, the Army was still developing Night Vision Goggle procedures, and many pilots held the opinion that flying unaided was safer than using NVGs. Since it was just getting dark, the two crews without NVGs left first. They flew back to Assembly Area Palm at fifteen hundred feet, following the natural gas 'tap line' back to camp. At that altitude, there were no obstacles in their path, and there were no other aircraft out flying. Both aircraft returned without incident.

Knowing we'd have about ten minutes for our turn, our crew took the time to don Night Vision Goggles – I'm glad we did. By the time we cleared the dust cloud and climbed to three hundred feet above the ground, I could see radio antennas spaced about every five to ten miles along our flight path. Will was flying, and I scrutinized the map in my lap. I'd highlighted all towers in the area with a red marker so that it would show up easily in the dim green glow of my 'finger light.' I couldn't identify one of the three hundred fifty-foot towers about fifteen miles away, even though the night was clear, with stars scattered across the sky. But the full moon hadn't come up yet, so it was dark. The obstruction lights must be out, so I made an adjustment to our route. "Sir, I can't see an antenna that should be just off our nose about ten miles. Can we come right about twenty degrees? I want to parallel the road with about a three-mile offset."

"Coming Right," Bill announced to our crew. "Clear Right," was their reply. I never saw that tower. Neither did the two aircraft behind me. The aircraft following me used a similar offset, successfully avoiding the unlit obstruction. But unfortunately, the commander, bringing up the rear, stayed at three hundred feet even without NVGs, and made no course correction. They were comfortable flying along the road with only a white searchlight to illuminate the way. Their choice would be fatal.

We wouldn't know they collided with the unlit antennae for several hours after they were deemed overdue. Of the five souls aboard, only one, the door gunner lived to tell their tale. He said the pilots discussed using NVGs but were confident that they were familiar enough with the area that the short twenty-minute ride would be fine without NVGs.

The last words from the cockpit were, "Oh shit. Where did that come from..."

I hoped that my life wouldn't end with those infamous words.

Chapter 27

A New Objective
(October – November 2004)

Oh, my aching back. I kept a tiny zip lock bag of 800 mg of Motrin in my shirt pocket. I ate them like candy. As a flight lead, I was a commodity in short supply, and I had to keep going until my replacement arrived. This particular trip provided more pain than usual. Before climbing into my cockpit for a flight, the medic would meet me at the ramp and give me a shot of Toradol to help with the discomfort.

Pain or not, I was flying. The SEALs I was supporting were a good bunch. Their intel guys were working overtime to find worthwhile targets, and one emerged from the target deck that held promise – Objective Grumbler.

Grumbler was a compound set high on a series of terraced fields. The walls had to be fifty feet high or more with numerous fighting positions along the long axis. This place was built with defense in mind. Sources indicated that an Al Qaeda personality was holed up inside running operations in the Tora Bora area. He was high enough on the target list that we dropped another mission to hit him.

We started with an offset infil of SEAL Recce and support elements. I placed them out of hearing range and returned to Bagram to pick up the assault force. The offset guys patrolled about eight kilometers to surround and cordon the fortress. Once satisfied that they were in command of the area and could control access in and out, they called for the main assault force to launch.

We were holding in the air about thirty miles away, waiting to be brought forward. The terraced fields were not favorable for what we called an air-land and would require a Fast Rope infil. I carried twenty-five SEALs, along with Chalk Two's twenty Rangers. I included a third helicopter, Maxim four-three. He had the responsibility of 'squirter' control. If someone ran and got through the previously set cordon, he'd chase them down and insert his small force of nine Rangers to capture or kill the fleeing individual.

This Objective was important enough for our commander to fly overhead in a communication heavy C-130, known as an Airborne Battlefield Command and Control Center (ABCCC). The AB-triple C, theoretically, could observe the battle from overhead. Commanders would be able to make timely and vital on-the-spot decisions. I was on the radio with our task force commander as we approached the target area. Only one ridgeline remained before my flight was exposed to the target and in the open. I finished my Before Landing Check. The crew chiefs made final preparations for roping the customers onto our specific terrace, just outside the fortress. We rounded the last corner – Tracer fire in all directions – inbound and outbound.

I couldn't believe the volume of fire.

My copilot spoke first. "Shit."

"*No kidding*," I thought. As a matter of fact, I remembered saying, "Holy Shit. Look at that." But during our after-action review, we played our VHS tapes, and I could clearly be heard saying, "target ahead... Gunfire two o'clock... Rope 'em in." I'm not sure how memory works in this type of situation, but I now wonder how accurate some witnesses accounts can be. If not for my recording, I'd swear I used the more expletive-laden comments.

In any case, we successfully put the entire force on the objective and picked up a three-mile orbit around the fortress. I didn't want to stay in the circle for long and changed direction twice before moving off for air refueling. Once gassed up, we returned for exfil. Objective Grumbler yielded our High-Value Target, troves of intel, and Night Vision Goggles. Exfil came at sunup as we squeezed onto the sloped terraces. The bearded warriors approached my cockpit with huge smiles. We returned to Bagram happy and successful.

I can't think of a better way to end a deployment than with a successful hit.

+++

Linda's knee held out long enough to perform the MCL surgery when I returned from Bagram. I don't know what it was with Linda's tendons and joints. They needed work every other year or so. Orthopedic doctors would assure Linda that she didn't need surgery; physical therapy would suffice. But she'd insist they take a look, always finding out that she, in fact, had a tear or other operable condition needing their skills.

The pain was always the amplifying factor in her numerous surgeries. From an early age, she'd taken big drugs for minor discomfort. Consequently, now that she had real pain, she required stronger medicines than your average patient. Her doctors usually were sympathetic to her plight. No pain was their goal – the same as hers.

I've got to give her credit. She blew right through physical therapy and was back doing projects around the house and at church. I couldn't get her to slow down; not even a little. Maybe she wouldn't get hurt so much with a slower pace. Slow and steady would keep her occupied and without injury. The downside to keeping her busy was that more she worked, the more medicine she needed to keep going.

+++

I was gone often, so when an opportunity popped up where I could take Linda along, I jumped at the chance. A trip to Savannah to inspect the Third Battalion's standardization program was the perfect opportunity. Linda spent most of her time at the beach while I pored over flight training records and administered tests to the pilots. These kinds of trips were enjoyable for her and provided a chance for us to share time together. Life was going well until March of 2005, until my dad died unexpectedly from a blood clot to his brain – No warnings, no hints, and total shock.

As I said in his eulogy, "I can't think of a better way to go. My dad sat down in his favorite recliner, dosed off, and never woke up." But I wasn't prepared to lose him so soon. His memorial service was amazing. His friends that I hadn't seen since I was a boy showed their respect as we celebrated his memory. The next day we ate my dad's favorite lobster rolls at the veterans' cemetery in his honor – my dad loved his lobster.

+++

We returned to Tennessee after burying my Dad, and time passed without a deployment. With more time at home, I noticed that Linda's chronic pain was becoming a problem. Doctor Parker tried to switch Linda back to non-narcotic medicine, hoping to manage her pain. But she'd always end up with opioids. Fentanyl patches were the worst. They proved to be too strong for her. She'd be speaking to me, then stop abruptly. I'd turn around to see her sleeping standing up. I called it 'human statue' syndrome, and I hated it.

He kept working through options, finally ending up with Methadone.

I didn't like her taking opioids every day, but this med seemed to work, and she didn't appear stoned like some of the other ones. Only in hindsight do I see how bad this was. But at the time, I just wanted her to be happy. As long as she was not in pain, she was satisfied, meaning I could continue my work overseas.

Chapter 28

Operation Red Wings and the Lone Survivor (2004–2005)

We still had helicopters at Kandahar, but Bagram was once again the central hub of activity in Afghanistan. Our focus shifted from the valleys of Jalalabad to the Kunar mountains. Just north of Asadabad, the Kunar was rife with Taliban fighting positions and observation posts. The area was ideal for enemy bed down locations (BDL). There were only three legitimate avenues into the Kunar by helicopter. The surrounding ridgelines were too high for a heavily laden helicopter to transit and were usually covered in thick clouds, keeping any aircraft without terrain following capabilities into the valleys. All three likely avenues of approach were overseen by Taliban members with allegiance to our targeted individual, Ahmad Shah. The Marines in the area wanted to mount Operation Red Wings to capture or kill him.

Our aviation task force at Bagram reorganized with a hybrid of airframes. Lieutenant Colonel Jed Dunham commanded our fleet of two MH-47Es from E 160th SOAR and seven MH-47D AWC variants from 3rd Battalion. Major Steve Reich, 'The Warden,' acted as the deputy, though he actually commanded the seven Delta model Chinooks. The AWC cockpits were more advanced than their conventional twins, the CH-47D, Though their capabilities paled in comparison the 47Es. They did have a distinct advantage over their sporty big brother. They had a larger lift capacity. A healthy rivalry was in play. The Delta Model guys touted their ability to lift more cargo or personnel, only to be countered by the Echo model guys saying, "it's great to lift more. But where can you take it if the weather is bad?" Both airframes had their strengths. Exploiting them was up to me, and the 3rd Bn Flight Leads, CW3 Charley Eider, and CW3 Cory Goodnature.

Cory and I often spoke about the best utilization of our individual airframes. As long as the weather was nice, his airframes were superior for what we were doing. The Marines' operation would require multiple lifts of as many men as possible. Overhead fire support and ISR would be needed, so the weather couldn't be an issue. Therefore, the 47Es had zero advantages.

The Delta models would take the lead.

Instead, I would relieve them of Quick Reaction Force duties a day early. We took turns sitting around our camp, waiting for some urgent and time-sensitive mission to pop up. The QRF stood ready twenty-four hours a day to respond immediately. I was paired with my FMQ co-pilot, CW3 Mark Tiderman. And riding in my jump seat was none other than Captain Marty Keiser. We had a saying, "QRF duty is boring until it isn't." Someone had to be having a bad day for us to fly.

Reich was ready to hand over the QRF duties to me, as they prepared for Operation Red Wings. But he wanted to hold on as long as possible – 11:00 the next morning.

+++

The plan for Redwings was straightforward, Charley would lead off the effort by emplacing a small four-man SEAL Recce team near the targeted area at night using Fast Rope. This team was not part of the SEAL unit we were assigned to. After infil, they'd position themselves to observe Ahmad Shah's village from a ridgeline above, trying to discern pattern-of-life and pinpoint Shah's location before the main assault arrived. The terrain was difficult to walk, and there was really no useful landing area in the tall trees atop the ridge. Elevation was another problem; the average elevation was over twelve thousand feet. Power wasn't a problem for the 47Ds. The Recce SEALs were the only element high up on the ridge. The hundreds of Marines that would follow-on to Amad Shah's home would land in and around the low-lying areas in the Kunar Valley.

Charley was the overall Flight Lead for the operation and worked diligently, putting the mission together with Marine and Navy planners. Night came, and the Recce infil began. We watched the SEALs infil on a live drone feed. There really was only one area suitable for placing them on the ridge – Landing Zone Thresher. Fast Rope was the only viable way onto the ground. The trees were very tall, requiring the use of our longest ropes, well over one hundred feet long. Charley explained to the team leader that the ropes might have to be cut away if they caught on foliage or rocks. The ropes were heavy and cumbersome, meaning the team couldn't carry them, and they didn't want to leave physical evidence of their arrival. If the crew cut them away, they'd need to stash them to avoid potential compromise. Which is precisely what happened.

The cutaway Fast Ropes lay on the ground in front of the frustrated team. Like every other group I've dealt with, nobody has any desire to manhandle FRIES ropes, especially one hundred-twenty footers. The SEALs didn't really have much of a choice. They gave a thumbs-up to the 47D. Satisfied the infil was completed, the now-empty Chinook returned to Bagram and a good night's sleep.

The SEAL's Fast Ropes were discovered at first light by curious locals. With their secret out and presence known, the SEALS had a choice, exfil immediately or hunker down for a fight. The Team Leader had the decision made for him, as the Taliban arrived in large numbers. Enemy fighters began to appear out of the woods. Future Medal of Honor recipient, Mike Murphy's calls for exfil went unanswered due to a communications breakdown at the CJSOTF. Thinking quickly, and mortally injured, Murphy grabbed his Iridium satellite phone and called for help.

+++

Cory and Reich were already in the planning area, getting things together to hand over to me for QRF. LTC Dunham found them and explained the dire situation at hand. Four SEALs needed immediate extraction under fire. The colonel asked if they should wake me up, but Steve Reich would not have it. They could get there faster than my sleeping crews. "No, Sir, we'll do the exfil. We're already dressed to fly and have already studied the area for the Redwings air movements. Getting Al out of bed will only slow down our response. Let us take the flight."

Reich made sense, and Dunham knew it. They'd easily beat my launch time by fifteen crucial minutes just by already being awake and dressed.

The 3rd Bn QRF formed and departed with a handful of SEALS to add guns to the fight.

The flight of two 47Ds, callsigns Turbine 33 and 34 was nearing the end of their roughly twenty-five-minute flight as I walked into the TOC. I had no idea of the unfolding drama as I poured a hot cup of coffee. I looked up at large-screen monitors mounted to the wall. Everyone in the room was watching intently. I quietly took my place at the field desk adjacent to the Colonel's and sipped my coffee. "Sir, what's going on?"

"The SEAL Recce team has been compromised."

"Oh," I looked around the room, then my watch. "How long until QRF arrives?"

"They should be there any minute."

"Sir, not to second guess, but shouldn't my team be flying this mission? We officially picked up QRF duties about thirty minutes ago."

"Reich made a good argument for his team to launch," he said.

"Okay." I'd just sit and watch the exfil. I didn't often get a chance to watch someone else get into and out of trouble.

The Turbine flight was speeding along at one hundred and fifty knots. A pair of AH-64 Apaches were sent to support, but couldn't catch the Chinooks, now running along the ridge at full speed. The Apaches called to offer their services, but they'd need the MH-47s to slow down. Reich asked where they were and wanted to know their ammunition loadout. He did not slow down. Knowing Steve Reich, he probably figured the Apaches weren't likely to shoot, even if needed, because of a very restrictive ROE. Instead, he drove on alone, expecting to insert his QRF SEALs.

He'd be in and out in less than forty seconds. Getting the QRF on-site was his priority.

Reich's MH-47D entered the video frame from the left, slowing as it neared Thresher. Reich instructed his Chalk Two to hang back and allow him to infil his SEALS so they could secure the landing zone for exfil hoist operations. Like the night before, air landing didn't look promising. Slowing to a hover, I noted his hot engine exhausts in the ISR feed. He was using every bit of power his aircraft could give.

Then a sudden, massive heat source appeared in the 47's Ramp area – Had to be an explosion. The Chinook, mortally wounded, tried to fly away, but the drive train had been compromised by an RPG. The front and aft rotors desynchronized causing the two rotors to mesh unforgivingly. The airframe, now without blades, dropped abruptly onto the steep slope, where it careened and bounced, littering the hill with pieces of aircraft and men, smashing its way to its ultimate resting place. A post-crash explosion filled the ISR video. *"Could anyone survive that?"* I wondered. *"Maybe if they were thrown clear."*

Turbine 34 witnessed the entire sequence. He called the TOC to inform us about what we already knew – Turbine 33 was down. Eight QRF SEALs from CJSOTF were aboard along with seven Night Stalkers from Third Battalion and one from HHC 160th SOAR. The man from HHC was my Standards NCOIC, and good friend, SFC Tre Ponder.

The crash looked unsurvivable, and we still didn't know the disposition of the original SEAL Recce team, and we wouldn't know until we put more boots on the ground.

LTC Dunham looked at me.

"Sir, I can take SEALs and infil them on the southern edge of the ridge out of sight. I can be in the air in less than thirty minutes."

He didn't say a word, just nodded his head. We rallied our SEALS and headed for the Chinooks. I sat in the bed of a pickup truck as our driver hauled ass toward the airfield. Bagram had become a rule-oriented, Air Force-run, pit of people who never left the wire. A courtesy patrol member armed with a notebook tried to take down our bumper number for a speeding ticket and safety violation for overloading the Hilux truck bed with aircrew. As we whipped past, I thought, *"not today, my friend, no ticket for us."* My Crew Chiefs were already at the aircraft and were set to go.

My co-pilot Mark was already in the right seat, running through the checklist as I briefed the crew. I slid my body armor over my head as the crew chiefs asked questions and confirmed the Rules of Engagement. I told them that once we entered the Kunar, they needed to engage any person, not wearing an American Uniform. There would be no friendlies or innocent bystanders where we were going.

+++

Once I strapped into the left seat, I cranked the engines and waited for a 'ready call' from Chalk Two.

In earlier times, we'd get priority for takeoff using only our callsigns. But now, Bagram was a busy airbase, with cargo and fighter planes taking off and landing every few minutes. As I worked the details of my departure with the control tower, I used hand signals to communicate with Mark. Not really necessary. He knew what to do.

Chalk Two called 'Ready,' and we pulled pitch on our way to Hell.

Mark nosed the aircraft over, accelerating till our cruise guide indicator needle hit the yellow range, meaning we should go no faster. I think we topped out at around one hundred and fifty knots. I ran through my cruise and penetration checklists. As soon as we rounded the first corner away from Bagram, I cleared the flight to test fire – this was gonna be a gunfight.

I selected guidance to an aerial checkpoint I'd created just southwest of HLZ Thresher. I was planning on approaching the Kunar from a slightly different angle than Turbine 33 had used. My mind raced with possible scenarios upon arrival. Would we see our friends alive? Would the enemy expect us so quickly? I thought about the embassy mission back in 2001. *"They'd never expect us twice,"* I thought. Who was I kidding? The fighters would be swarming the hill looking for survivors, and we'd be lucky if we didn't suffer the same fate.

My SATCOM radio came to life. LTC Dunham instructed me to divert to our Forward Operating Base (FOB) at Jalalabad. The SEALS there wanted to join our QRF. I was pissed at the delay, yet grateful at the same time. Maybe getting a chance to rethink how we'd get everyone on the ground safely was a good idea. The navigation system now directed us toward JBAD.

Once on the ground, we shutdown to our Auxiliary Power Units, keeping all systems up and operating to facilitate a quick departure. Mark stayed in the cockpit, and the crew tried to relax while I went inside with the SEALS.

+++

The troop commander met me as I entered the tent. The tall Samoan shook my hand as we walked to a map tacked to a nearby wall. Lieutenant Commander 'Henry' ran his finger across the terrain feature he'd like to use for landing. We'd have to use Fast Ropes, probably a one-hundred-foot slide. He grimaced but nodded his approval. Leather gloves or not, their hands were going to take a beating going down those ropes. 'Henry's' next question was how many men could we carry? The ridgeline was roughly twelve thousand feet high. If I dumped fuel on the way, I could probably hover with about eighteen men. He wanted more, but I couldn't give him what he wanted. As in most Afghan scenarios, aircraft performance was the problem. And as we saw with Turbine 33, the ground still has a PK of 100%.

Our only real decision was whether or not we wanted to wait until dark. The weather was supposed to be rainy with low cloud cover. I voted on flying in the bad weather to exploit the 47E's strengths. No enemy, no matter how tough, likes to hang out in the rain; we could use the precipitation to our advantage.

The point became moot when I received a phone call from LTC Dunham. "Al, I want you to hold at JBAD. We're coming up with a plan here."

My feelings got the best of me, "We've got a plan here. We've got an HLZ at the southern end of the 'Thresher' ridge to rope-in thirty-six SEALS. And we're ready to go."

"No," he said. "I want to use 3rd Battalion assets. You stay there as QRF. We'll brief you on the plan once its solidified." Not wanting to hear my opinion, he hung up.

"*Fuck*," I thought. I was here – only a fifteen-minute-flight away. What kind of plan could they have? We sat around, waiting for instructions. Darkness fell along with misty fog. Whatever their idea was, it wouldn't happen that night. Weather sucked – D models couldn't get there, but mine could.

The FOB radio operator called me over to his station. "Hey Chief, I just got a call on Line-of-sight from Turbine 31. He's got a flight of Three MH-47Ds landing in about six minutes. They're going to kick off Red Wings early."

"What?" I couldn't believe my ears. "There's no way a flight of D models is going to make it in this weather," I said.

Lt Cdr 'Henry' didn't know the difference in aircraft and didn't care. He rounded up his guys and headed outside to join the incoming helicopter force.

I got on the landline to Bagram. I spoke with the battle captain, "Sir, what's happening? You guys were supposed to 'read-us-on' to the plan. Yet, I just found out you've got D models coming here in six minutes."

"Calm down, Al. Charley is the Flight Lead for Red Wings, and he's familiar with the area and the overall plan – he's just going to execute a day early. By the way, LTC Dunham is onboard. He'll get off at JBAD to monitor the infil from the FOB."

"Okay," I said and hung up the phone. I really wished I'd been consulted. I was confident I could get the guys in using radar and Digital Map; the D models had neither. I was convinced there was zero percent chance they'd even get near Asadabad, let alone into the Kunar. But it was out of my hands.

I settled into a chair, sipping a bottle of chilled water. The humid air in the tent made my clothes feel sticky and heavy. And now that I had a chance to relax and take in the scene, I noticed the odor of perspiration – my body armor stunk. My friends are dead, more are about to go into the Kunar without me, and all I can focus on is the stink of my equipment.

Turbine 31 and his flight of three MH-47Ds departed with my SEALs and headed to the Northeast. I looked over at the SEAL Master Chief. I pointed to a spot on the map, indicating where I estimated they'd turn around. And wouldn't you know it, I was pretty close. Charley wasn't too proud to admit he couldn't get through that weather, and turned around.

As the night went on, the storms worsened to include thunder and lightning. Now, even an 'echo' model would not succeed. Our window of opportunity to get boots on the ground that night was closed. We'd have to wait for the storms to pass.

+++

With all of our Chinooks at the FOB, we brought everyone inside. We were going to have to wait for several hours. LTC Dunham decided it was too dangerous to fly during the day, so we'd wait till the next cycle of darkness. If that was the case, I wanted to take everyone back to Bagram for quality sleep and to regain the use of our best planning tools and imagery. "Sir, we can't do anything from here for several hours. Let us go back to Bagram. We can come back before it gets dark." The commander wouldn't have it. He felt it sent the wrong message if we left our forward location to sleep comfortably in our beds.

The only air-conditioned building or tent with room to sleep was the gym. I propped my body armor and flight vest against some weights and used them as a pillow with my patrol cap over my eyes. The hard rubber floor was at least cool. Outside, the temperature was uncomfortably hot. No one slept, though I suppose you could say we rested.

+++

After a short nap, Charley and I put our heads together. We needed to infil as many men as possible in one lift. The rainstorms would start again. We figured we'd have just one shot at getting friendly reinforcements on the ground. Charley would bring his force into the Red Wing HLZs through the lower mountain passes. My wingman and I would TF over the cloud-shrouded western mountains to rope our SEALs to the upper ridgeline. We'd meet back at JBAD to re-evaluate the weather and enemy situation to see if we could do another lift.

We departed at first dark. I went west, circling around for my ingress, Charley went east. The Rules of Engagement were now 'Hold.' We had too many friendlies on the ground in different uniforms. We'd have to be engaged with a weapon to fire back. The situation reminded me of Anaconda. *"We're all gonna die,"* I thought. But I couldn't quit; too many people were counting on me.

My flight-of-two broke out of the fog roughly two miles out, allowing us to tighten up, for a simultaneous infil at two separate but nearby clearings. I could see Chalk Two come to a hover as his crew kicked ropes. Mark was slowing our helicopter to a hover. Unfortunately for him, the nose of our Chinook was hanging out over a several thousand-feet drop, giving him no visual cues to help hold his position. I still had good visual references, so Mark relinquished the controls. "You have the controls."

"I have the controls... give me directions, guys."

"Sir, you're in a position to rope," I heard over the ICS.

"Ropes, ropes, ropes," I called.

"Standby, Sir, start coming down." My crew talked me through a slow descent, enough that the ramp height was only fifteen feet.

"Roping in progress." The SEALs were all on the ground in less than thirty seconds. My guys pulled the hundred-foot ropes inside, and we rejoined Chalk Two. We joined just as a torrential downpour blanketed the area. We could barely see the terrain ahead, as our radar painted the rain and mountains. The storm scope displayed thunderstorms in all quadrants. There wasn't much to see as we matched nearby terrain features to our digital map. To say the 'pucker factor' was intense would be an understatement. We were gonna die; no question about it. *"Not gonna make it this time,"* I thought.

Maybe it wasn't so bad. I looked down and to my right front. There was a small draw leading further into the Asadabad valley. The rain lessened some, and I was able to speed up before we were hit with the next wave of storms.

We'd used our only window of opportunity for that cycle of darkness. It'd be another twenty-four hours for the next lift. Now that we'd put reinforcements into play, LTC Dunham felt more comfortable letting us go back to Bagram for the day. We needed sleep; this was going to be a tough week.

+++

Air Force Search and Rescue assets were brought in while we slept. A-10s flew overhead, trying to contact any survivors on the SAR frequencies. Emergency beacons were popping up in several directions from the crash. Survivors might have made it out. But it was more likely the Taliban had picked through the aircraft rubble and pilfered the aircrew survival radios and infrared beacons. We'd have to be careful not to be lured to false signals. If anyone were still alive, we'd bring them home along with our dead. We just had to find them. More troops were needed if we had any hopes of covering enough ground to find our friends.

+++

Each night we struggled to identify the right time to launch. The summer storms were the worst I'd seen in years, and they did not relent. We had to time the flights between storms, usually providing one lift, then return to JBAD to wait for another opening. When or if a gap in the storms occurred, we'd put another group in.

The Marines were trying to conduct Red Wings but couldn't move quickly through the rugged terrain. So we ran a parallel operation. I can honestly say this was the most emotionally charged mission I'd ever been part of. There were only three ways into the Kunar by helicopter, and one was perpetually cloud covered. The Delta models could carry over one-thousand pounds more than my Echo Models, so they were the primary lift birds. Each Echo model led a flight of Deltas into and out of the valley. I lost count of how many times the MH-47Ds went inadvertently into a cloud. They'd announce, 'blind alley' and climb to fourteen thousand feet to clear all terrain in the area. Once they broke out, they'd find a 'sucker hole' and descend back through the clouds to rejoin our flight. We put over a hundred men into the area in no time.

Now we had to wait for them to work. The Air Force resupplied the teams in the field with GPS-guided-steerable-airdropped pallets. Most of them worked – the ones that failed ended up smearing the steep slope with water, MREs, and batteries.

Rangers and SEALs recovered several bodies, and we brought them back to Bagram for a return to the Mortuary Affairs Division in Dover, Delaware. And while we waited for another survivor or deceased friend to be found, we rehearsed carrying caskets for a 'dignified transfer' of our fallen comrades to a C-17 headed home.

I was one of the pallbearers for my friend SFC Tre Ponder, who I'd known since 1995. He was not only my Standardization Instructor but a close friend... I was going to miss him.

Marty Keiser found me at the rehearsal. "Al, come with me to the JOC. We've got a survivor." Someone else took my place on the casket as I ran to the Rescue Coordination Center in the JOC.

Tom, the PJ commander was in charge of the rescue plan. "We have proof of life for Markus Luttrell, one of the original SEALs. He seems to be the lone survivor. Right now, we've got an Afghan team led by an SF Sergeant moving on foot to secure him until we can pick him up." Tom looked around the room to let that sink in. Aerial photos and satellite imagery of Luttrell's location were scattered across the planning table. According to the Afghan who alerted us, the SEAL was in grave danger. The Taliban knew he was in a little farmhouse at the base of 'Thresher Ridge.' Terraced fields surrounded the house, and thick woods bordered the fields. The imagery analyst mensurated the products before printing them for distribution. Dimensions and elevations were clearly marked in the high-quality photos. A Chinook would have no problem landing in even the smallest of fields – I was ready to go get him.

Tom continued, "The weather forecast is the same as it's been every night this week. We've got one window of opportunity to snag the survivor. We're going to have the SAR 60 from Kandahar pick him up."

I couldn't believe what I'd just heard. They wanted the Air Force Blackhawk to fly in and scoop him up. I knew the elevation was too high for the HH-60 and voiced my opinion angrily. "No way."

I got everyone's attention. "There's no way a sixty has the performance to pick him up."

Tom interrupted me, "They've stripped it down. No armor, no guns, they assure me they'll be able to get Luttrell."

"No way the Air Force is gonna traipse into our backyard and pull out our guy. They're not familiar with the area and could end up shot down themselves."

Tom's diplomacy was spot on. He knew what he was doing. "Okay, Al, you can go get Luttrell. But realize that means you'll be utilizing our one weather window for the night. We've still got men unaccounted for in those mountains, and if you don't bring in reinforcements tonight, we won't be able to bring more until the next period of darkness."

You could have heard a pin drop as everyone waited for my response.

There was really no decision to be made. "Fine – the 60 guys can pick up Luttrell, and I'll bring more troops to 'Thresher,' but I'm gonna plan their fuckin' route... AND... I'm gonna plan the Fires and control the timing."

A collective sigh of relief came over the room. Tom knew I'd put my emotions aside and made the right call.

+++

I sat down with the CSAR crew and apologized for being a dick. They understood and were glad I was helping them. I showed them using a 3D program called 'Top Scene,' how to avoid suspected enemy positions, and facilitate my Fires Plan. Then I visited the A-10 and AC-130 pilots to discuss the ROE, munitions, and timing. The choreography of overhead CAS, HH-60s, Chinooks, and ground forces, was in my humble opinion, a masterpiece. We still didn't know where potential friendly survivors might be. And the lawyers wouldn't allow me to pre-emptively bomb someone for lurking on an overlooking piece of terrain, so I got creative.

During the day, Unmanned Aerial Vehicles scanned the nearby ridges looking for fighting positions or people. I was satisfied that no significant concentrations of the Taliban were present on the key terrain, and if there were any undercover, we'd take care of them in due time.

Ten minutes before exfil, the AC-130 began to hit templated enemy locations on key terrain with 105mm and 40mm weapons. The intent was terrain denial and provide a suitable diversion for the HH-60s approach. Three minutes out, A-10s dropped 500 lb. bombs for the same purpose. At one minute out, the fires stopped and shifted to the vicinity of my HLZ high on the ridge. The HH-60 helicopter landed in a cloud of dust. Luttrell climbed aboard under his own power – the 60 lifted off. Then the CAS lifted and shifted fires along the 60's egress route.

As the fires shifted away from my HLZ, I hovered over the opening in the trees.

"Sir, Clear down left."

"Clear down right."

I settled down among the two-hundred-foot-tall trees to deliver another group of Rangers to reinforce the SEALs already on station. As I climbed above the trees, I could see the HH-60 was gone. The Lone Survivor was safe, now we just had to recover the last of our missing men. I banked the helicopter toward home and dove down the mountainside for a low level run back to Bagram. Luttrell's rescue may have been my finest plan in all my years with the 160th.

+++

It wasn't long before we pulled the last bodies from the mountains and began retrieving the hundreds of men we'd inserted. Once the last helicopter landed, we cleaned up and held a small memorial service. I stood stoically in formation as each of our men was eulogized. I fought back the occasional tear and lip quiver. I wanted to be an example... we have our losses, we lose our friends, but we keep fighting – we don't quit.

When the service ended, I slipped away from the crowd and found a dark area between two buildings. I'd been operating like a robot devoid of emotions and showing no fear for my crewmembers. With my back against a wall, I slid into a sitting position and cried like I've never cried before. I shook and sobbed, pouring out withheld emotions. I didn't want anyone to see me. I tried to stop the 'waterworks,' but I couldn't. Even Anaconda hadn't pushed my emotions this far.

Underneath the tough exterior I was grateful to be alive.

+++

Several weeks after Operation Red Wings and our recovery and rescue efforts ended, I hopped on a plane headed to the States. One of my junior Crew chiefs, Specialist Jones, was my travel partner. During a layover in Amsterdam, I dragged him to an airport bar and bought him a beer. We sat quietly as the foam settled in our glasses.

Jones broke the silence. "Sir, I just want to tell you that when we were hauling ass to rescue Turbine 33, I was scared." He was embarrassed to share his fear but needed to tell me. "I didn't know what we were gonna do when we got there, and I didn't want to die."

I looked him in the eyes and said, "Well, I was fuckin' scared, too; for all the same reasons you were." I raised my glass to toast. "Here's to doing what we're scared to do – Night Stalkers Don't Quit."

Chapter 29

Linda's parents – a disaster (2005)

Afghanistan was in the rearview mirror, and I was already hitting the road for training. We embarked on the USS *Bataan* for a week, supported contingency planning in Tampa, and eventually worked my way to Thailand. Linda was doing okay considering Red Wings took our mutual friend Tre earlier that year. Linda knew Tre's daughters and wife. Dealing with the deaths of unit members is tough enough, but much worse when you're more than acquaintances. Linda's therapy sessions were helping her deal with emotions, and she was working through recovery from two recent knee surgeries. With a bottle of Oxycodone to buoy her nerves, Linda flew out to visit her parents in California. I didn't think that was a good idea. Her mother had never treated her well without me nearby.

I couldn't get away and asked Linda to delay the visit. "Let me go with you," I said.

"No. I want to do this myself; I'm strong enough now... I need to do this on my own. If you go with me, I'll never know if I did it myself or because of you."

"What kind of flawed logic bounced between her ears?" I thought. *"Just delay your trip for two weeks, and I can go with you."*

She wasn't giving in. She had plans to take her mother out to eat, they'd walk on the beach, maybe go to Knotts Berry Farm, and eat fried dough. I finally gave her my blessing for what was surely an ill-fated venture. But I had to admit, Linda had been doing well. She might make it through the week.

+++

Linda's first day with her parents unfolded as she'd planned. Her mother was accepting, loving, and a gracious host – that was day one.

The second day began with Linda's mother Daisy scolding Linda for ruining her life. She felt Linda was the worst child of the family. She was the cause of everything that ever went wrong, and Linda belonged in Hell.

She began to throw household items and dishes at Linda and threw her out of the house, disowning her as a daughter. She wanted her gone – immediately.

Linda was shocked. This was a terrible setback. She called me in tears as she drove away from the house. She asked me to make hotel reservations and arrange for a return flight to Nashville as soon as possible.

Linda was an emotional wreck. It seemed my instincts had been correct. Her parents were horrible humans. How could they be so mean and hateful? I'm pretty sure Daisy suffered from some undiagnosed and, therefore, untreated mental illness, such as Bi-polar or Borderline Personality Disorder. But regardless of why Linda's mother treated her poorly, the effect was the same.

She settled into a room that I'd booked at the airport Marriott and proceeded to get very drunk. I hoped she'd make the next morning's flight.

Linda returned to Tennessee surprisingly chipper. It seemed to me that she'd made up her mind that since she was banished from her mother's life, she wouldn't have to deal with the attitude and pain any longer. Linda was going to approach this flare-up, differently than any other time that Daisy gave her hell – maybe Linda was getting stronger with therapy. This would be good because I was about to spend another Christmas overseas – this time in Iraq.

Chapter 30

Operation Iraqi Freedom (2005-2007)

Christmas at Al Assad was anti-climactic compared to my other holidays spent away from home. Nothing special or significant occurred other than we were chasing Abu Musab al-Zarqawi, the leader of Al Qaeda in Iraq. He was responsible for beheadings and other gruesome murders. As is the case with most intel driven missions, there were plenty of 'dry holes.' The near misses were frustrating, but he'd get his comeuppance within the year. Zarqawi was sneaky, slippery, and careful, but even he couldn't avoid a JDAM with his name on it. There's a saying used mostly by the AC-130 crews: "You can run, but you'll only die tired."

Violence in Iraq continued as the Shia and Sunni sects fought for predominance. I could tell I was going to be back several more times. The highlight of Iraq for me was that it was much easier to fly there in the relatively flat terrain vs. the mountains of Afghanistan.

+++

Between my Al Asaad deployment and my first turn at Balad, Linda and I took our sons skiing in Colorado and bought my first boat. I wasn't going to waste time. I lived by the saying memento mori – remember your mortality. I was going to make sure my sons had great memories of me. So, we spent as much time together as possible

About that time, we began fielding the replacement for our venerable MH-47Es – the 47G, or 'Golf model.' It was supposed to be an improvement – not so much at first. The aircraft didn't have any increases in capability but did have growth potential, where the 47E was a technological dead end. The IAS software was a maxed-out hodgepodge of patches and add-ons. Its black boxes, designed in the eighties and fielded in the 90s, couldn't accept any new programming, so a change from IBM to Rockwell was the fix.

The Golf model software, when introduced, was a miserable joke. The code writers tried to mimic the IAS but couldn't replicate the functions. Rockwell had to go back to the drawing board, eventually producing a slick, efficient product that we came to love. I was one of the first to receive an MH-47G qualification as the Regiment Standardization Instructor Pilot. I also had a significant say in how the software and displays were tweaked. It was going to be a while before the Gs were ready for combat, so I kept my focus on 47Es for the time being.

Busy as always, I embarked again on a Navy LHD, this time the *Bon Homme Richard*. Then bounced back to Thailand, flew desert training in Albuquerque, and attended school in Alabama before leaving for Iraq.

Balad was different than my other deployments. Speed was a key component during this phase of operations. Our two MH-47Es had to launch within twenty minutes of an identified High-Value Target location. Five Blackhawks and two Chinooks would rapidly depart for our nightly target based on intelligence that I can't describe.

In order for me to keep up during a rapid launch sequence, we had to improvise. A Chinook takes longer to start than a Blackhawk unless we've already flown. The MH-47 checklist has items and actions that can be skipped if already completed during the first flight of the day. So, at the beginning of each duty cycle, we'd preflight, run-up, and conduct hover and engine health indicator tests before joining the other pilots for our first meal of the day – dinner.

Balad missions were fast-paced, exciting, and mostly landed in large vegetation-covered fields along the banks of the Tigris and Euphrates rivers. Vegetation meant no dust during landings; no dust meant we could land in smaller areas and set-down closer to buildings, known as landing to the 'X'. These pinpoint landings are the most exciting missions, only eclipsed by vehicle interdiction, which is essentially a moving 'X.'

Suicide bombers, bomb makers, and violent extremists were the bad guys in Iraq. And I was adapting to a different enemy and environment. My friends and I were continually pushing the flight envelope to catch the enemy by surprise. I carried as many troops as I could fit. Engine performance was rarely a problem in Iraq. And I wanted to give the 'customers' everything they asked for. In my opinion, speed, and violence of action, coupled with as much deception as I could muster, helped me stay ahead of bad-guy bullets. More troops on the ground meant more guns – more guns translated to fewer friendly injuries and more enemy deaths.

Eventually, the enemy adapted to our speedy assaults and found other ways to communicate – of course we could adapt as well.

+++

Upon my return to the States, Linda underwent yet another knee surgery. Though painful, I swear she liked the attention, and maybe the prescription pain pills that came along with the recovery. But all-in-all, I thought Linda was doing well, even with another series of training trips to Savannah, Fort Bragg, Fort Lewis Washington, and another embarkation of the USS *Bataan*. I couldn't expect any better from her or my sons. Only looking back, can I see that things weren't going as well as I thought. I was fooling myself – a classic enabler.

Chapter 31

So, my Sons don't have to... (2007)

The attacks of September 11, 2001, were six years behind us, and the deployments were starting to take their toll on the force. The Army loosened its stop-loss requirements. Soldiers could retire, but they needed to give two years' notice compared to the one year that used to be required. Several of my friends submitted their paperwork to get out once they passed the twenty-year mark. They saw the writing on the wall. Deployments would continue, and the training trips in between were only going to increase as old guys left, and new guys filtered in. I was asked on more than one occasion, "Al, why don't you retire? You've paid your dues several times over. Why not quit while you've still got your health."

My response was always the same. "I do what I do, so my sons won't have to." And I meant it. I honestly thought we could finish what we started in Afghanistan and Iraq, but only if we kept up the pressure on the enemy.

I was an aggressive Flight Lead, more so than many others. I gave everything I could offer to the ground forces I supported in the hopes that we'd accomplish missions that could break the back of terror groups. I wanted to destroy Al Qaeda's global reach and disrupt new groups from gaining footholds. I didn't want Stephen or Andrew placed in harm's way, so I was going to fight till I couldn't.

Both of my boys had other plans.

+++

While I was away on my most productive OIF deployment, both boys secretly spoke with military recruiters. Stephen wanted to fly Navy jets, and Andrew joined the Army as a Chinook crew chief. I was proud of their intentions but didn't want them in the fight. I was carrying our family's load. It wasn't fair that they would join me overseas.

Stephen's timeline had an automatic delay built-in, he still had to finish college. He'd found a program that allowed him to enlist as an E-4. He didn't have to go to basic training until he completed college and went to Officer Candidate School. But in the meantime, he had all his medical benefits and pay. All he had to do was graduate. I hoped he'd take his time, but he wanted to get into the fight so bad he took extra courses to include summer classes, allowing him to graduate in three years instead of four. I was trying to keep him out of the fight. What the hell was he thinking?

Andrew took a different approach. His enlistment was like something out of the movies, he walked into the recruiter, took his ASVAB test, got results the next day, signed up, and was scheduled to leave on a bus, only days later – I was not happy. But I could not stop him from half a world away. Andrew entered basic training as I was running around Iraq with one of my favorite Ranger Companies, Alpha Company 1/75.

+++

I'd taken a liking to the A Co. Commander on my first Zarqawi raid. Major Dave and I got along great. He and his company were in the middle of Ramadi, about a thirty-minute flight from Balad. During this particular deployment, I spent almost every night, landing at HLZ stork, shutting down and heading inside for my nightly assignment. We spent so much time there, I had one of our mission planning computers installed in their TOC.

One night we had a tip that a particularly nasty Shia militia was operating in the area, so we headed out to disrupt and destroy their organization.

The mission was straightforward. We'd fly both MH-47Es to the 'X.' The objective was a series of small buildings grouped together within a compound wall. My imagery analyst knew just what I was looking for in a product. His mensurated photos included not only length and width dimensions but with his tools, he could even determine wall or pole heights. Major Dave wanted to land as close to the main building as possible, preferably with the ramp facing the front door.

Somewhere to the north would be good.

I know he was thinking outside the main gate, but I was leaning toward inside the compound. The dimensions were sufficient to place my Chinook smack dab in the center, and the Rangers wouldn't have to breach the steel gates. Chalk Two would land outside the walls to the southwest several hundred meters away. We each carried a load of fifty Rangers. A Chinook at sea level elevations can lift just about anything that can fit inside.

After briefing my crew, we headed to the helicopters. And in keeping with my tradition, I searched the sky looking for the constellation Orion.

There he was, high in the sky.

This was gonna be a good night, I could feel it. I took a deep breath as I slid into my seat and cinched my lap belt a little tighter than usual. I was going to plop us down right next to that asshole's building.

A slight tailwind caused warm fumes from the massive turbine engines to waft into my cockpit as I 'cranked' the engines. And after running through the required checks, we departed Ramadi as a flight of two. We turned west and accelerated; we didn't have far to go. The trip would be short, so I checked in with the overhead stack as soon as I could change frequencies. Our ISR platform was controlling the potpourri of air platforms circling high above our target buildings. Their part in the assault was to observe and protect us. The special Blackhawk was outfitted with enhanced sensors and a crew of highly motivated operators.

"Eagle Eye 21, this is Sumo 41 on fires." I didn't have to wait for a response. They were expecting us.

"Sumo 41, Eagle Eye 21, go ahead."

"Eagle Eye 21 confirm you have mission products to include GRGs – Break – send SITREP when able."

"Sumo 41, all players in the stack have products. Prepare to copy SITREP..."

I rolled my handy number two pencil between my fingers, waiting to copy the pertinent conditions of our target. Eagle Eye rattled off his data: "Three sleepers on the rooftop of building ten, there's one sleeper on the south side of building two – two movers walking south to north along the east wall – No lights visible on target. How copy?"

I repeated back the information to confirm I got it correctly noted – all was well. A 'Bing bong' alarm went off in my helmet.

I glanced at my clock. "Six minutes," I announced to the crew.

I could hear the Rangers yelling it back over the sound of the helicopter. I was flying from the left seat with my window open. I closed it to avoid dust in the cockpit. Even after all the missions I'd done, I still felt the urge to pee just minutes from landing.

"Three minutes," I said.

We crossed our release point, and I slowed to eighty knots. I'd memorized the area from imagery, and I was looking for a distinctly shaped silo... "*there at one o'clock.*" I picked up my target without any trouble. I was flying low, brushing my aft landing gear across the roof-top television antennas, when the crew called me clear. I lowered the thrust – dust kicked up as we touched down.

With the ramp down, the Rangers emptied the airframe.

Less than fifteen seconds later, we were on our way.

"Ramp up, aft ready."

"Forward ready, clear for flight."

And just like that, we were out of the compound and on our way to a ground laager site to await the exfil call or a potential CASEVAC or another emergency.

The Rangers made short work of the target, calling all secure within minutes. They were already conducting Sensitive Site Exploitation before we sat down to wait.

Time passed, and we were called back for their ride home to Ramadi. Not only had we nabbed our targeted individual but had a lead on a torture chamber not far away. Major Dave didn't want to conduct a follow-on until he had a chance to evaluate intelligence and hit the target deliberately. He wanted to make sure our rescue didn't kill the very people we intended to rescue.

+++

In the next cycle of darkness, I was back in HLZ Stork, waiting for Alpha Company to load. There was no need to meet inside because this mission was 'in the can.' We repeated everything except routing from the last night's assault. This one had higher stakes. The man that gave up the information about the torture cell said that several of the occupants were scheduled to die within the next twenty-four hours – three of them were going to lose their heads.

We landed to the 'X' then air-loitered nearby for a quick response. The Rangers blasted a hole in the wall and flowed through. They shot everyone that fought back.

The Ranger medics rendered first aid to as many torture victims as they could, but there were some gruesome injuries. One man had his kneecaps drilled through with a hand drill; another had his ears burned with a blow torch. *"What kind of animal does these horrible things to other humans?"* I thought.

Once the objective was secure and the SSE complete, we were called in for exfil. I watched as the Iraqi hostages walked toward the back of my aircraft. There had to be over twenty of them. I can't describe the looks on their faces – shocked but happy?

Like many of our missions, this one made national news about a week after we'd conducted it. And in the coming weeks, we were all over the place, disrupting enemy activities. The pace was fast and furious. The missions were all high profile, sporty, successful, and best of all, no friendly losses.

Chapter 32

MH-47G sees combat (2007)

Early in 2007, the Regiment decided to add the Golf model Chinooks to the overseas fleet. 4th BN, 160th SOAR had just finished fielding their aircraft and were working the bugs out of the software. CAAS (Common Avionics Architecture System), the replacement for the 47E software, known as IAS, was still in its infancy. The Regiment's Third and Fourth battalions raced to gain proficiency so they could deploy their airframes.

Flight Leads qualified in the 47G were few and far between, so I was asked to join the fight flying G models with the guys at Fort Lewis. Knowing I was weak with the new CAAS software, I went to Lewis for two weeks of intensive immersion training. I worked with several pilots that were well versed in how they wanted to use CAAS. I offered no opinions and just listened. Funny how fast you can learn by just paying attention – I should try it more often.

+++

Autumn in Kandahar is seasonally windy, driving sand into the air. Visibility generally hangs around two miles with suspended dust particles. We got plenty of experience with the MH-47G Multi-Mode Radar. Procedures were the same for this version of the MMR as the 47E, so the learning curve wasn't too steep.

Equipment and hardware are a combat enhancer, but the people you work with makes all the difference. I enjoyed working with the Fourth battalion. The guys were fun, had a great attitude, and were highly professional. One example of their bravery was a CASEVAC about an hour south of Kandahar. A British SAS soldier was bleeding from several holes and needed advanced medical care. We flew into the teeth of the enemy as they directed RPG and heavy machine gun fire at our helicopters. CW3 Cal Dockery set down under extreme conditions to evacuate the critically injured soldier. Cal's flight medic kept him alive during the long flight to a critical care hospital at Bastion FOB. Not only did he live, but he wrote us a heartfelt thank you letter from England.

One of our strong suites since the beginning of hostilities was CASEVAC. Our medical staff and augmentees from the Surgical Resuscitation Team (SRT), had fantastic field-portable capabilities. I don't know how many lives they saved in the back of our helicopters, but I know it's no small number.

I usually assigned my Chalk Two aircraft as the medical platform. Never once did a crew in my flight hesitate to launch into any maelstrom, no matter the quantity or intensity of the enemy fire. We saved a lot of guys. And I can't say enough nice things about our medical staff.

+++

Before going home, I needed to get past Objective Moto. A terrorist bombmaker hid in the mountains west of Ghazni, Afghanistan. Our flight of five Chinooks would land to the 'X' in varying locations around our High-Value Target. Moto's series of walled compounds were spread around a narrow valley. The strategic situation was not lost on me. The surrounding mountain ridges were too high for most helicopters to fly over, and the approach to the north was narrow, winding, and restrictive. The canalized terrain limited ingress to only one good way into the valley, making it easy to defend. Early warning posts and anti-aircraft guns could be oriented primarily toward the southern approach.

Our orbiting AC-130 gunship provided diversionary fires when our helicopters were about six minutes out from landing. I was tucked in formation as the fifth aircraft. My friend Ed was leading the flight with LTC Jed Dunham as the air mission commander. My duties in the trail aircraft would be to follow the flight, provide backup navigation, and land in my assigned HLZ. As usual, I started shifting uneasily in my seat as we neared the target area. 'Bitchin' Betty' gave me a 'Bing Bong' chime. "Six minutes," I announced over the intercom. The calmness in my voice didn't betray how nervous I was. The moon hadn't come up yet, and there was a slight overcast in the sky, eliminating starlight. With no cultural lighting, it was doggone dark. Previous missions in the region proved to have tricky landings in the dusty rolling terrain. This target had a determined enemy that was going to fight as soon as they encountered us.

"Three minutes," I said.

My crew responded, "Three minutes, aft ready."

"Three minutes, forward ready."

The landing area was in sight. Brad Duco was on the controls and set-up for his dust landing.

"Heavy Dust forming at the ramp... dust mid-cabin..."

"Heavy Dust cloud at the cabin door."

Brad focused his attention on his hover symbology and made final adjustments. We touched down in one of the thickest dust obscurations I'd seen. I coughed as the smell of the talc-like dust permeated the cockpit and settled on every surface.

Twenty-five Rangers we'd lifted onto the target ran down the cargo ramp and moved toward their assigned compounds. We 'called out' and departed for holding five miles to the south. The radios came alive as the fight rapidly progressed.

It was apparent that the enemy was fighting a delaying action as the HVT tried to getaway. Bad guys ran from the Objective, forcing the ground force commander to commit the Immediate Reaction Force to chase 'Squirters.'

Once the IRF was on the ground, our entire flight moved to a ground laager site about twenty miles away to await the exfil call and provide CASEVAC.

Once at FOB Ghazni, we topped off on fuel and listened to the fight on the radio. The Rangers were tangling with a determined foe. The enemy soldiers were not giving an inch without giving their lives. They were protecting their leader, whom the IRF had cornered about a half-mile away.

Time is one of the critical factors that affect missions. Time on station, time en route, sunset, and in this case – sunrise. LTC Dunham's concern for the safety of our helicopters relied on the cover of darkness. He was dreadfully nervous about exposing our Chinooks to daylight, a noble motive, but in my opinion, poorly misguided. He ordered us to retrieve the Rangers with enough time to return to Kandahar before sunrise. That would mean leaving before the mission was complete. I argued against prematurely withdrawing – I was overruled.

The Rangers assembled at the extraction HLZs and waited for us to arrive. The ground force commander, still fighting with the HVT's security force, decided to stay in place without the main force. The IRF had just captured Moto but was not ready to leave. We could delay our departure and arrive back at base after sunrise, or they could hold up in their location until the next cycle of darkness. LTC Dunham was firm in his convictions... We'd leave.

I was pissed.

We couldn't leave them behind. I was sure a counterattack would happen once the sun came up. That meant we'd have to come back and pull them out under fire. My opinion didn't matter; we returned to base.

Not long after arriving at Kandahar, my fears were realized. The IRF was receiving indirect fire from mortars. The ground force commander was wounded by rocket fragments almost immediately. It looked like we were going to have to launch right then, in broad daylight. The colonel looked at me, trying to make sense of what was happening. "They'll be okay," he said.

My frustration and anger were building. "No, Sir, they won't."

I knew we shouldn't have left them behind. Ed and I started formulating a plan for exfil. But Dunham was holding on to a night-only flight. AH-64 Apaches were sent to keep the enemy from advancing on the IRF's position, ensuring they'd be alright until darkness fell. With gunships providing support, Dunham made us get some sleep.

We ended up sleeping in a large tent with bunk beds placed neatly in two rows. The lights were out making it tough to find my bed. I swept a small flashlight around looking for my rucksack. There, in the corner, it was hanging from a bedpost. The other pilots, knowing that I'd be one of the last to get some sleep put sheets and blankets on my bed. I was relieved and thankful that I could just slide beneath the clean cotton sheets and doze off. Dunham was only about five minutes behind me. Nobody had taken the time to set up his bed.

His flashlight beam swept the area. It was painfully apparent to him that he hadn't been taken care of. He sighed and sarcastically mumbled. "Thanks, guys."

We slept until just before dark, got an update on the situation, and modified our extraction plan. Ed and I agreed that we'd use only two Chinooks to pull the pinned down Rangers from Objective Moto. Surprise, shock, and speed would be our best defense. Even with A-10s and an AC-130 overhead, we needed to arrive unnoticed, a difficult task in a pair of loud Chinooks.

Our circuitous-routing around the far-western mountains added forty-five minutes to the flight, but it allowed us to approach from the more difficult and less likely direction. Under the cover of darkness and moderate southern wind, we could conceivably arrive undetected until the last minute – we could only hope.

Ed led us through the narrow mountain passes, and I followed as closely as I dared. The outnumbered Rangers reported that they were now under heavy concentrated fire. The exfil was going to be 'hot.' I knew it was going to come down to this. My adrenalin was spiking. This was gonna suck, but the draw toward the enemy fire felt good. We were going to get our guys, and Moto.

"Three minutes," I said.

At one minute from landing, we emerged from the mountains. I could see the friendly markings and adjusted my approach. Based on the previous night's landing, I knew the dust would be bad. But I was prepared and would rely heavily on my crew to guide me to a safe landing. The sequence of events happened quickly – very quickly.

"Heavy Dust forming at the ramp – dust mid-cabin."

Then before the next series of crew coordinated calls, our Miniguns opened up. The roar was deafening, flames from the six rotating barrels making it difficult to see.

The crew, focused on their gunnery tasks, were not going to assist in landing. Brad and I were on our own.

My approach was faster than usual, mostly out of excitement. Then I felt the landing gear plow into the dirt, and I stomped on the brakes. I sat still, waiting for our passengers to load. I could feel the concussions of their M-4 rifles as they covered their movement onto my aircraft. I saw a man firing an AK-47, then as he swung his rifle in my direction, the left Minigun spit thousands of 7.62 mm rounds toward him. Chunks of clay and wood flew as the outgoing bullets met his cover. He disappeared behind the wall, waiting for our guns to silence. A short pause in our firing must have made him think it was a good time to try again. He leaned out from his cover and aimed at me again – I was helpless. I could hear the dreaded incoming rounds hitting my aircraft. "Tink,tink,tink." Minutes passed – no – only seconds that felt like minutes. Another burst of Minigun fire and the enemy soldier disappeared in a pink mist.

Then all at once, it was time to go.

"Aft Ready."

"Forward Ready, clear for flight."

Our flight departed, Miniguns killing enemy soldiers still trying to take us down. I accelerated as soon as I cleared the dust cloud. Our successful exfil surprised even the Rangers. They knew what time we'd land and still didn't hear us coming until the final approach. We sustained no injuries or significant equipment damage, though we were struck with several AK-47 rounds, some coming dangerously close to vital components and fuel lines. Another night of cheating death.

November had arrived, and I was ready to go Stateside for a rare holiday at home with my family.

We'd earned it.

Section V

"Be still my heart; thou hast known worse than this."
                                                    – Homer

Chapter 33

Should have Quit (2008)

The war had been going on for seven years. Action overseas seemed to be calming down. And many of my friends made the decision to retire from the Army to salvage their marriages. The choice was not easy, but several of my peers called it quits to stabilize and preserve their family life. I discussed leaving the military with Linda. Surprisingly, she wouldn't have it. The conversation as I remember it was similar to others we'd had: "Hey Linda, let's talk."

"What's up?"

"Dave just dropped his retirement paperwork today. It's been relatively quiet in Afghanistan. Maybe this is a good time to quit. What do you think?"

She didn't take long to respond. "No. Absolutely not. You'd only be quitting because of me, not because you wanted to."

"No, I think it's time. We've been at war for seven years. Don't you think it's time someone else rowed the boat?"

"No. If you leave the Army right now, you'd reveal me as a failure. I'd never recover."

This was a no-win situation for me. If I 'got out' and worked as a Civilian Mission Instructor at Fort Campbell (CMI), I'd be home all the time, but she knew I wanted to be in the fight. I knew it too but was willing to cut away the deployments to save my relationship. But conversely, if I kept deploying, I wasn't sure how much longer she would last. She could probably hold her own and maintain the status quo, which wasn't too bad. But if her depression and loneliness picked up, she might never recover. I had to wonder if she was setting me up. A suicide attempt wouldn't be abnormal for her when things got challenging.

Linda just wouldn't let me quit. So, I shoved my negative feelings down deep and decided to make the best of our situation. If I weren't going to deploy anytime soon, I'd spend as much quality time with my family as I could. Maybe I could strengthen Linda's support network. She'd pushed away friends and family that tried to help her throughout the last several years. And I hoped it was possible to help reconnect people she'd emotionally cutoff. It was worth a try.

+++

Spending more time with Linda started out great that winter. Her favorite drink was 'Sex on the Beach.' Her version consisted of Vodka, Peach Schnapps, Orange

Juice, and a splash of Cranberry. I'd join along with Bourbon and Coke. We didn't do much, mostly watched movies on DVD. At some point, I noticed that her drinks were going down quicker than mine – much faster. For every glass I put down, she had two.

By springtime, she wouldn't let me mix her drinks, claiming they were too weak. Admittedly, I did attempt to water them down. But now I was going to lose the ability to keep track of how much she was drinking. I was afraid her tolerance had increased so much that she needed more. And I finally discussed it with her.

"Linda, I want you to stop having alcoholic drinks during the work week."

"What?"

"Yeah, I think we've been drinking too much. Maybe we should back off a bit. At least for a while."

She was offended and let me know it. "I'm fine. It's you who have a drinking problem."

She really knew how to play me.

She let me have it. "I only drink because you do. Maybe you should just stop completely. I think PTSD is making you feel guilty."

Post-Traumatic Stress Disorder? Where had that diagnosis come from? I'd seen and done some wild things in combat, but I'd never even considered myself to have any mental or emotional issues. It was time to fight.

Linda turned the whole argument away from her alcohol habit to me needing to see a psychologist. I had no idea this was just the tip of the iceberg. Things between us were going to get much worse before they'd get better. So much for my presence being a stabilizing factor.

+++

The sound of ocean waves calmed us both. An opportunity to bring her along to Savannah, Georgia, on a work trip presented itself. So, we drove together, staying near the beach. I knew this was a golden opportunity to improve her mood. Her back and knees ached, and she was clamoring for surgery again. I hoped that some happy times on the waterfront would improve her mood, making her a little more tolerant of her physical discomfort.

I spent my days at the third Battalion hanger checking flight training records and written policies. Linda spent time in the sun on Tybee Island. Two days passed, and things were going well between us, and her mood was pleasant and happy. I couldn't have been happier. Until the third night.

We spent the evening in a riverside Irish bar known for good beer and an upstairs memorial dedicated to local military members who died overseas. They had a beautiful collection of photos and plaques from families and units that had lost people. The memorial was somber enough when sober, but adding alcohol brought my brooding to the surface.

I knew most of the dead men. And as we climbed into a taxi headed for our hotel, we argued. She irritated me, and I don't remember why. Funny, because most people would describe me as a happy drunk. But that night I was mad – I just wanted to fight. Maybe Linda hadn't shown enough remorse about my friends' deaths. We went back and forth with nasty comments. Months, no, maybe years of mutual frustration were bubbling to the surface.

She'd had enough – I was the problem, not her. She demanded I see a psychologist.

But in my opinion, she was the 'nutjob.' I was fine.

The hotel kitchenette wasn't well-stocked, but one thing it had was a block of knives fit for a restaurant. We continued name calling until Linda withdrew a French knife and pointed it at me. I'd never seen her act that way. "What the hell are you doing?"

Her right hand shook as she threatened me with the knife. "You've got PTSD, and I can't take it anymore."

I wasn't scared. I was pissed. "Put that thing down – Now. You're not going to hurt me with that."

"Okay, maybe I won't. But I'll kill myself."

Alcohol clouded my judgement. "Go ahead... do it."

She screeched and lunged at me like a scene from a movie. I deflected the knife and grabbed her by the throat. A raspy gurgling noise could be heard as I tightened my grip and shoved her on the bed. In combat, I was never mad at my enemy, even as we tried to kill each other. It was just business. This was different. I wanted her to feel pain. At that moment, I truly hated her. I squeezed harder, then abruptly let go.

She wasn't sad or crying. And once she caught her breath, she smugly pointed out that I must have PTSD. I slept on the couch and considered her comment – maybe she was right.

She later told me that she baited me into that violent response, wanting to push me away.

I don't remember how we returned to an amicable state, but the drive home was fine. Apparently, we both needed to vent and let off steam. The insanity of dealing with an alcoholic can twist your own insights. Now I was worried that I might be the problem, not her.

+++

Life got better after the Savannah incident, or so it seemed. I made a concentrated effort to keep my anger under control and ignored or downplayed Linda's drinking. I didn't have to witness her slow downward spiral, thanks to more trips to Tampa and Virginia Beach. I called Linda often, usually catching her sober during the day. I don't think she'd have her first cocktail until after 6:00 pm.

I prayed that things would improve. My faith in God was strong, and I felt we were in good hands with him watching over us.

God filled Linda's heart one weekend that I was away supporting a NASCAR race in Kansas City. She called me unexpectedly and announced that she was done drinking. She'd had enough and admitted there was a drinking problem. I'd been right all along, and she apologized for flipping the responsibility on to me. I have to say I was very proud of her. Even though she didn't quit drinking altogether, she cut back tremendously.

She should have stopped.

In the fall, God graced us with a new family member. We welcomed Stephen's girlfriend Tiffany into our family. I always wanted a daughter, and she was amazing for him. We welcomed her into our family with open arms. Her family was initially less accepting. Why wouldn't they be? Stephen was going to head off to US Navy Officer Candidate School shortly after their wedding. Upon completion, he'd take her away from Tennessee for the foreseeable future. My son was a threat to their family.

They'd get over it eventually and welcome him.

+++

Christmas came, and we got a visit from Stephen. Officer Candidate School was in Rhode Island, so my mom's house in New Hampshire was the logical location for us to all meet. Tiffany flew in, and Linda and I drove from Tennessee. He'd lost a ton of weight in just two months, but it was good to see him. And after he returned to class, Linda and I went home, just in time for me to attend another school at Fort Rucker.

When I got back, I took Linda to Las Vegas for some fun in the sun. Life was good. Our relationship felt better than it had in a long time.

Chapter 34

The End of Normal

I'd always wanted a dog, but Linda wouldn't give in. I was gone too often to give one proper love and attention, and she wanted nothing to do with caring for a dog. So, imagine my surprise when I returned from Colorado and was met at the front door of my home by a tiny puppy, only four weeks old. Scooter was a Jack Russell and Beagle mix, known as a 'jackabee.' We didn't know it, but this little bundle of fur would be the glue that kept us together for years to come – especially when things got worse.

+++

My son's OCS class was over, so Linda and I proudly drove to Rhode Island to attend Ensign Stephen Mack's Navy OCS graduation. What a wonderful event. I had the privilege of running along with his class during morning PT before their ceremony. And I got to have breakfast in the dining facility and watch the officer candidates eat while getting yelled at. Good times... Memories of Warrant Officer training flooded my mind with fond emotions. The next morning would be the final ceremony. Since I was a commissioned officer, Stephen had arranged for me to swear him in and perform his commissioning in a private setting behind the main auditorium. I couldn't wait.

Before we left our hotel, it seemed to me that Linda may have been drinking discreetly. She had a funny look in her eyes – either stoned or drunk, but I'd been with her the whole night.

"Linda, have you been drinking?"

She looked baffled that I'd asked and answered without irritation. "No, but I did take extra methadone. My back and knees are bothering me."

Ah, methadone. I wasn't happy that Linda was taking an opioid again for minor pain. I didn't like her taking the pills at all. And she was totally out of it if she drank even small amounts of alcohol while taking them. Her lack of short-term memory was the most noticeable side effect. And it was about to play out big.

As long as she didn't have any booze, she'd just be a little stoned at the ceremony. We'd attend, and I'd get her out of there before anything embarrassing could happen. And like the good flight lead I was, my mind churned out potential scenarios, courses of action, and contingencies. But I hadn't anticipated what was about to come – and there was nothing I could do to stop it.

The drive was quiet until we entered the hotel parking lot.

Imagine the conversation as Linda asked me how she looked. "Is my dress okay?"

She looked beautiful in her red dress. "You look great. Why do you ask?"

"Well, I was going to wear my white dress, but it turns out Tiffany is wearing white. I came this close to packing it. I love that white dress, but could you imagine how bad it would be if Tiff and I wore the same dress?"

"Disaster" was the first word that came to mind. Then I remembered Linda telling me weeks before that she would wear white even though she liked the red dress better.

"No," I thought.

"Wait. Didn't you tell me she was wearing red and you'd wear white?"

"Nope. She's wearing white. I'm sure of it."

Oh, my God. Tiffany stepped into the parking lot wearing a gorgeous red dress, almost identical to Linda's. This was not going to go well.

We got through the day uncomfortably. Tiff's icy stares and cold demeanor were something I'd like to forget, but the memory is etched in my mind forever. She was mad, and rightfully so. Even though this day was important to us, it really belonged to them. I didn't have any idea that this was the first of many mind-slips, mental reversals, and eventually outright hallucinations to come.

Chapter 35

Bergdahl tips the scales (2009)

Linda's drinking seemed under control, but she was taking more pain medicine than I thought she should, but we could deal with that when I got home. For now, it was my turn at FOB Sharana. I'd pretty much had the whole year off, and other guys had been picking up the slack. So, I hopped on a C-17 to Bagram Airbase; followed by a C-130 transport on a 'Ring Route,' to Sharana, my favorite Forward Operating Base. I was scheduled to lead flights from April through the middle of July, then my friend Chad Dominique would replace me.

I always liked Afghanistan in the spring. The temperature was cool but not cold, and the weather patterns were generally pleasant in our Area of Operations. The Taliban, IMU, and Al Qaeda tended to lay low in the winter, making targeting more difficult. But once the snow melted, the bad guys came out to play. One of the interesting aspects of FOB Sharana was its altitude. Chinooks were the primary Special Operations Air Platform there due to the area's high elevation and lack of proximity to aviation fuel. The power and range of the MH-47 made it the perfect tool for transporting our usual 'Customers.'

This particular rotation, I was supporting SEALS and Rangers. I mentioned earlier that though I'd like to claim to be the best Flight Lead in the 160th, the truth was I was no better, but in my humble opinion I was much more aggressive than most. The SEALS liked that. And they were waiting for me because they knew that the command would let me execute missions that others weren't allowed to do – Vehicle Interdiction being one.

VI, as it was known, was customarily accomplished with smaller airframes, not Chinooks. But because of the elevations in our area, no other rotary-wing platforms could perform the mission. And the SEALS were under the impression I'd be allowed to support their plan – they were right.

After striking a few low-level Taliban commanders, we set our sights on bomb makers. Improvised Explosive Devices (IED) were probably the biggest threat to conventional US and Afghan forces. Taking out the suppliers made everyone safer, so we focused on them. The details on how targets are identified and followed are for another conversation, so the start point for this discussion begins after a target is identified.

The SEALS gave me a military grid, direction of travel, and estimated speed. After a quick couple of taps on my calculator, we had a maximum load to carry and a fuel endurance number. Then we'd run down to the helicopters, brief the crew, crank, and depart as quickly as possible. The goal was to catch the target vehicle while they were in the open. We wanted to avoid built-up areas to reduce or eliminate the chance of collateral damage to non-combatants.

Our first VI mission came just after dark. The sky was clear, but the wind was blowing hard from the west. It wouldn't slow us down, but it would make for a bumpy ride. The terrain along the route was slightly hilly throughout the central valley. The target-vehicle was transiting a bumpy dirt road tucked up against a two-thousand-feet-high ridgeline to the west. Most areas the road passed were unpopulated and covered with sparse vegetation.

Our flight of two forty-sevens flew a loose formation as we chased our quarry to his ultimate stop. We had enough fuel to fly for about two hours with twenty-one assaulters. Jackson, the SEAL troop commander, was in my aircraft, and we were working together to coordinate our strike.

Our ISR chase aircraft, callsign VB-123, was flying high overhead, keeping tabs on the target, reporting their position every three minutes. The white SUV, a Toyota Fortuner, churned up a cloud of dust, making it easy to follow. Our eyes-in-the-sky passed a SITREP: "Thunder two-one, VB-123 on 'Fires.' The target vehicle just crossed over a stream and is approximately five miles to your south, heading southbound on a single-track dirt road... estimated speed is 25 mph. No other vehicles in sight. You are clear to engage."

I responded on the UHF radio. "VB-123, Thunder two-one, I copy all. Pass vehicle coordinates when able."

The overhead sensor operator sent the unwitting driver's coordinates. "Thunder two-one, vehicle coordinates to follow, prepare to copy... 42SVB06505945 – How copy?"

"VB-123, Thunder two-one copies all – turning to engage. Prepare to laze target vehicle."

The sensor operator acknowledged; we were ready to go. Lieutenant Commander Jackson patted me on the shoulder and took his place looking over the right gunner's shoulder.

Our flight-of-two continued south in a tail-chase. We wanted to achieve surprise by approaching the SUV from behind. Hopefully, in the dark, they wouldn't see us coming, and the road noise and strong wind would mask our sound until we could see inside the vehicle windows. By then, the occupants would feel the heavy thump, thump, thump of our rotors, but there'd be no escape.

Our procedure was to maneuver into a position above but slightly offset to the driver's left, and fire warning shots in front of the SUV. The Minigun noise alone would freak most people out. Add the visual display of tracers, ricochets, and smoke, and hopefully, this would cause the driver to stop. Then we'd land peacefully and relieve them of their precious cargo.

If they didn't stop, my right gunner would unload a burst of 7.62 MM into the hood of the car to disable it. If, at any time, weapons were brandished, we would engage the gunmen directly and take them by force.

+++

VB-123 continued to update the target vehicle location and speed, allowing us to quickly overtake them.

We were still undetected as we eased alongside the driver's side of the truck and looked down into the windows – no weapons yet. I gave the order to fire warning shots. "Go ahead and attempt a stop."

"Roger, Right Gun hot. Right Gun engaging."

We were using A165 7.62 MM ammunition, otherwise known as Day-Tracers. The bright red stream of bullets from the electric gatling gun was an utter surprise for the driver, but he didn't slow, not even a little.

Jackson spoke: "The occupants are looking out their windows. They're looking up at us."

"Do you see any weapons?"

"No weapons at this time."

"Go for the engine – Disable the vehicle."

"Right Gun Hot, engaging target." My gunner's voice was calm and consistent throughout the engagement. He moved his gun aft and walked his rounds into the hood of the fleeing vehicle. The hood came off violently, with what looked like a series of small explosions, which were the bullets ripping through the sheet metal and chewing up the engine block. The engine immediately quit, and the SUV coasted to a stop.

"Thunder two-two, Thunder two-one. The vehicle is disabled –we're pulling away – you're clear to infil." I looped back around to watch the assault.

Thunder 22 started his approach as we banked left. Their dust cloud was very dense and obscured the vehicle. I could taste the soil even from my orbit, noting the grit in my teeth.

We circled overhead, providing security while the Chinook was on the ground, and the ground force approached – weapons at-the-ready.

Two men threw open their doors and rolled out of the truck with AK-47 rifles. They started to fire but were both dead before they hit the ground... Target secure.

We had several more missions with successful results. And as the weather warmed up, I knew my time was nearing the end. My replacement would be there by the end of the first week of July. Our target set was complete, and the intel guys were working up new targets, which wouldn't mature until I was gone. I should be able to spend my last couple of weeks with easy offset infils and reconnaissance missions. This deployment had been long, but Linda was holding up; I was looking forward to going home.

+++

My 'easy days' were not going to happen thanks to Private First-Class Bowe Bergdahl, who walked off his post at the end of June. Stories vary on why he left and how he was captured, but none of them change my responsibility to help rescue him as quickly as possible. Every unit in theater dropped whatever they were doing to retrieve the missing soldier.

We ramped up our VI missions going after couriers known to be involved with his captors. None of them ever stopped. They always fought. And they were always on the losing end of an M-134 Minigun. But time passed, and although we came close to grabbing Bergdahl a couple of times, we were always a step behind. Occasionally we found physical evidence left behind. We found his underpants on one target and his socks at another. The poor bastard was going to be sorry he walked off his post, of that I was sure.

But it was time for me to leave. CW4 Chad Domeeka showed up and was chomping at the bit to chase our wayward PFC.

Bergdahl was no traitor. I'd describe him as a misguided idiot. We'd risk anything to get him back alive, but I'd leave that up to Chad and the guys as I boarded a C-130 to Kandahar. My ride home on a C-17 bound for the States should depart as soon as I cleared customs.

+++

So, there I was, standing over all of my clothes, military gear, and toiletries as a customs agent searched me for contraband. I was always insulted by this gesture of mistrust. But occasionally, I heard about someone trying to sneak mines or grenades back home.

Only one thing could make that moment in customs any worse…

"Is there a Chief Warrant Officer Alan Mack in the room?"

That was odd. Very few people would know I was here.

I raised my hand. "Here."

"Sir, you have a phone call in operations. I'm told it's urgent."

My mind went right to Linda. I thought she was doing well, but my imagination went into overdrive. I worried more with each step toward the phone. "Hello. This is CW5 Mack."

The OIC of our Sharana Task Force was on the other end. "Al, we've got a problem. Chad just died of a heart attack…"

"What? Say that again, please."

The young captain repeated his comment then filled me in. My replacement, a fitness guru, went to the gym as soon as I left Sharana. That in itself shouldn't have been a problem, but after a vigorous workout, he returned to the planning area and suddenly and unexpectedly fell onto the floor dead. He hit the ground, not breathing and with no pulse. He had a massive coronary event. Luckily, his story didn't end there.

Sitting only a few feet away were two pilots certified as EMTs and one of our best flight medics. Not only did they start CPR and rescue breathing, but they summoned the Surgical Resuscitation Team (SRT) playing cards one tent away.

Quick reactions, skill, and a little luck ultimately brought Chad back from the dead, though he 'flatlined' three more times during his CASEVAC. A quick flight to Germany and he'd eventually recover to fly again. But in the meantime, sources indicated Bergdahl was about to be moved from a compound just to our south. If we moved quickly, we might have a chance to grab him. Therefore, I needed to get back to Sharana as soon as possible. I jumped aboard an MH-47 from our sister company, and they brought me back to my team.

As we headed back to the FOB, I pondered my predicament. We might rescue that moron, but at what cost? Linda was expecting me home in twenty-four hours. She was not going to take the news very well.

Well, one step at a time...

+++

The S-2 NCO finished briefing us on Bergdahl's suspected location. A large compound in an isolated area among large, gently rolling hills. The SEAL's imagery analyst assured us that the building had plenty of open areas in which to land helicopters. My experience had shown that if an area around a compound had no buildings or trees, it was either a cemetery or the terrain was too steep to build on. The SEAL Command Master Chief tapped his pencil on a printed image on a nearby table. "I want to go here."

I expressed concerns about the degree of slope. "Chief, I might not be able to land there. It might be much steeper than it looks."

"Al, you've got to take us right to the front door. This isn't a Kill/Capture mission where we can afford giving the enemy time as we make our way to the building – this is hostage rescue. If we don't get through the doors quick enough, the enemy will execute Bergdahl." He let that sink in.

"Okay, I'll do what I can."

I assigned landing areas to my other two Chinooks and headed for the door, only to encounter my imagery analyst.

"Mr. Mack, you can't go. I re-looked the terrain. The slope around the compound is over twenty degrees. There's nowhere to land; I don't think fast rope is an option either. The ground is like talcum powder. This is a bad idea."

"Thanks, Jay, I'll pass that on to the SEALs. And I'll figure something out – I always do."

The assault force stood firm – the front door or nothing.

The forty-minute flight to the target passed quickly, as my crew and I discussed options for alternate landing areas. The SEALs eavesdropped as we rounded the last ridgeline, bringing the landing area into view.

'Bubbles', my copilot spoke. "Crap. There's no way to land there. That slope is way too steep."

I took the controls to land the helicopter myself – I knew what I had to do. "Okay, I have the controls – set the brakes... Gentlemen, we're going to land to the upsloping trail leading to the front door."

"But, Al, that's too steep."

"I know. By the way, any of you guys ever heard of Son Tay?"

My right gunner understood the reference. "Wasn't that a prison camp raid during the Vietnam War?"

"Yup."

"Didn't they crash a helicopter into the camp intentionally because there was nowhere else to land?"

They understood the concept.

"Yup. Hold on."

It was too late now; I was going to stick my MH-47 onto an uphill trail only feet away from the target building. I would be successful or crash onto the objective. Either way, we'd be where the SEALS wanted to go. I flexed my hand to tighten my flight glove. "One minute," I announced as I eased back on the cyclic and lowered the thrust. The helicopter nose came up in a decelerative attitude. I focused on my hover page as the dust enveloped the cockpit. My decel angle matched the landing area slope perfectly. All four landing gear hit at the same time and the aircraft stuck like Velcro.

We made it.

The landing was soft, I have no idea how close my rotor blades came to the berm along the landing area. We took off, the same way we landed in a cloud of thick dust. The assault force breached the doors, killed the guards, and searched the premises. Unfortunately, it was another 'dry hole.' Bergdahl's DNA was all that was present. He'd been there recently, another near miss. The longer he was gone, the less likely we'd find him alive; I wasn't going home any time soon.

I called Linda to give her the bad news. There was nobody to replace me. I'd have to serve Chad's deployment. And instead of being home in twenty-four hours, I'd be delayed for another ninety days... She assured me that she'd make do.

If I had to a mark on the calendar the ultimate turning point of her descent into emotional hell, this was the day.

When people I meet thank me for my service, I get slightly embarrassed. After all, I've just been doing my job. Flying into a hail of bullets, risking death was exhilarating. Flights in weather not fit for man nor beast were challenging but exciting. And pulling off missions that no one else will try, was what I signed up for – I enjoyed my job. What I didn't account for was the toll my commitment to the Army placed on my family. Not only did I miss many of life's opportunities with my two sons, but my wife had to pick up the load. And although she meant well, she was not emotionally equipped to carry the weight and responsibility of being a single mother and potential widow. The sacrifice to my family, not me, is the real cost of my service. They deserve thanks more than me. But I wouldn't figure that out for a few more years...

Chapter 36

Emotional Darkness (2010)

Living up to the Night Stalker's creed can be tough to follow.

The first paragraph reads: Service in the 160th is a calling that few will answer for the mission is constantly demanding and hard. And when the impossible has been accomplished, the only reward is another mission no one else will try.

It was an admirable lifestyle for me – not so much for Linda. 2010 was a busy year; busier than most. Within a week of coming home from nearly seven months in Afghanistan, I was deployed to Africa for an unrelated mission. This deployment was different than most. We had yet to settle back into our married routine, and I couldn't tell her where I was going, what I was doing, or how long I'd be gone. To top it off, my son Andrew, now a full-fledged MH-47 mechanic, would join me.

Linda put on a good show of supporting us, even though her melancholy demeanor was not hard to miss... She assured me she'd be fine. And if I were gone too long, she'd visit my Mom in New Hampshire. I hadn't seen a vodka bottle around the house since my return, which was promising. Maybe she no longer needed alcohol. She'd been jumping from doctor to doctor trying to get enough Methadone to achieve a pain-free life.

Pain clinics prescribe higher doses of opioids and narcotics than most general practitioners are willing to accommodate; they also have strict rules on usage. Most clinics keep their patients honest with unannounced pill-counts. If the amount of pills in the bottle don't match up with expected count, they assume they've been abused or sold. They drop the patient immediately. No excuses or begging will change their minds. And Linda had already been let go by the three practices in town; there were no more chances locally. A forty-five-minute drive to Nashville was the next closest clinic. I could only hope Linda would listen to the doctor's instructions this time.

+++

Andrew and I deployed to parts unknown and returned within two weeks. The expected long deployment was short and sweet. So, I tried to reconnect with Linda as quickly as I could. I'd found it got harder as the years went on. Long separations used to end with reunification, an argument or two, and a loving embrace. Now our deployments ended without any show of emotion. She didn't seem to care whether I was there or not. She behaved how she wanted. I didn't factor into the equation.

I had thirty days to rekindle and stabilize our relationship before another Christmas deployment to Afghanistan. I didn't want to go. The weather was expected to be gloomy and overcast, not suitable for flying drones, fighters, and of course, helicopters. This trip would be a waste of time, effort, and family collateral.

Before I left, I could at least enjoy Thanksgiving at home. Linda wanted to host a traditional turkey dinner at our home in Clarksville. We had excellent family participation. Stephen and Tiffany came, Linda's sister Anna was present, the group was rounded out with Andrew, his fiance Justine, and me. A holiday spent with family was a treat that I'd been missing. Linda did most of the dinner preparation. My role was to entertain everyone – so I did. But in doing so, I missed Linda's stealthy drinking.

Her bottle was in plain sight on the kitchen island for all to see; she wasn't drinking much at all.

None of us knew she had a second bottle in an under-sink cabinet. That bottle was empty by dinner. Linda was totally inebriated without anyone really noticing, not until dinner, that is.

She was drunk, but so were most of us. The commotion came after we ate. I was clearing plates from the table when I heard my daughter-in-law Tiffany scream in pain. I leaned into the dining room to check on the problem.

"What's goin' on?" I asked.

"Linda stabbed Tiff's hand with a fork," someone said.

I looked around the table. Facial expressions said it all. Something wasn't right. Tiff wouldn't have complained for no reason.

Linda was claiming innocence.

What the heck could have actually happened. There had to be a misunderstanding. There wasn't.

Linda, for some reason known only to her, stuck her fork into the back of Tiffany's hand, and claimed she hadn't. A clue that our situation at home might be deteriorating was obvious now, but I chose to ignore the warning signs and chalked the whole situation up to a misunderstanding.

I should have looked closer.

As time passed before my deployment, Linda's vodka bottles were starting to show up again. When I complained, her drinking went 'underground.' I didn't realize it at the time, but she was hiding small flask-like bottles of vodka around the house for ease of access. If I were at the east end of the house, she'd secretly pull her drinks from a western closet, and vice-vera. Searching for these elusive bottles would, unfortunately, become an obsession and the bane of my existence.

+++

Christmas in Sharana in 2010 was uneventful for me. The Taliban was quiet, the weather was indeed as bad as forecast. And we sat around watching movies and playing Call of Duty. Linda traveled to my mother's house in coastal New England while I was gone. Usually, this would be an excellent experience for her. This time she had a synthetic leash – a limited supply of Methadone. Her pain clinic doctor restricted her prescription to one week with no refill. His intention was for her to return to his office within the week to renew her supply of pills. Linda was determined to stay in New Hampshire as long as she could. So, she adapted by breaking her tablets in half and reducing her dosage. By all accounts, she began experiencing withdrawal symptoms. She offset her lack of pills by self-medicating with vodka.

Linda hid her drinking. My mother knew something was amiss, but, like me, she couldn't put her finger on it.

I called Linda on my satellite phone to see how she was doing, and I remember the surreal conversation vividly to this day.

"Hey, Linda, how're you doing?" A long pause with no answer concerned me. Maybe she couldn't hear me. I adjusted the antennae and handset and tried again. "Hey Linda. Things are quiet here, and I miss you. How are things?"

It was like we had two separate phone calls; Linda sounded concerned as she responded with an off the wall response. "Oh, baby, don't cry."

Was she talking to me? "Linda, what are you talking about? I'm fine."

She continued – "It's okay baby, I'm fine. Please don't cry."

I could only imagine my mother, nearby, hearing one side of an imaginary conversation. And I was getting pissed. "Linda, what the heck is going on? I'm fine – I am NOT crying."

The crazy conversation continued until I couldn't take it any longer and just hung up. What the heck just happened? This was the first of many made-up conversations, hallucinations, and false memories her mind generated thanks to prescription drug withdrawal.

My stress was building, and I had no way to relieve it. At least if we were out flying missions, I could take out my burdens on the Taliban or Al Qaeda. But with the poor flying weather, we were stuck at the FOB. The guys in the planning area took the brunt of my fury. I chewed them out over stupid stuff. I was a complete asshole.

After several similar calls home, I quit trying. She should have gone to a local doctor but was determined to hold out as long as possible before returning to her pain clinic in Tennessee.

Then one day, she just left and headed for home.

+++

As Linda made the long drive to Clarksville, I routinely logged into the Find My iPhone APP to check her progress. She ignored my calls, texts, and e-mails as she trekked back to the south. Linda later confided that she was 'plastered' with vodka. She would only pull over to rest or sleep after scraping her car along the interstate guardrail several times. To this day, I can't believe she made it without a self-destructive crash or a police stop. She had no memories of the trip except for one night. It was 2:00 AM when she took Scooter for a walk and became disoriented. She was drunk, withdrawing from her methadone. And it was 20 degrees outside.

She said that she couldn't find her way back to the hotel in the dark, so she sat down in the snow. There's no telling how long she was there as Scooter whined, barked, and pulled at his leash until her eyes opened. She was freezing but wanted to stay put. She'd die right there on the icy sidewalk unless she could think of a reason to go on. The dog was the answer. He coaxed her to her feet and led her to the hotel. She'd live another day, but only because of Scooter.

God, angels, or luck? How she made it home is a miracle.

+++

When I arrived, I was shocked to find her semi-demolished car. Both sides had scrapes and dents, the side-view mirrors were missing, and the grill was smashed. Of course, Linda played up the winter weather and claimed a plow had damaged her car. Deep down, I knew better, but went along.

+++

Taking my frustrations out on the guys overseas had a cost.

My Battalion Commander witnessed my temper and behavioral changes and assumed PTSD had taken its toll. I needed a break. He was right, but not for the reasons he thought. Linda was falling apart, and by this point, even I had to admit that.

The colonel reassigned me to the Special Operations Aviation Training Company (SOATC).

A job in the training company was either a reward, a break, or a punishment. It was all in how you looked at it. I wanted to be in combat, so this was a punishment for me. But I decided to make the best of it. The time at home was valuable. Now I'd have time to reacquaint myself with my wife and fix her problems. This was the point in our relationship where I finally saw how bad things had become. Linda was sober when I went to work. She passed out on the living room floor by the time I came home. It was apparent she needed help with her addiction. *"How hard can it be,"* I thought.

Time for an intervention. She agreed to attend Alcoholics Anonymous – she'd even go that night. I couldn't be happier. She was willing to work things out right now. It was plain for me to see – AA was the answer. We were going to fix her.

I sent Linda to her first meeting with a happy kiss. I knew she'd return with the answer to her problem. But hours passed, and no word, text, or phone call came to indicate she'd be late. She didn't answer any of my calls, and I began to worry – she should have been home hours earlier. Finally, a strange man answered one of my frantic phone calls.

"Hello, this is the Montgomery County Jail, how may I help you?"

Jail? Had they found her phone? "Hi, this is Alan Mack. Why are you answering my wife's phone? "

"Sir, this is Deputy Frank Jones, I'm afraid your wife has been arrested for Driving Under the Influence."

"There must be some mistake," I said. "She was at an AA meeting, there's no way she was drunk."

"Sir, I'm sorry to say, the AA folks turned your wife in. She was drinking at the AA meeting, even though they asked her to stop. When she tried to drive her car away our officers arrested her. She was very drunk."

"Can you tell me where the car is so I can go get it?"

A quick taxi ride later and I had the car back home. She'd hit a curb, requiring me to change the tire before I could drive; she must have been drunk even before the meeting. I was dumbfounded. AA was supposed to fix her, not put her in jail.

I still had a lot to learn.

Chapter 37

The Ship (2010-11)

In my mind, I was still keeping a wrap on Linda's problems. Nobody knew she'd been arrested. And her newest stint in Rehab was as secret as any special operation I'd ever participated in. We had the situation fixed; I thought Rehab had fixed Linda. In order to keep her secret, I kept attending out of town training, known as TDY (Temporary Duty). The training company may not have put me in the enemies' gun sights, but it had its share of high adventure.

Night Stalkers are trained, qualified, and certified in all operating environments such as desert, mountain, and overwater. The Special Operations Aviation Training Company (SOATC) is designed to train all aircrew to operate in these very distinct environments. All new pilots and crew chiefs spent their first several months in the 160th in Green Platoon. Not only did they get training in advanced first aid, and shooting, but they endured long hours of cross-country flights with complex scenarios requiring them to utilize all of the special mission equipment built into their sophisticated helicopters.

Exposing the students to extreme flight conditions that might someday confront them during a mission was supposed to provide 'stress inoculation.' It wouldn't make them immune to spacial disorientation, air sickness, or feelings of boredom and fear, but it would make them aware and potentially anticipate them.

One of my favorite SOATC tasks was ship landings. We taught our new crew members how to operate around and on US Navy air-capable ships. Only certain vessels are certified for MH-47s to land on their helipads or decks. We could easily land on multi-spot ships like LHDs and their older brethren LHAs. These ships were essentially mini-aircraft carriers. Helicopters, vertical takeoff and landing, like the V-22 Osprey, Harriers and the newer F-35s could launch and recover near simultaneously.

Single-spot ships like LPDs were a little more difficult to learn due to their smaller size. Both classes of ship required significant practice to become qualified and periodic currency landings, known as 'bounces' to remain proficient. The USS *Nassau* was going to be off the East Coast conducting Hovercraft (LCAC) training and V-22 shipboard certification.

With no Marine air squadron onboard, they offered us a unique opportunity to embark with our students for a week. SOATC had never stayed on a ship before. I had the benefit of operating from ships several times during my time with the Regiment. Some of my fellow instructors lived on the USS *America* during the Haiti invasion of 1984-85. These same air crew were part of my Task Force Dagger counterpart to the South after 9/11. Some of their lessons-learned could only be taught by immersing ourselves in Navy culture. Embarked air wings and squadrons are often at odds with 'ship's company.' We were no different. Learning how to coexist in their world was my goal.

I boarded the USS *Nassau*, LHA 4, in Port Canaveral, Florida. The little aircraft carrier was moored, and the crew was making ready to depart. I hurried along the pier trying not to be late. My duffel bag and backpack were heavy slowing me slightly. The warm salt air smelled wonderful, and the morning sun warmed my face as I looked at the cloudless sky.

"This was going to be a fun excursion," I thought.

+++

I usually flew onto a ship; boarding it in port was something I'd only been told how to do. Now I was going to give it a go. I wanted to portray myself as experienced and professional as I walked up the ramp to the Officer of the Deck. I knew I had to salute the US flag, but which one? There were three. One next to a podium at the top of the ramp, one hanging inside the hanger deck, and one toward the back of the ship at the fantail. The officer I was addressing looked at me impatiently. I picked one and whipped out my best salute.

"Sir," I said. "Chief Warrant Officer Five Mack, requesting permission to come aboard."

This was going perfect – was.

My duffle bag hadn't been used in years. I hadn't noticed that dry rot had taken hold. I really should have used another bag.

The strap running across my shoulder snapped abruptly. The heavy cylindrical bag dropped to the no-slip ramp and took off downhill. Navy crew members walking up yelled and jumped out of the way. I turned and sprinted to catch it before it hit the pier and bounced into the bay. Realistically there was no way I could catch it.

A passing Master Chief took pity on me and intercepted the wayward duffel just before it went 'feet wet.'

"Sir, you might want to keep better control of you personal affects onboard," he said with a smile.

Embarrassed, all I could muster was a quick "thank you," as he handed it back.

"You better get going Sir, it looks like they're waiting for you, so they can put to sea."

I repeated my performance with the Officer of the Deck, minus the bag debacle.

+++

I found my cabin with no trouble. The cramped quarters had four beds, and I had the benefit of being there before my roommates. The choice of 'rack' would be mine.

After unpacking my gear, I headed topside to observe our departure from port.

The sun was still shining bright as the tugboats pulled us from our mooring and set us on our way out to sea. I figured that I should probably meet up with the ship's operations officer and the 'Air Boss' to see how they wanted to handle our helicopters arrival the next day. In the meantime, I needed coffee.

+++

I walked into the officers' wardroom from the starboard side and spotted a cook restocking condiments on a table to my left. Our eyes met, and we nodded simultaneously in greeting. Army pilots on a Navy ship were an oddity, but the cook had seen weirder things and went back to work.

The gentle rocking of the ship made me assume a bit of a waddle to keep my balance as I walked. The deck constantly tilted back and forth ever so slightly.

A Navy chief unexpectedly stopped me as he left 'Officer Country.' "Sir, you might want to consider a trim," as he gestured toward my mustache.

"Thanks Chief, I'll keep that in mind, but for now I've got a job to do. So, please step aside."

I could tell the Chief wasn't happy with my response, then he looked at my rank insignia.

"Sir, pardon my asking, but what rank are you?"

"CW5."

He looked perplexed at first. "As in Chief Warrant Officer Five?"

"Yes. Never seen one before?"

"Never. You guys are like unicorns; you hear they exist, but you never see one."

As I turned to resume my journey to find coffee, I acknowledged his luck at meeting a unicorn. "I've heard that. Take it easy Chief."

His mood had improved after talking to me. "Yes Sir. Enjoy your time aboard."

Before I proceeded further into the spacious dining room, I stopped in front of a full-length mirror placed near the entrance in proper Navy fashion. Customs of the Mess required me to look like a proper gentleman, even in my two-piece Nomex flight suit. The camouflage pattern hid the oil stain I'd picked up on deck an hour ago. I tugged at an exposed thread and applied pressure to a Velcro patch on my sleeve. My thick brown mustache had drawn the Chief's attention. I wasn't going to trim it, but I could at least ensure my uniform looked good.

The aroma of cooking bacon permeated the air as I walked further into the room. I love that smell. I couldn't wait for chow to start. Marine Corps Major Bill Greene sat across the table and slid a mug of steaming coffee in front of me.

"Mister Mack, here's a cup of 'joe' for ya."

"Thank you. Please call me Al."

"Okay Al. After we finish our coffee let's talk about tomorrow's arrival."

We discussed what spots the helicopters would end up on and the best way to get everyone below decks to their quarters. Once everyone settled in, he wanted to present an overview briefing. He wanted to emphasize the Captain's pet peeves with 'Helo' operations and how to keep the Air Boss happy – good information to have.

+++

I slept great. The hum of the ship's machinery made great 'white noise.' My cabin was dark except for the glow of luminescent exit markings; it was hard to tell the passage of time. I left my wristwatch on the desk across the room. I didn't want to get out of my 'rack,' but I didn't want to be late for the 'fly on.' 07:00 – time to go.

After a hot shower, I headed for the wardroom for breakfast and coffee. The ship's crew was moving quickly getting ready to receive the incoming Army Chinooks. I pushed through the 'chow line,' then made my way up the control tower. On a ship the tower is named Primary Control, otherwise known as 'Pri Fly.' I would accompany the 'Air Boss' as a unit liaison, colorfully nicknamed the 'tower flower.' I could translate Army-speak to Navy and vice-versa.

I climbed the steep grated stairs and ascended the last ladder leading to 'Pri Fly.' A smiling Commander John Williams was waiting for me.

"Good morning Mister Mack. It's a pleasure to make your acquaintance. I don't think I've ever met a CW5 before. I bet you hear that a lot."

"Yes Sir, that is true. Do you have any questions about our aircraft before they get here?

"No, I've worked with your unit before."

"Okay then, let's have some fun," I said.

Commander Williams scanned the horizon with his binoculars. "Do you think they'll come from the north or west?"

"I looked at a copy of the arrival plan my guys sent. I think they'll come from the southwest. They're going to hit an Air Refueling Track off the coast of Georgia before they head our way."

Williams answered a phone call from the Helicopter Direction Center (HDC). On a deck, well below us, they monitored the ship's radar and were already talking to the MH-47 Flight Lead, callsign Raven 41. He had a flight of four helicopters cruising along at three hundred feet above the water at a speed of one hundred and thirty knots.

He holstered the handset and renewed his search of the horizon. "There they are."

I looked out the large windows eventually picking them up visually.

HDC pushed the incoming flight to Pri Fly's frequency.

"Tower, this is Raven 41, flight of four MH-47s, five miles off your port beam. We're inbound at Cherubs three with two hours to splash, requesting to land, chocks and chains for shutdown and passenger offload."

"Raven flight, cross the wake and call the numbers."

They answered and flew around the back of the ship, turning left and passing the ship's island.

"Tower, Raven flight passing the numbers."

"Raven flight, you're clear to cross the bow."

I looked toward the front of the ship and watched as the flight, spaced about three rotor disk lengths entered the 'Charlie pattern' for landing. Commander Williams assigned each aircraft a landing spot. I don't care what anybody says, the Chinook is a graceful beast. I admired their lines and movement as each aircraft banked in our direction.

As they neared the deck, they slowed and followed hand signals from the yellow shirted LSEs. As the nose of each Chinook approached the flight deck, they pivoted on their nose until they were parallel with the *Nassau*, then slid sideways over their assigned landing spot. There were nine total, but only a few were suitable for multiple MH-47s. Once on deck, the wheels were chocked, and chains fastened to landing gear.

Forty-five minutes later all the aircraft were 'put to bed,' and the crews situated in their cabins – not a bad showing for the United States Army.

+++

The next day we began night operations, so we got to sleep in. As with the night before, I slept great. I can't say everyone in our group fared as well. Two of our crew chiefs were hopelessly seasick. I don't think I've ever seen the shade of green their faces produced. By all accounts they were vomiting all night and couldn't eat. They just wanted to get off the boat and into the air. But we still had several hours until dark.

Classes and briefings rounded out the day in the 'Ready Room,' until the Captain announced flight quarters over the ship's 1MC intercom. So, I headed topside to walk the flight deck looking for debris known as FOD. Once completed, we donned our gear, conducted our crew brief and I climbed into the left seat of my MH-47G. Our callsign for the evening would be Raven Four-One. Our mission was to get six takeoffs and landings for both my students. My first copilot was CW2 Ron Chase and my second was CW2 Dominick Goodie. I'd flown with both on several occasions. Not only were they both skilled and experienced, but they were a lot of fun to fly with.

We needed to run through the startup checklist, and we'd be on our way. We'd get our bounces out of the way quickly. Working on a Navy ship meant following their procedures. We couldn't just crank the engines. I needed permission for everything we did. The night began with a friendly wave to our assigned LSE. The 'Yellow Shirt' was standing about fifty feet to our right front waiting for my hand signals. I flashed three fingers representing our Auxiliary Power Unit. He turned to face Pri Fly and got the Air Boss's attention. When he turned to face me, he already had his thumbs up ready.

The whiney turbine engine wound up, it's high-pitched screech filled the air making converasation impossible without the inter-crew communications system (ICS).

"Tower, Raven 41, spot seven, winds for engine start and rotor engagement."

The Air Boss was ready to go. "Raven 41, clear to start engines and release rotor."

The LSE was waiting. I held up one finger, representing the number one engine.

Thumbs up.

The engine roared to operating speed, but the massive rotors stayed put. Our rotor brake kept them nicely in place. I repeated the signal for number two, then spun my index finger in an overhead circle as if I had a lasso.

Thumbs up.

Ron released the brake, and our synchronized rotors began to spin. I always like this part of the flight. Going from quiet stillness to the repetitive thump of the blades ripping through the air and the roar of the powerful T55-L714A engines boosted my adrenaline. I loved my job, and we hadn't even got to the fun part yet.

More hand signals to breakdown the chocks and chains and the 'Boss' had us bouncing again and again. The other helicopters got into the game minutes later. Without any cargo, we carried a full load of fuel giving us a little over five hours of flight time. Once our currency iterations were complete, I wanted to leave the ship and head about ten miles to the east for our crew chiefs to work on their hoist skills.

If there's one group of guys that make things happen and don't get the credit they deserve it is our enlisted crews. Not only do they bust their butts to get our helicopters ready to fly, but they've got their own set of skills to stay proficient at. Gunnery and hoist are probably the two most important. We didn't have any ammunition with us, but our M-134 Minigun were installed to pretty much get in their way.

We left the pattern, headed east and descended to one hundred feet above the water. Ron was on the controls. The crew chief instructor tossed an illuminated chem stick into the ocean to act as an imaginary swimmer. The crew chief manning the cabin door gave instructions to Ron.

"Sir, swimmer is at our three o'clock, outside the rotor disk. Slide right seventy-five."

Ron complied.

"Swimmer still at three o'clock. Slow your slide. Continue to your right twenty feet... ten feet... five, four, three, two, one, hold your right. Position looks good. Door plug coming out – hoisting out." The external rescue hoist cable paid out as fast as he could control it.

Ron held his position using his hover symbology. He was focused entirely on his inboard MFD. He was rock solid.

"Hoist is five feet from the swimmer. Hoist is in the water. Swimmer has the hoist in hand and is securing himself."

Ron hadn't moved an inch.

"Hoisting in – cable coming tight in three, two, one. Hoisting in – hoisting in."

I could tell Ron was getting tired. He started to move to our left as he flexed his hand.

"Hoisting in – swimmer is five feet from the probe. You're drifting left. Come right two."

Ron listened and did what he was told.

"Swimmer is at the cabin door. Recovering swimmer – swimmer secure. Door plug reinstalled."

The crew chief at the right ramp station chimed in quickly. "Aft Ready, clear for flight."

The front chief finished it off. "Forward ready, cleared for flight."

Ron announced he was looking outside again and was accelerating.

"Very nice iteration," I said. "Okay, lets swap out and do it again."

My copilots changed positions while I flew.

Dom was ready to go, and I relinquished the flight controls. We had another hour of fuel to expend, so we kept at it. The full moon had been high in the sky up until that point. Eventually it hid behind some clouds as it made its way below the horizon. No moon and overcast sky made for a dark night. It was becoming difficult to discern the horizon, which could be a problem.

"Guys, it's getting dark. Pay attention to cues for spatial disorientation. If you feel the onset speak up immediately."

Everyone acknowledged. The last thing we needed was to finish our night running into the water disoriented. It's more common than you might think. I thought it prudent to return to the *Nassau*.

"Lets go Dom. Turn right to heading three zero zero and speed up to one hundred knots – maintain three hundred feet."

He did as he was told but he didn't roll out on the assigned heading. He kept turning, his angle of bank increasing.

"Dom, are you okay? You're passing zero one zero and descending."

"No, I feel funny. I'm kind of dizzy and I..." He was suddenly silent.

"I have the controls," I announced.

"You have the controls Al. Holy crap I felt like I was flipping end over end and rotating sideways all at once."

The instructor in me couldn't help myself. "And what illusion is that?"

"Coriolis illusion," someone yelled from the back.

"That's right, and it's a pretty nasty one. Wouldn't you agree?"

"Heck yeah, that sucked. I could have flown us right into the water."

"Yes, you could," I agreed. "We've lost crews to that very problem. Remember how it felt, and next time you feel it coming on, pass the controls and make your crew aware you're not operating at full capacity."

Not a bad night of training. Not bad at all.

+++

Our week on the ship was coming to an end. I'd tried to call Linda every day, but she wasn't answering the phone. I resorted to email, but she wasn't responding to them either. I started to worry that she might have fallen off the wagon again. I tried to compartmentalize my feelings. This environment was too unforgiving to not pay attention to the details at hand. Besides, how much trouble could she get into in a week?

Lucky for us, not too much.

Tiffany and Stephen told us that they were expecting a son. My God, could it get any better? A grandson was on the way. This could be the catalyst that pushed Linda to get her act together.

My grandson, Cason, was born in January. And we were excited to see him before another winter deployment to Sharana.

+++

My three-month winter deployment was uneventful and passed without any excitement. I hopped onto a C-17 hoping for quick transit home. But a maintenance delay in Germany yielded timing problems at home.

Linda, not able to wait, hit the vodka and was arrested again for drinking while driving.

When was this going to end?

I got her back into Rehab even though our medical benefits were starting to dry up. The therapist was good. Linda did well. I was happy with her progress.

Twenty-eight days went fast. She could have used more time, but that was all our insurance could give. Rehab was complete – her third attempt. This time, I was sure she was going to make it.

Chapter 38

Attempting to Regain Control (2011)

I was convinced Linda's treatment was working, so I went back to work in time to meet Ross Perot Jr., a frequent benefactor and donor to our wounded soldiers. He visited our compound, and I was chosen to fly with him in the MH-47 Combat Mission Simulator. A typical 'Dog and Pony Show.' I'd show off all the gizmos, bells, and whistles and let him give it a try. After all, he was a rated pilot who'd set a world record circling the globe in a helicopter. I thought he'd enjoy the machine. His two assistants climbed aboard for a dry run and had a blast.

The realistic flight simulator sometimes seemed like an expensive video game. I could place the cockpit anywhere in the world for mission rehearsals. I taught the two gentlemen how to aerial refuel, land on an aircraft carrier, and land in a visually obscured environment. They smiled and laughed for forty-five minutes. They assured me the boss would love the same routine.

When Mr. Perot climbed into the cockpit, I started in with some polite small talk to break the ice and ran through the same routine. He had more difficulty than I expected. And I think I may have embarrassed him, because when the period ended, he climbed out of his seat without a smile, and without a thank you or goodbye. He didn't seem happy with me or maybe his performance. I don't know for sure, but I think I unintentionally insulted or embarrassed him. That's unfortunate, and I'll never have the opportunity to apologize, not that he needs one.

+++

Linda was doing the best I'd seen in years. The last rehab must have stuck. I was confident that I could return to the training schedule. The year was busy, as usual. I went to Virginia Beach for ship landings, traveled to the southwest for desert and mountain practice, and air refueling in Dallas.

Her progress stopped, and at some point, Linda answered texts but not phone calls. This was a pattern I'd seen before. Sure enough, I came home from a trip to find her passed out on the living room floor, incoherent and combative – so much for Rehab.

The roller coaster of success and failure was taking a toll on me. I had to regain control. Something had to give, so I called a marriage counselor and offered to request reassignment to Fort Rucker, Alabama. If I moved there, I'd stay home and never have to leave again. But Linda would not budge. She wanted to stay in our house. She loved Tennessee and would not leave.

Linda's behavior was becoming more erratic at home. She would punch walls for no apparent reason and try to draw me into a fight. She broke her hand punching through sheetrock. A wall stud didn't move... Each injury brought pain pills from the emergency room doctors. That is, until one day, someone called her on it. A doctor we'd never seen, flipped through her medical records, and listened to her proudly exclaim how many surgeries she'd endured. He said that he knew she was lying. She was 'doctor hunting' to get pain pills.

I hadn't even considered that.

She was outraged and demanded to see another physician.

"No," he said. "I'll not let you drag this practice into your problem. You can NOT see anyone else, and if you persist, I'll notify the police."

She was pissed, and so was I. He didn't know her. She had real pain, or so I thought. I was definitely enabling her.

Without more Methadone, she increased her vodka intake. I knew it was wrong, but she hurt. The paradox was taking its toll. I couldn't sleep because Linda would slip out of the house to go to a liquor store or bar. I knew if she went out, she'd be driving drunk – always a problem. And she was operating on a restricted license. Another arrest would mean a total loss, and maybe jail. I considered turning her in to the police myself. She was going to kill someone if left unchecked. Dents and unexplained scratches covered her car. The time was nearing that I had to make a choice: Report her to the police or roll the dice and hope she had no more accidents.

Not only couldn't I sleep, but I was continually searching for vodka bottles. I'd find them in the weirdest places, like under furniture, in sock drawers, behind books, and under her car seat. I was nearing emotional collapse. I started thinking about leaving her, but we'd been together so long and through so much. I needed help, and I needed it quickly. So, I called upon our Regiment Psychologist. The young doctor didn't seem old enough to impart any life wisdom or direction, but I was willing to listen.

Lucky for me, her professional manner, and willingness to listen, earned my trust. So, when she advised me to look into ALANON, I did.

The easiest way to describe ALANON is that it is the companion program to Alcoholics Anonymous, but for family members. If I can pinpoint Linda's accelerated destructive spiral to my attempts to rescue Bowe Bergdahl, I can say my initial ALANON meeting was the point where I first felt some stability and control – not much, but some.

I arrived early in the church parking lot and watched as other cars pulled up and offloaded their passengers. I don't know what I expected to see, but these folks looked normal. They weren't dirty, or shaking, nor did they look scary. They looked like me, but happier. So, I worked up the courage to find my way into the ALANON meeting.

+++

I introduced myself and wanted to know how to fix my wife. "I'm a soldier. I must deploy and can't leave my wife behind, especially without a driver's license. I'm sure without me, she'll miss her probation meetings. One miss and she'll go to jail. She's hiding her drinking, lying to me regularly, and is a danger to herself and those around her." I wanted a fix. "How can I get her to stop drinking?"

The reply from the group was simple... "you CAN'T fix her. ALANON has an acronym to cover that facet of the problem – You didn't Cause the problem, you can't Control the problem, and can't Cure the problem."

But I wanted a fix – something quick and effective.

The group would help me get my emotions in check so I could help MYSELF. After all, how could I even think of helping Linda when my health and mental state were diminished by letting her behavior control ME.

Yes, this group was going to help, but I wasn't sure how.

+++

Not long after my first couple of ALANON meetings, Linda noticed that I was doing better. She couldn't get me mad as quickly, and I looked like I was sleeping better. She'd been trying to push me away, hoping I'd leave her. A divorce would prove how much of a failure she was, thus living up to her mother's words.

Twice a week, I met with my support group. The friends I made were crucial to my emotional and physical survival.

Linda's drinking kept up, and she coerced another doctor to perform ankle surgery after she broke it again, kicking our living room wall in a drunken rage. And of course, the injury needed fentanyl patches and methadone to keep her pain under control – a little excessive in my opinion.

Then one day, she floored the accelerator and squirted from her parking spot at Target. The passing car she hit didn't stand a chance. Both vehicles were total losses. Linda's car, once her pride and joy, would never drive again. How the responding police officer couldn't tell she was under the influence is beyond me. Our insurance company covered the damage but promptly dropped my policy due to excessive damage claims to Linda's car. Not only was I out a $2,000 insurance deductible, but I was embarrassed. I'd been with my Insurance company for over twenty years, never needing their assistance, that is not until Linda's addiction set in.

Angry doesn't adequately describe my mental state. Not only was Linda irresponsible and unsafe, but she didn't care. "Just buy a new car," she said. "It's not really a big deal."

Oh, it WAS a big deal. We fought, and it was ugly.

She told me to leave and let her live the way she wanted. Or better yet, I should hit her as punishment for her mistakes. But, thanks to my ALANON teachings, I walked away, taking the dog to our guest room, and locking the door. We both needed to cool down. She wouldn't be able to drive away without a car, and she wasn't getting my keys. But it wasn't long before the front door closed with a resounding slam; she'd called a taxi and was on her way to a bar – I honestly could not control her. She was trying to force my hand, but I couldn't quit. We were going to work through our problems – I knew it.

+++

Believe it or not, a new car was in the cards for Linda, whether I liked it or not. I wasn't going to let her drive my truck, and the unit would have me traveling before I wanted. Unless I wanted her addiction known, I was powerless to resist new car shopping. She wasn't going to walk.

Linda loved the color red. Put that on a shiny Ford Taurus with leather seats and I knew she'd smile. I loved seeing her happy and the car was a thing of beauty. *What the hell was I thinking?*

The salesman had the contract ready to sign. The car was hers. My daughter in law, Justine wanted to celebrate Linda's new purchase. She suggested we meet for lunch at a local steak house. Before we left the showroom, the salesman pointed out features that he thought Linda would like. She fidgeted and squirmed. She'd seen enough and wanted to hit the road in her new car. She had to use the restroom at the restaurant. I pointed to the dealer's bathroom, but that wouldn't do. She was anxious to drive the new Taurus. The salesman was happy to see her excited to drive her new car. "Okay. We're nearly done, take it for a spin, it's yours."

I finished the deal as she drove off the lot headed for our restaurant with a blank look on her face. It's as though she wasn't really there mentally.

Our salesman, Jack, noticed my concern. "She'll be fine," he said.

"I'm not so sure, Jack. Something seems a bit off."

"Well, the car is yours. Enjoy it," he said with a genuine smile.

"Alright," I thought, let me get to the restaurant and see what's up with her. *"I hope she likes the car."*

+++

I stood next to Justine in the parking lot of the Longhorn Steak House. Linda left before me; she should have beaten me to the restaurant. And she wasn't answering texts or phone calls – something was amiss.

A flash of red passed from my right. I glanced up just in time to see Linda attempting to turn into a parking spot at a high rate of speed. She had to be doing forty miles an hour in the lot. I could see a look of terror on her face. The car was traveling too fast, and she couldn't slow it down for some reason. To her credit, she didn't hit any other vehicles as she weaved between them. But her luck didn't keep her from slamming into the side of the restaurant. Her newly purchased Ford Taurus didn't penetrate the building or hurt patrons inside, but its front end was crushed – we'd owned it a mere twenty minutes, or less.

Maybe Linda had a stroke and lay dead in the driver's seat.

No. She was unhurt, but in shock. Her foot stuck to the accelerator, and she couldn't use the brake. I looked helplessly at her ankle cast from the recent surgery. I wanted to cry, and I wasn't even sure my new insurance company would cover the damage to her car or the restaurant.

A crowd formed as the 'rubber-neckers' came to see what happened. The blank look on Linda's face and lack of remorse tipped me off that she was drunk. She was late because she made a pit stop at a liquor store before our celebratory lunch. Even though my frustrations were at an all time high, I didn't turn her in, and the police officer must have thought her emotionless expression was due to shock, not alcohol, and prescription pain medication.

+++

If not for my ALANON supporters, I might have gone over the edge. My inability to control my situation led to frequent anxiety attacks and difficulty breathing – I didn't think I could go on much longer.

Several days and many arguments later, Linda quietly threatened me out of the blue.

"Alan, I think you should leave the house. If you don't, I'm going to slip into the garage while you sleep to find the perfect tool."

She looked into my eyes. "I'm going to kill you with a hammer. If you sleep, you'll die in the worst way I can imagine."

The calmness with which she made the threat was the scary part. She seemed to have made up her mind that I needed to die violently and horribly, like something out of a movie. I probably should have left the house, but instead, I calmly picked up Scooter and went to the guest room. I didn't know it, but I'd be spending a lot more time there. As I closed the bedroom door, I realized the flimsy lock would be insufficient to stop her if she actually came after me with a hammer. I had to improvise, so I wedged a chair under the knob, poured a glass of bourbon, and retrieved my .45 from my safe. If she tried to get in, I'd call the police, but if she breached the door, I wouldn't hesitate to shoot – that's how far we'd fallen.

Needless to say, I didn't sleep well that night, but a drunken Linda slept nicely. And when I spoke with her in the morning, she had no memory of threatening me. I was really beginning to wonder whose mental state was worse, hers or mine. She pointed out that she was fine, but maybe my PTSD was causing hallucinations. Once again, she accused me of being the problem.

I was starting to believe her. Was I losing my sanity?

Her spiral just picked up steam – another parking lot accident; Linda staggered out onto the asphalt to survey the damage, gave a thumbs-up to the other driver and left the scene. She headed to a nearby liquor store for more vodka. The other driver wasted no time providing Linda's license plate number and description to the police. They found her about an hour later, drunk in a bar and charged her with Driving Under the Influence (DUI) and leaving the scene of an accident. This time I made my stand. I refused to bail her out of jail, but she didn't need my help. She called a bail bondsman and was home within three hours, now madder than ever that I left her in lock-up.

She wanted me to hurt her.

We argued in one of the most bizarre conversations I've ever had.

"Go ahead, beat me again," she yelled defiantly. "Hit me in the face. My lawyer has photographs from the last time, and he'll release them if anything happens to me."

"What the heck are you talking about?"

"The pictures are in his safe. I told him to send them to the press, the police, and your unit."

I couldn't believe my ears. There was no lawyer, no safe, and no photos. It was like she was acting out an episode of her favorite cop shows. She was losing control over me. By not bailing her out, it was obvious I was was starting to think on my own. She was losing her manipulative control. She needed something to hold over me and was determined to push me.

She was close.

No, she was there – I shoved her onto the bed by her throat. I'd kill her if I didn't reign it in – I thought of my sons. Frustration was overwhelming. "Linda, you need to go to rehab tomorrow," I yelled at the top of my lungs.

"Fuck you," she said. "I just need another drink."

I watched her slide a hidden bottle of vodka from under my pillow – mine.

I could take no more. I couldn't breathe. I grabbed Scooter and retreated to my sanctuary in the back bedroom. I secured the door and slipped beneath the covers, pistol in hand. There was no hiding my grief. I cried myself to sleep.

Linda and I had drifted apart considerably and, in my opinion, to the point of failure. However, in a surprise move three days later, Linda told me she wanted to try rehab for the fourth time. She said she didn't like who she had become. By this time, I was skeptical. What the heck, if she wanted to get help, that was fine with me, but I really didn't care. At least if she was there, I didn't have to deal with her bullshit.

+++

Twenty-eight days later, Linda emerged healthy, happy, and with a new direction. I'd seen this before, but for the first time she'd come clean about her habits, lies, deceit, and attempts to get me to fight her. I couldn't have been happier. My persistence, love, and support carried us through.

Life it seems is like the instructions on a shampoo bottle: Lather – Rinse – Repeat.

Chapter 39

Nearing the edge (2012)

Several months had passed since rehab. Linda was drinking in moderation. She claimed she still needed it for pain control. I didn't like it, but she was behaving. Winter ended, Spring was upon us, and the warm sunny weather helped put us all in a good mood.

Then we got a call we always knew would come, but you never actually are ready for – Linda's father, Gerrit, died.

Even though he was abusive throughout her life, she craved his elusive love and respect.

I always knew she'd take his death hard, but I didn't know how hard. Within days, she tried to overdose with pills.

One-month later Linda's mother Daisy died – both parents gone in the blink of an eye.

Weeks passed with no sober moments in our house. Empty vodka bottles littered every room. I could not keep her sober. I hadn't had a coherent conversation with Linda in days.

Then one day I caught her driving drunk – the sin I warned her about.

I let her have it with more expletives than I'll portray here. My screaming had to be heard throughout our neighborhood. "What the Heck, Linda!"

"You promised me that you'd be sober today!"

"How hard is it to NOT drink?"

"Just don't drink!"

Her slurred response only made me angrier.

"I'm a loser," she said. Her expressionless gaze told me she was too drunk to argue with.

"Just go away," she pleaded.

I snatched the newly acquired gallon of cheap vodka from her hands and poured it in the kitchen sink.

"NO," She wailed. "Just leave me alone."

I dragged her by the arm to our bedroom. "Go to fucking bed," I said.

"Just hit me. I deserve it..."

A pang of compassion returned, and I softened my tone. "Look Linda, you can do this. Just don't drink again. You'll be sober when I get back from work and we can get you back into rehab."

"Okay," she said, and closed her eyes.

I tucked her under a fluffy down comforter.

I returned to work and pretended nothing was bothering me. The phone interrupted my serenity. Linda hadn't gone to sleep after all. She'd been busy since I left the house. She scanned my alert roster for phone contacts. She started at the top and went down the list, calling each number. She complained to each person that I should not go home. The last person she called was my friend Chuck, who subsequently called me.

Embarrassment? Anger? How should I feel? Maybe betrayal.

The cat was out of the bag now. There was no turning back; she had crossed the Rubicon.

I sped home – I was done.

I was moving out.

Chapter 40

Over the edge (2012)

After moving out, I kept up my psychologist appointments and ALANON meetings for fear I'd give in and repeat my enabling ways. Linda wanted me to come home. Linda texted or called several times a day asking me to either come home or bring Scooter back; she missed him. She was mad that I refused to tell her where I was and that I wouldn't move back in. I still had a streak of compassion. I made one last effort to get her into rehab, paying a visit to the Tri-Care Insurance counselors at Fort Campbell. As I feared, Linda's options were limited. She'd burned through our allotment of compensated visits, and she needed a twenty-eight-day visit, followed by a year in an assisted living 'sober house.' But we had no benefits remaining.

I begged the ladies in the office to find an exception, or in my opinion, Linda wouldn't live past six months. Unfortunately, they couldn't help; their hands were tied. Over the last couple of years, we'd squandered our medical benefit and were now left without options.

Dejected, I went back to my hotel for the night.

+++

I started the next morning with a hot cup of coffee and a new attitude. My day was going well. Linda hadn't texted me all day. My phone sat quiet. I decided to check up on her. I dropped what I was doing and headed across town. If she was fine, I could use the opportunity to empty the mailbox.

Butterflies pounded my stomach as my creative imagination ran through scenarios. I needed support. No way I could do this alone. I dialed my son in Virginia. "Hey Stephen, I'm driving to the house to check up on Mom. Can you stay on the line when I go in?"

"Yeah. Sure, no problem."

"I'm almost there. Maybe two minutes out."

"Okay," was all he said.

"I'm at the front door; it's unlocked." The house was eerily quiet. Most other times, the television could be heard in the background. "I'm in the kitchen, and there's no sign of Mom."

Empty vodka bottles littered the counters; there had to be thirty empty gallon bottles. I kept moving forward toward the ajar bedroom door. I eased it open.

The air conditioner was blasting frigid air. At first glance, she wasn't there – maybe in the bathroom – No. The down comforter on the floor was covering someone – Linda.

"Alright, I found her. She's sleeping on the bedroom floor."

"Linda," I said, trying to wake her. Uncovered now, she wore only her underwear, and her body was bruised everywhere.

"Oh, Linda. What have you done?" Her shoulder was cold to the touch – Ice Cold.

She was dead.

+++

I'd seen my share of dead bodies overseas; they were a curious sight. But seeing my wife of twenty-six years lying lifeless on the floor, upset me. The love of my life departed this earth rather than sober up.

I needed a drink of water...

The neighbors came out to see what was up as the ambulance and police cars rolled up – lights flashing. Those who'd tried to help her in my absence cried. "She just wouldn't listen," they told me. And I knew that they finally understood what I'd been dealing with.

An hour passed before the police let me back into my now-empty house. I poured a tall glass of ice water, sipped it slowly, and sobbed.

Several days later, Linda's memorial was well attended. If only she'd known that she was loved by so many people, maybe she would have made other choices. Alas, my wife was hell-bent on self-destruction, especially after her parents died. Linda found love and happiness with me and our sons for a finite period in her life; unfortunately, her addiction to pain medicine, and eventually, alcohol, was stronger than her love for us.

Section VI

"A man who has been through bitter experiences and traveled far enjoys even his sufferings after a time."

– Homer, The Odyssey

Chapter 41

West Point – Headed for Happiness

The 160th SOAR, a volunteer organization, is known for allowing Warrant Officers to stay within its ranks indefinitely. Not many pilots leave, and if they do, we always joked that their peers tend to feel betrayed unless you die, get medically grounded, or are dragged away to another assignment at the behest of the unit. I am grateful that the unit took care of me when I needed a change.

The 160th offered me desirable positions both internal and external. I could stay within the community or transfer to the regular army. I'd served the Regiment faithfully, and they were willing to reward my loyalty. This was going to be a tough decision; I needed time to think. In the meantime, I was asked to help unveil 'America's Response.' The beautiful bronze statue of a horse mounted by a Special Forces soldier stood at the site of the Twin Towers of the World Trade Center. The newly constructed Freedom Tower stood tall in the background.

Since I was the Flight Lead of SF ODA 595's mission responding to the attacks of 9/11, I had the privilege of attending the unveiling ceremony at New York City's Ground Zero.

I'd never been to NYC. And they rolled the red carpet out for us; not to mention interviews with NY1, Fox and Friends, and other local outlets.

New York may have some things to offer that Tennessee could not. I wondered if the West Point Flight Detachment job was still an option. After all, I'd be closer to my mother and brother, who still lived in New Hampshire. My friend John was the outgoing Detachment Commander. So, I called him to see how things might work if I threw my name in the hat to be his replacement.

+++

After the unveiling, I returned to Clarksville where my mood took on a certain melancholy. Memories, good and bad overwhelmed me. They all equated to sadness. Everywhere I looked held some emotion from my past. Happy memories made me sad because of how Linda's life ended. And memories of things that should make me sad, definitely put me in a sour mood.

The decision was simple; I needed a change of venue. New York was my next objective.

Assuming I could land the job, I'd need to sell my house quickly, find lodging in Orange County, New York, and learn to fly West Point's helicopters. I'd flown over 6,000 hours in Chinooks but now I'd need to qualify in the LUH-72 Lakota. Was I getting ahead of myself?

I still needed to get selected by the West Point Superintendent.

In preparation, I cleaned house. I donated Linda's best clothes and accessories to a battered women's shelter. I offered up my pool table and gym equipment to my friend Charley who stayed with me the night Linda died. Not only did I make daily runs to the county landfill, but I was active online selling or giving away almost all of my possessions.

Once the bills and administrative requirements of Linda's death were resolved, I put my home up for sale with an amazing realtor. Dorothy, my realtor, instructed me on what minor improvements to make and how to dress up the house for sale. It sold within a week. The sale worked out good for me because I got my wish – reassignment to New York. I took a quick trip back to NY for house-hunting. I found the perfect home in Orange County. The beauty of the Hudson Valley caught my eye immediately. I was searching for happiness – there could be no other outcome.

I wasn't going to quit until I found it.

+++

Leaving Clarksville and Fort Campbell was tough. I'd spent roughly seventeen years of my army career there. But now the sometimes-grueling journey to redemption began. I drove across the country to see my sister-in-law, both my sons, my grandchildren, my mother, and brother. I attended flight training in Pennsylvania and arrived at my ultimate destination to close on my new home by early June. Of course, learning a new flight area, local regulations, and establishing myself took time and a slight mental toll; I didn't realize how much until my household goods and furniture arrived on a moving truck. The oppressive summer heat and humidity squeezed sweat from my pores, as I carried box upon box into the house. I'd just re-carpeted the entire place, replaced the appliances, and best of all, added air conditioning. Now I directed the movers where to place the seemingly endless supply of moving cartons. I tried to get rid of as much stuff as I could before the move, but I still had tons of acquired junk. In many cases, boxes from my garage or attic arrived untouched and unchecked, from Tennessee.

Even with a warm sunny day to set the mood, the tasks of starting over were piling up. For the first time since I was nineteen, I was doing this alone – no wife, no family, no friends – just my dog scooter. And without opposable thumbs, I can't say he was much help.

Unpacking was slow-going and toilsome. Blasting music kept me motivated, but it was tough. I'm not known for my patience with tedious jobs, so I shifted gears and tossed a dog toy across the room to get Scooter riled up. I think he was still in shock from our move and just looked at me. Controlled breathing might be the key. I gave it a shot – in and out – slow and steady. Sad thoughts were still there but I tried focusing on the good. I reached into another carton and removed a small fleece blanket from one of the many containers littering my new living room. A gentle thump on my bare foot startled me... What appeared to be an empty plastic vodka bottle bounced off my toes and skittered out of view. So, down I went onto 'all fours' to search the shadows...

I found it... a flask-like bottle with an all-too-familiar vodka label.

I thought all the offending empties had been discovered and discarded before the move. But no, lying on my floor, was a persistent reminder of the lies, deceit, and sadness that ultimately defined my life before Linda died.

I wasn't going to quit, no matter how sad. I'd changed my location, job, and lifestyle. This was a new start.

Redemption and happiness were real and I reminded myself, they were mine for the taking.

Chapter 42

Parachute Team and Executive Travel

A helicopter pilot scared of heights? Yes, that would be me. Flying is fine, but put me on a ladder or balcony, and I get nervous fast... Ironically, flying the West Point Parachute Team would be the first step toward the return of my self-respect and ultimate happiness.

My LUH-72 was a beautiful green Eurocopter operated by the Army for administrative environments. The medium-sized utility helicopter was made almost entirely of plastic and had no combat role, armor, or survivability equipment. Later in my career, I'd refer to it as the 'mighty Lakota,' a mild jab at its capabilities. "The LUH will give you everything you need, but just *barely*," I'd say with a squeaky emphasis on barely. Though not a Chinook, the feisty utility helicopter was fun, easy to fly, and perfect for the academy mission.

The United States Military Academy (USMA) Parachute Team jumped four to five days a week from our LUH-72s and from a civilian airplane on the weekends.

The warm August was pleasant, especially with our doors open. The aroma of the end-of-summer foliage filled the air as we circled the parade field, known as the 'Plain.' Historic buildings, looking like medieval castles, surrounded the landing area, giving me goosebumps. Our flight checks were complete, and I headed in for a landing.

The helicopter shuddered as I slowed to a hover over the greenest grass I'd ever seen. The 'Plain' doubled as a parachute drop zone and a parade field. The beauty of the campus and the surrounding area distracted me from noticing the large group of cadets milling around near the bleachers.

After shutting down, I walked toward the coaches. Two cadets stepped into my path. "Good afternoon Sir, I'm Cadet Dave Caskey, and this is Cadet Chris Smith. We've heard so much about you and have been looking forward to meeting you." The polite young men waited patiently for my response.

"The pleasure is mine," I said. "What can I do for you?"

"Sir, we'd like you to be our leadership mentor."

I had no idea what that entailed. I wanted to help, so I casually agreed without really thinking it through. "Sure. I'd love to."

They scurried back to the safety brief so we could start jump operations.

I gave my copilot an inquisitive glance, to which he responded with a shoulder shrug. He didn't know what I'd signed up for either.

+++

The Lakota is capable of carrying eight passengers, but just like any aviation platform, performance is based on elevation, temperature, and weight. The first several skydiving 'lifts' carried only four jumpers. As we burned fuel, the passenger number increased to the eventual number of eight.

Each 'lift' was the same. We'd accelerate to our best climb airspeed before clearing the trees at the end of the 'Plain,' then get to forty-five hundred feet and turn into the wind at eighty knots. The cadet Jumpmasters ran the show. Once at the proper altitude, speed, and azimuth Jumpmasters gave the signal to exit the aircraft, usually with a flashy backflip or funny face. I smiled so much my face hurt. After each lift, I'd circle the last canopy down and follow it to the DZ. Once on the ground, I'd slide open my window and wait for the next group. The jumpers approached my helicopter smiling and ready for an obligatory fist bump. Then we'd repeat the process until fuel was expended or the sun set. These kids were professional, happy, and energetic; my God, their attitude was catchy.

+++

It turns out that being a leadership mentor consisted of sharing life lessons and Army experiences. Cadets were inquisitive, especially regarding how to handle Warrant Officers and NCOs as a new lieutenant. I loved answering their never-ending questions. Their youthful exuberance rekindled my love for the Army. If all West Point Cadets were like these two, the future of the US military looked bright. The Cadets tried several times to get me to try a tandem skydive, to share the experience of freefall. No way that was happening. I'm scared of heights.

+++

Most of my flying involved executive travel. My boss, Lieutenant General Robert Caslen, the Superintendent of West Point, made frequent trips to Washington, D.C., to meet with military and civilian leadership. If he didn't spend the night, we'd usually wait around for him by touring the D.C. area. A quick change of clothes at the airport and we'd be on the Metro to see the sights. By the end of the day, we'd reposition to the Pentagon for a quick pick up and return the General to New York.

If I wasn't flying to our nation's capital, I transported VIPs from West Point to New York City or vice-versa. The scenic flights along the Hudson River provided an opportunity to point out historical landmarks and points-of-interest to curious passengers. Easy to see from the air and interesting to discuss were Bannerman Island Arsenal, Sing Sing prison, Piermont docks, Alpine tower, Grant's tomb, Yankee stadium, Freedom Tower, and of course, everyone's favorite, the Statue of Liberty. If I made a return flight, there'd be nothing left to talk about so, I'd test the gullibility of anyone interested to listen about made-up sites. My favorite was the old Hudson River Slinky factory. Everyone remembers the coiled metal spring toy marketed to kids since 1943. I remembered television commercials while growing up portraying children happily watching the flexible helical walking down a set of stairs to its familiar jingle:

♫ "It's Slinky; it's Slinky. ♫
For fun, it's a wonderful toy.
What walks downstairs, alone or in pairs
And makes a slinkety sound…

I'd sing the lyrics while pointing out a bare concrete pad on the eastern shore of the river just north of Manhattan. A factory of some type stood there long ago, so I'd weave it into my story. "This place was thriving in the 1940s. Look. There to the right. See those stairs? That's the original slinky test track."

Appropriate oohs, and aahs came from gullible passengers.

My crew chief, aware of where I was going with the tall tale, would egg me on. "Sir, what happened to the factory?"

"The Second World War ended, and we needed to reconstitute Japan's manufacturing base, so we moved the plant to Nokia. This one fell into disrepair, especially after the company switched from metal to plastic."

Everyone nodded their heads as if to understand the historical implications.

Then I'd let them off the hook with a giggle and a smile. Storytelling was in my nature, and it was reawakening as happiness and stability crept back into my day-to-day life.

+++

Regaling the skydiving team with 'there I was' war stories and other tall tales kept them interested. And my friendship with the cadets grew enough that I agreed to a tandem skydive before they graduated. The month of May rolled around, and I found myself sitting on the floor of a Lakota helicopter. The parachute team coach, Tom Falzone was the tandem master to whom I was attached. He sat behind me as I squeezed between his legs – pretty much in his lap. And as he tweaked and tightened my harness, I looked out the open cargo doors. The terrain dropped away as we climbed to our jump altitude of 13,500 feet. I can't describe how scared I was, though as my crew looked on, watching for fear or weakness, I put on my best 'brave face.' Go Pro cameras were on everyone's helmets to record my first jump for posterity. The cold started soaking into my uniform as we climbed through 6,000 feet. The spring sky was clear and sunny; I can't imagine a better day. Tom tapped me on the shoulder to indicate a final adjustment. He cinched the final straps, and we 'scootched' toward the right-side cabin door.

My pulse quickened, and my heart raced as I swung my feet outside the helicopter and onto the skid. No two ways about it, I was scared.

As we tipped forward to exit the safety of the aircraft, I was head-to-earth – too late to quit.

We planed out, falling belly-to-earth. I admired the view as I looked around. The initial shock wore off almost immediately, and the cadet jumpers swooped in from above to fist bump and take pictures. The freefall portion of the jump lasted about a minute before we opened our chute and sashayed across the sky, taking in the beauty of the Hudson Valley. Within minutes we slide onto the grass at West Point amid cheers and laughter. I was lucky not to break my smile muscles – what a fantastic feeling.

By the next school year, I'd earned my skydiving license and enjoyed feelings of accomplishment as I fell from the heavens. Commanding 2nd Aviation Detachment provided the opportunity, and the cadets gave me the courage to try something new. I will be forever grateful for their trust and friendship.

+++

I'd like to think my soldiers and their families enjoyed their time in 2nd Aviation Detachment as much as me. Our missions ranged from parachuting, VIP, Aerial Fire Fighting, and helicopter hoist rescues. Our unit was located on a valuable plot of land at Stewart International Airport in New Windsor, New York. The hangar once housed an entire battalion of airplanes and helicopters and now was home to two Lakotas and a pair of Cessna 172s.

Along with my equipment, I leased part of my hangar to the New York State Police Special Operations Response Team (SORT). The aging structure was old but spacious and well cared for. It held a kitchen, gym, sauna, shower, and bunk facilities. I frequently sponsored pot luck picnics with beer, accompanied by a blazing fire pit in the center of our recreation area. We shared the cost of renting inflatable jumping playgrounds for the numerous children in our midst. Good times were upon us all – no deployments, nobody getting shot at, and no one to shoot at. I had just enough stress as the commander to keep me intellectually stimulated, the unit mission was fun, and I enjoyed the people I worked with. But something was missing...

Chapter 43

Happiness Found

A little over a year had passed since Linda's death. Single life wasn't too bad, though popular online dating sites made it better. *Match* and *Plenty of Fish* provided leads to some wonderful women, but I hadn't found my 'special lady friend' yet. Dating was fun, and I'd do it again and again, as much as I needed to. Each night, I'd flip through messages from prospective ladies. Those that caught my fancy maintained running conversations. Eventually, one woman made an impression that produced an undeniably, unique friendship. Patti Lestrange, a divorced mother of three teens, liked that I was primarily seeking a friend, not necessarily a romance.

We took it slow – we took it easy. And our friendship grew as we spent more time together. Patti's infectious smile and positive outlook charmed me with ease. My past as a Special Operations Pilot intrigued her, especially when I spoke of the Horse Soldiers infil after 9/11. She'd lost her stepbrother in one of the collapsing towers and had no idea that as a nation we'd retaliated so quickly.

I introduced Patti to a military world that she could never have imagined without opening her heart to me. At some point, I realized I liked her a lot and told her so. Lucky for me, she felt the same. So, life continued day-to-day, and our relationship grew.

+++

Seemingly meaningless events can happen in life that later turn out to be significant turning points; the New York Airshow was one of those moments.

The summer of 2015 was quietly nearing the end when a forwarded e-mail from LTG Caslen named me the point of contact for Steve Neuhaus, our County Executive. I was instructed to assist in any way possible; he wanted me to help facilitate the show as best I could.

Originally scheduled to be hosted by New York City on Coney Island, the performers were coming, the promoter had committed, but sixty days out, the deal fell apart and landed squarely in the lap of Orange County, just fifty miles north of the city. Steve Neuhaus knew what he wanted... the show at Stewart Airport. My first act was to provide my hangar and ramp for a press conference announcing the shift from Coney Island to our sleepy facility. I enjoyed working through problems and logistics to help make the show happen. I reached out to the

10th Mountain Division at Fort Drum for helicopters to place on 'static' display. The show, headlined by the F-22 Raptor and F-18 Demonstration team, was a great success.

Working with the show, airport, and county, I met some wonderful people and made lifelong friends. And we'd do it again next year – I couldn't wait...

+++

Life was good. Patti and I were no longer just friends, we were husband and wife near the end of 2015. But then the Army decided I'd been at West Point long enough. The Aviation Branch thought three years was long enough for me to command the detachment, and they informed me of my impending move. They offered me several lucrative jobs, mostly back in Special Operations. But Patti had never lived outside New York and all my potential assignments were either in the deep south or at the Pentagon. She agreed to go wherever, but my sons had other ideas. "Dad, you're going to take her away from the only home she's ever known to a completely different region, to a military base, with a lifestyle that will be foreign to her, and then you'll go on the road or deploy, leaving her alone. She'll hate it."

Their advice was sound. And after talking it over with Patti, I declined reassignment and retired from active duty just shy of thirty-six years of service. But what to do about a job? I could fly for a nearby Air Ambulance Service; I could fly New York executives, or give aerial tours. The choice seemed simple; flying was the most natural progression to civilian life. But my back, shoulder, and hips hurt from nearly seven thousand flight hours. I thought a new path might be more suitable.

The County Executive offered me a job working for the Department of Emergency Services as the Emergency Manager for the county, a job I happily accepted. I think that leaving the Army to work in public safety is comparable and an easy transition. Instead of serving America's citizens, I work to protect my community. My entire adult life has been about serving the public in some way. And I'll keep at it because I love it.

+++

My home's back deck looks out over several acres of woods. I love sitting outside drinking either coffee or bourbon. At night, a clear sky full of stars is unimpeded by a lack of cultural lighting. Most evenings I can look above the treetops and Orion stands as a symbol for me. Just like that first infil of Enduring Freedom, and many subsequent deployments – everything is going to be alright.

Stepping away from the Army after such a long career was challenging. Military life is the only environment I've known since graduating from high school. I've traveled the world on business, and for pleasure. I've lost one wife and gained another. My blended family and grandkids bring great joy to my life. By not quitting, by not giving up, I've achieved a sort of calm and comfort that I could only dream possible.

My advice to anyone facing similar life circumstances is to keep a good attitude and keep God in your heart – optimism is healthy.

Night Stalkers Don't Quit!

Glossary

AAA	Anti-Aircraft Artillery. See also ADA.
ADA	Air Defense Artillery — Weapons and equipment for actively combating air targets from the ground. See also AAA
AFSB	Afloat Forward Support Base. An aircraft carrier or LHD is used as a base of operations to launch and recover special operations missions from offshore locations.
Amphib-1	A maneuver where an MH-47 helicopter infils special operations troops and/or boats into a body of water from a ten-foot hover.
Amphib-3	A maneuver where an MH-47 helicopter infils and/or exfils a high-speed boat with crew onto a body of water using slings, fast rope, and rope ladders.
APU	Auxiliary Power Unit – A small turbine engine that provides electrical power and hydraulic pressure before the helicopter's main turbine engines run.
AOR	Area of Responsibility — The geographical area associated with a combatant command
	Air Control Point — A geographic position along a flight route marked by coordinates
	Call Sign — Any combination of numbers or pronounceable words, identifying a unit, individual, or aircraft maintaining communications.
CAAS	Common Avionics Architecture System. The pilot/user interface for MH-47G and CH-47F helicopters. The software developed by Rockwell used technological improvements to improve upon IAS (see glossary). It allows data input and flight/mission queries to assist in mission completion.
CASEVAC	Casualty Evacuation mission. Similar to MEDEVAC, but is usually embedded within a flight and is not dedicated to an entire area or theater.
CDU	Control Display Unit. Located on the MH-47 cockpit canted console. A soft-touch key pad allows pilot's data input or information queries tied to the Integrated Avionics System (IAS) and the Common Avionics Architecture System (CAAS).

CHAFF	Radar confusion reflectors, consisting of thin, narrow metallic strips of various lengths and frequency responses, and are used to reflect echoes for confusion purposes.
Charlie Pattern	A helicopter pattern used to control air traffic flow to and from an LHD.
CJSOTF	Combined Joint Special Operations Task Force. Combined utilized elements of other country's military organizations. Joint represents multi-service US forces.
CRRC	Combat Rubber Raiding Craft. A rubber zodiac-style boat utilized by special operations forces for maritime infils.
Delta Pattern	A helicopter holding pattern for US Navy air-capable ships.
EOD	Explosive Ordnance Disposal.
EOS	Electro-Optical Sensor. A sensor similar to but technologically superior to a FLIR (see glossary). It is primarily used by aircraft to see terrain, vehicles, and personnel using differential temperature and/or fused I-2 systems (NVG).
E2	Radar Exponential Elevation display used with IAS and CAAS.
Flares	Anti-missile countermeasures used to decoy infrared/heat-seeking missiles.
FLIR	Forward-Looking Infrared. A thermal imaging sensor is used primarily by aircraft to see terrain, vehicles, and personnel using differential temperature.
FOB	Forward Operating Base.
HAR	Helicopter Air Refueling — The refueling of a helicopter in flight by a C-130 aircraft.
HAS	Hardened Aircraft Shelter – A concrete bunker used as an aircraft hanger and bomb-resistant shelter.
HEEDS	Helicopter Emergency Egress Device. A small self-contained compressed air supply for emergency crew egress for a sinking helicopter. Usually carried in a flight-vest pocket during overwater flight.
HLZ	Helicopter Landing Zone – A location designated for landing a helicopter.
HOS	Helicopter Oxygen System – A console that provides supplemental oxygen to aircrews above 10,000 feet MSL.
IAS	Integrated Avionics System. The pilot/user interface for MH-47E and MH-60K helicopters. The software initially created by IBM allows data input and flight/mission queries to assist in mission completion.
IED	Improvised Explosive Device.

INFIL	Abbreviation for a helicopter infiltration of friendly forces through, into, or onto enemy-controlled areas or denied terrain. Special operations forces recognize three distinct categories: 'X:' This is a helicopter landing as close as possible to a target objective or individual; it may be as far as 300 meters away. The aircraft is well within small-arms range. 'Y:' This is a helicopter landing no closer than 300 meters from a target objective or individual but no further than 1 Kilometer. This is intended to remain clear of small-arms range. 'Offset:' This is a helicopter landing no closer than 1 Kilometer to a target objective or individual, and usually no further than 10 Kilometers. The concept is to land undetected.
JTTF	Joint Terrorism Task Force.
JSOC	Joint Special Operations Command.
LHD	Landing Helicopter Dock (LHD) amphibious assault ships. Similar to an Aircraft Carrier. Launches and recovers helicopters, vertical takeoff, and landing airplanes (Harrier, F35, and V-22). In addition to aviation operations, the 'well deck' can launch and recover Landing Craft Air Cushion, aka hovercraft (LCAC).
LNO	Liaison Officer – A unit representative who is a subject matter expert for a supported organization.
MANPAD	Man-Portable surface-to-air missile. Examples include SA-7, HN-5, and Stinger. This heat-seeking (IR) lock-on and tracks aircraft heat sources until impact. Sometimes they are equipped with counter-countermeasures to defeat aircraft defensive decoys.
MFD	Multi-Function Display. Located on the MH-47 instrument panel. Essentially a video screen constituting a 'glass cockpit;' the MH-47E utilizes four and the MH-47G five. All flight information is presented to the pilots, and different modes of equipment are selected here from a soft-touch bezel key surrounding the unit.
MMR	The AN/AQ174B, made by Raytheon, is a pod-mounted radar equipped with multiple modes such as terrain-following (TF) and terrain-avoidance (TA), ground mapping (GM), and weather detection and avoidance (WX).
M-134 Minigun	A six-barreled 7.62 MM electric 'Gatling gun' style machine gun capable of firing several thousands of rounds per minute.
M-4	A magazine-fed, 5.56 MM rifle with a collapsible stock carried by the US military.
M-9	A magazine-fed 9 MM pistol made by Berretta carried by the US military.

NVG   Night Vision Goggles. A device usually in a binocular form used to amplify ambient and artificial light in the near-infrared range to enable pilots to see in low-light conditions (Night).

ODA   Operational Detachment – Alpha. A US special forces team consisting of twelve soldiers. Their primary missions include Direct Action (DA), Unconventional Warfare (UW), and Strategic Reconnaissance (SR).

RPG   Rocket Propelled Grenade. A Warsaw Pact weapon designed to destroy tanks. Has many unintended uses as a direct-fire explosive round often used against trucks, structures, and helicopters.

SECDEF   Secretary of Defense.

SERE   Survival, Evasion, Resistance, and Escape school for high-risk-of-capture personnel such as special operations forces.

TF   Terrain Following Radar. Mode used to fly low-level around, over, and through rolling or mountain terrain with limited or no visibility.

TF   Task Force – An adhoc organization created with units not typically assigned together working for a single commander in a unified manner.

TUG   An aircraft tractor capable of towing airplanes and helicopters. Usually painted bright yellow or flat green.

USSOCOM   Special Operations Command.

USASOC   United States Army Special Operations Command. An Army organization commanded by a three-star general. Subordinate units include but are not limited to Rangers, Civil Affairs, Special Forces Groups, 1st SFOD-D, and 160th SOAR.

VI   Vehicle Interdiction. A helicopter stalks a target vehicle, usually with the assistance of an aerial surveillance platform.

VSI   Vertical Speed Indicator – A gauge or cockpit indication that displays an aircraft's rate of climb or descent.